FIGHTING HOOSIERS

FIGHTING HOOSIERS

INDIANA IN TWO WORLD WARS

Edited by

DAWN E. BAKKEN

INDIANA UNIVERSITY PRESS

This book is a publication of

Indiana University Press
Office of Scholarly Publishing
Herman B Wells Library 350
1320 East 10th Street
Bloomington, Indiana 47405 USA

iupress.org

Manufactured in the United States of America

First printing 2021

Library of Congress Cataloging-in-Publication Data

Names: Bakken, Dawn E., editor.
Title: Fighting Hoosiers : Indiana in two World Wars / Dawn Bakken.
Other titles: Indiana in two World Wars | Indiana magazine of history.
Description: Bloomington : Indiana University Press, [2021]
Identifiers: LCCN 2021001355 (print) | LCCN 2021001356 (ebook) | ISBN 9780253056832 (hardback) | ISBN 9780253056849 (paperback) | ISBN 9780253056856 (ebook)
Subjects: LCSH: World War, 1914-1918—Indiana. | World War, 1939-1945—Indiana. | Soldiers—Indiana—Biography. | United States—Armed Forces—Biography.
Classification: LCC D570.85.I6 F54 2021 (print) | LCC D570.85.I6 (ebook) | DDC 940.4/12730922772—dc23
LC record available at https://lccn.loc.gov/2021001355
LC ebook record available at https://lccn.loc.gov/2021001356

To all the editors, associate editors, assistant editors, editorial assistants, and interns who have kept the Indiana Magazine of History *alive and thriving for 117 years as the journal of record for Indiana history.*

CONTENTS

FIGHTING HOOSIERS

Introduction

DAWN E. BAKKEN, EDITOR

THE FIRST ISSUE OF THE *Indiana Magazine of History* (*IMH*) appeared in print in 1905. The *IMH*, a peer-reviewed journal sponsored by the Indiana University (IU) Department of History, is one of the oldest continuously published state history journals and now operates as part of IU's ScholarWorks. The journal publishes articles by academic scholars and independent researchers; its archive is also filled with original diaries, memoirs, and letters. Many of those primary source documents were written by Hoosiers on the battlefront—from territorial days to the twentieth century—and by their loved ones back home.

This collection showcases seven articles on Hoosiers in the two world wars of the twentieth century. Four reproduce original diaries, letters, and memoirs. Readers will meet, among others, Alex Arch, a Hungarian-born immigrant who was the first American to fire a shot in World War I; Guy Connor, a radio operator on convoy duty in the Atlantic; Maude Essig, a nurse serving with the Red Cross in wartime France; Kenneth Baker, who crawled across French battlefields (sometimes over and around dead bodies) to lay phone lines for military communications; and Bernard Rice, a combat medic who witnessed the liberation of Dachau.

Twelve years after the *IMH* began publication, on April 6, 1917, the United States entered the Great War. Among the first who registered for military service were 260,000 Hoosiers. By the end of the war, 400,000 more had registered; more than 3,000 Indiana men and women had died.[1]

One Hoosier soldier played a prominent role at the outset of American involvement in the war. On the night of October 22, 1917, members of Battery C of

1

the US Army's Sixth Field Artillery, with the loan of shells from a French unit and some assistance from a French officer, dragged an artillery piece through the mud into an abandoned gun pit and, at 6:05 a.m. the next morning, fired toward German troops. On October 24, US newspapers reported that a young soldier had fired the first American shot of the war. The early stories described a redheaded sergeant from South Bend, Indiana, as the man who had pulled the lanyard. The unnamed soldier had told a reporter that he hailed from "South Bend and proud of it!"

The ensuing media frenzy to determine the identity of the soldier is described by authors Greta Fisher and Lauren Kuntzman. In their extensive survey of period newspapers, they found that readers, newspaper editors, and local boosters were quick to fill in the story with their own details. One South Bend newspaper promoted a local man who had worked at the city's Oliver Chilled Plow Works before the war. The War Department, however, identified the soldier as a corporal who had been wounded and, not coincidentally, was headed back to the States for a government-sponsored tour promoting Liberty Bonds. In September 1918, nearly one year after the incident, the commanding officer of Battery C publicly confirmed the identity of the Hoosier soldier who had fired the first shot. Intense media coverage, public spectacle, and misinformation (at least some of it deliberate) are not the sole purview of modern times.

Many other Hoosier soldiers served no less bravely but without media scrutiny. Guy Burrell Connor enlisted in the US Navy in June 1917. After a short duty aboard the battleship USS *Pennsylvania*, Conner was transferred to the USS *New Hampshire*, assigned to transatlantic convoy duty. Connor was an electrician first class, who manned the ship's radio and fixed electrical equipment when needed (including going aloft to fix a broken antenna).

Connor's first experience of convoy duty took place in September 1917, when eleven transport ships, one cruiser, two destroyers, and the USS *New Hampshire* convoyed more than twenty thousand American troops across the Atlantic. His diary captures the challenges of naval warfare in the early twentieth century. Communication by radio meant that as his ship sailed farther into the Atlantic, the radio signals from the United States grew weaker. As the *New Hampshire* approached Europe, Connor could contact the naval base in the Azores, which served as an important refueling stop and shore leave destination for American ships and soldiers.

The *New Hampshire* was powered by coal, and Connor relates the tedious, multiday process of "coaling" the ship, both in the Azores and in New York. Through mechanical problems, an Atlantic hurricane, and the outbreak of the

Spanish flu, the *New Hampshire* continued its duty until the Armistice, which Connor notes in his diary entry for November 11, 1918.

Guy Connor returned to his home in Indiana after the war; in July 1919, he married his sweetheart Alice Scott (also mentioned in the diary, since her letters to him arrived in batches only when his ship reached the US shore). The Connors lived in Auburn, Indiana, where Guy worked as a coremaker in a foundry. Connor was forty-seven years old when he was issued his World War II draft card, although there is no record that he was called up for duty. Connor died in December 1968.[2]

Maude Essig, born near Elkhart, Indiana, in 1884, served as an American Red Cross nurse during World War I. In 1919, after her return home, she compiled an account of her experiences based on letters and a diary; the memoir was not found until her death at age ninety-six in September 1981.

Essig left New York City on a crowded transport in December 1917. Her unit of nurses, recruited from central Indiana, was bound for the French resort town of Contrexéville, which had been designated as a base hospital. Several large buildings were assigned to the hospital's use, but Essig and her colleagues arrived to find their workplaces filthy and in poor condition. Nurses spent weeks cleaning, setting up equipment, and hauling water in cans up flights of stairs, as the water pipes had burst in the freezing weather.

Essig worked at a base hospital, which was intended to be removed from the battlefield. Wounded soldiers were first treated at field aid stations and then were supposed to be moved to field hospitals and thence to evacuation hospitals. Complex surgeries and long-term care would take place at the base hospital. But by spring 1918, Base Hospital 32 was receiving soldiers directly from the front; after the Second Battle of the Marne that summer and the Allied Meuse-Argonne offensive, the hospital was overwhelmed with casualties.

Of one day in late July, Essig wrote: "Our patients are coming directly from The Front and they say it is terrible—lying there waiting for help to come—All come in awful condition—no previous care has been given to their wounds—It takes a lot of soaking to clean their wounds, dried blood, filth and dirt and lice." Essig and her colleagues became accustomed to nursing soldiers who had been gassed—60 percent of the hospital's patients had been injured by gas, and their lungs and respiratory systems often barely functioned. Many soldiers had serious head injuries, had lost limbs or eyesight. By autumn, the Spanish flu sickened nurses, doctors, and patients alike. It was mid-January 1919, two months after the Armistice, when the hospital discharged its last patients; the USS *America*, carrying Essig and many of the other Base Hospital 32 nurses, along with one thousand injured soldiers, docked in New Jersey on March 13.

After the war, Essig worked at hospitals in Indiana and Illinois as a director of nursing and as a hospital administrator throughout a long career. She retired to live at a veterans center in 1952.

Essig, like so many other nurses who wrote about their wartime experiences, spent little, if any, time complaining about the conditions in which she worked. Comparatively few accounts by Red Cross nurses have revealed the condescension that professional nurses often faced from male doctors and commanding officers. In contrast, many soldiers were less circumspect in writing about their treatment by, and general disdain for, officers. One of those men was Kenneth Gearhart Baker, who, long after the war, began to write his memoirs. Baker's writing was unfinished when he died in 1984 at age ninety-two.

Private Kenneth Baker was a member of the Signal Corps and part of the Army's Thirty-Second Division in World War I. In a distinctive voice, Baker begins by recounting his training at Camp Douglas, Wisconsin: "After having been in camp all of half an hour we were lined up again and my name was called and I was advised that I was on guard duty. That was what you got for having a name that started with a letter at the first of the alphabet, B for instance. Later we decided the reason for this was that most sergeants had never learned their 'letters' in school beyond C, so each day in making up details they always started with A and rarely got beyond C." After Baker and the rest of his company arrived in England, on their way to France, Baker was left behind in the hospital with a throat infection. He endured weeks of duty as a "casual," which he pithily described as "just another way of saying you are going to get the dirty end of a lot of work details."

When Baker finally caught up to his company in France, he went to work installing telephones at battalion and company headquarters in the field and was also tasked with laying and maintaining the lines between those headquarters. Baker describes crawling across fields in all kinds of weather and at all times of the night to replace circuits and relay bales of telephone wire. He writes of following wires that ran under the bodies of dead soldiers and lying flat when machine-gun fire and shells went over and around him.

The technology of telephone communication in World War I was also hampered by the fact that artillery pieces were often pulled by horses and mules. Telephone wires caught on horseshoes and tangled around animals' legs. Baker found one of his lines cut "into six inch pieces" by French soldiers trying to untangle their horses and the axles of their wagons.

Kenneth Baker returned home after the war to attend Purdue University and earn a degree in electrical engineering. He worked for the Wagner Electric Company in Indianapolis and also served in World War II, working in base supply for the Army Air Forces—this time as an officer.

The war memoir of another engineer begins the section of this volume devoted to World War II. Bernard Rice had retired from a career as a chemical engineer when he decided to write an account of his war experience as a combat medic. As a young man, he had fallen in love with flying and dreamed of joining the war as a navigator or a pilot. But Rice was drafted into the Eighty-Second Armored Medical Battalion of the Army's Twelfth Armored Division and became, in his words, "a pill roller."

Rice and the Eighty-Second Medical Battalion first saw action at Herrlisheim in January 1945. The Twelfth Division sustained massive casualties as they engaged with German troops trying to retake Strasbourg. Rice recalled that "the Hell of Herrlisheim lasted eight days before troops from the 36th Infantry Division relieved us. In memory, everything runs together, but [there] are incidents I cannot forget." One night, Rice and the aid station's surgeon tried to treat simultaneously a lieutenant whose arm had been blown off and a soldier with "so many holes" in his belly that Rice feared he would die at any moment. Instead, as they worked on the young soldier, the lieutenant, whose shoulder had been treated and bandaged, dropped dead behind them. "At Herrlisheim," Rice wrote, "hell and health met at the hands of the combat medic and were forever after united."

In March 1944, the Eighty-Second Medical Battalion became part of George Patton's Third Army and their drive into Germany. Rice writes of crossing the Rhine on a pontoon bridge and the dangers of being part of a reconnaissance squadron that often traveled miles ahead of the main body of troops.

Then "on April 26," Rice remembered, "strange people wearing ragged clothing began straggling to the 12th Division's rear." As Rice would soon learn, they had escaped one of Dachau's "satellite" concentration camps as German troops retreated. "Even our bloodiest battle," Rice wrote, "could not prepare us for Dachau." Rice still vividly recalled piles of charred bodies and also remembered, with palpable anger, the "good German" civilians who were brought to the camp to view the dead, all the while protesting their ignorance of what had gone on there.

Rice remained on duty in occupied Germany until February 1945. He reunited with his wife in California the next month, and they returned to Indiana. He did not attend a reunion of the Eighty-Second until 1980. He did not complete his memoir until 1997, noting that "for the first thirty-five years after the war, I tried desperately to forget. I was only partially successful; there was much that refused to be forgotten." Rice died in February 2014 at the age of ninety-one.

World War II was also fought behind the front by the Allied intelligence services. Bloomington, Indiana, native Lawrence B. McFaddin enlisted during his junior year at Indiana University and became a member of the Office of Strategic Service (OSS).[3] McFaddin was first stationed in England and later in Germany. In October 1944, he and three of his friends embarked on a seven-day furlough. They took in the sights in London and then boarded a train for northern Scotland. The four men stayed at a lodge in the Cairngorm mountains.[4] They hiked, rested, and ate. McFaddin wrote of the first afternoon: "When we went down [to the farm's dining room] there were milk and gingerbread waiting for us—real milk—that wonderful cow!" He wrote as a young man eager for adventure but also longing for peacetime and home: "It was a wonderful feeling of being completely away and yet closer to the things I consider priceless than I had felt for weeks."

McFaddin's second letter described his time in St. Ives, an English seaside resort in Cornwall, during an eight-day furlough in May 1945. During a week of what he described as "contented laziness," he enjoyed afternoon tea each day and sat on the beach under "a glorious English sun." Lulled by the warmth of the sand—and perhaps unaware of the water temperature on an English spring day—McFaddin ran into St. Ives Bay one afternoon and "emerged, dripping, and a ghastly shade of blue."

The two letters somehow made their way to the editor of the *IMH*, who published them in the journal's September 1945 issue with a somewhat apologetic editor's note: "Our average reader may question the propriety of printing these two little gems in a historical magazine, though surely no one would question the desirability of having them in print."

During the same year in which McFaddin traveled to Cornwall and his letters were published in the *IMH*, he met Marian Shotter, a London native, who worked at Bletchley Park as a code breaker. The two wrote to each other for five years after the war ended and McFaddin had returned to the United States. They married in 1950; McFaddin became the director of development for the National Bureau of Economic Research. He died in 2009. More than seven decades after they were written, McFaddin's letters give a glimpse into the wartime experiences of a young Hoosier soldier discovering a world beyond Indiana while longing for home.[5]

This volume concludes with a look at the Hoosier home front. Despite significant increases in US military spending under the 1937 Protective Mobilization Plan, the federal government was forced to begin a massive mobilization effort after President Franklin D. Roosevelt declared war in December 1941. A major part of that effort was the manufacture of ordnance. According to Brig. Gen. James Norell, chief of military history for the US Army, "the munitions manufactured by and for the Army's Ordnance Department during

World War II exceeded the output of all the other technical services of the Army combined."[6]

During the course of the war, seventy-two ordnance plants were built across the country. In 1941, the federal government opened the Kingsbury Ordnance Plant in LaPorte County in northern Indiana. The complex covered twenty square miles, with eighty miles of surrounding railroad track, so that railcars could bring in all the necessary materials. Workers filled bullet shells, artillery shells, and bomb shells with explosive materials and added the fuses and detonators; then the ordnance was shipped out. At the height of production, the plant employed twenty thousand workers. Over the time that Kingsbury was in production, the female workforce rose from one-third of the total to 45 percent.

Wartime factories needed women workers, and many women were eager to sign up, not only for the satisfaction of working for their country and the war effort but for the good wages. Like all other parts of US society, however, the plant was segregated. Although Kingsbury had to bring in all of its workers from surrounding towns and rural areas, it recruited only a comparatively small, set number of African Americans. Two of the nine production lines were staffed by black women; the remaining seven were staffed by only white women. Black women who applied and were qualified for office jobs were offered janitorial work. Every position in the plant was coded either male or female, as well as black or white. African American women who worked at Kingsbury took their breaks and lunches in segregated rooms, used segregated bathrooms, and were assigned to separate air raid shelters. When housing was finally built near the plant, only white families were allowed to live there.

In response to such overt discrimination, African Americans wrote to the president's Fair Employment Practices Committee (FEPC), a federal agency created during the war, seeking the opportunity to be hired and allowed to do the work they were qualified for. Many black women wrote directly to President Roosevelt and to Eleanor Roosevelt, believing that the president and first lady were sympathetic to their plight. Women described their past work experiences and their skills; they told the Roosevelts about husbands and family members serving in the military; and they asked for fair treatment and equal employment. Pernellia Hull, in a February 1942 letter to the president preserved in the National Archives, ended by describing herself as "a law abiding citizen with our country at heart and our boys on the front."

—◊—

Hoosier men and women have served with bravery and distinction in wartime since the Indiana Territory became a state in 1816. In the twentieth century, tens of thousands of Hoosiers served on the battlefield, behind the lines, and on the home front. The articles that follow offer just a few of their stories.

NOTES

1. Connor McBride, "Indiana in World War One," United States World War One Centennial Commission (website), accessed October 13, 2020, https://www .worldwar1centennial.org/index.php/indiana-wwi-centennial-home.html.

2. This information does not appear in the original article. World War II Draft Card, 1930 and 1940 U.S. Censuses, ancestry.com.

3. In the original 1945 article, the author was listed as Lawrence C. McFaddin. The middle initial was corrected in the journal's index.

4. McFaddin called the property Lynchurn farm. The house, recently restored, is now Sky Mountain Lodge and is once again open to tourists. Their website includes McFaddin's 1944 description.

5. No information has been found in *IMH* files as to how editor John D. Barnhart obtained the letters. Postwar information is taken from "Marian Shotter McFaddin," *Lake Placid News*, December 10, 2015.

6. Foreword, Harry C. Thomson and Lida Mayo, *United States Army in World War II: The Technical Services: The Ordnance Department: Procurement and Supply* (Washington, DC, 1991).

ONE

Pride, Patriotism, and the Press

The Evolving True Story of the First American Shot of World War I

GRETA A. FISHER AND LAUREN E. KUNTZMAN

ON OCTOBER 23, 1917, ALEX Arch from South Bend, Indiana, a member of the 6th Field Artillery, Battery C, fired the first American shot of World War I. Everyone involved was aware of the historical importance of the event, which announced that the United States was officially in action at the front and also stood as the first action by an American force in a European war.

As news of the first shot spread, the press routinely misreported details of the story, sometimes through lack of understanding, sometimes willfully as brazen untruths. The U.S. government, when in a position to clarify the facts, instead chose either to deny any knowledge of the details or to manipulate the facts to suit its own agenda. With more than a century elapsed since the "first shot," it has become clear that many factors—including censorship, pride, patriotism, profit, and propaganda—influenced the reporting and recording of the historic event. As a result, every aspect of the story—including the date, the location, the name of the unit, and the name and description of the man who pulled the lanyard—would appear incorrectly in news across the United States for years and decades to come.

The basic facts of the story are these:

Artillery units were the first American troops on the ground in France and were strategically placed with French units in quiet sectors for training. Near the front, a small group of Americans, mostly officers, were frantic to fire the first shot. Despite lacking literal horsepower, a dozen men worked through the night of October 22, 1917, at the invitation of their captain, Idus McLendon, pulling an artillery piece through a muddy valley and into an abandoned French gun pit. "It was the hardest, nastiest, most back-breaking toil I had ever seen," McLendon later wrote.[1] He managed to persuade the reluctant French officer in charge to let the Americans fire. Unable to master the foreign paperwork required to be issued ammunition, they borrowed twenty-four shells from a French unit and, with a French officer present to record the official time, at 6:05:10 a.m., they fired towards the German positions. U.S. Army officials, understandably, did not want to publish the details of their troop deployments; the only information that made it through the censors to the American public was when the shot had been fired and the fact that a "Red headed sergeant" had pulled the lanyard.[2] When asked where he was from, he had answered, "'South Bend, Indiana and Proud of it!'"[3]

Censorship was the first factor to impact the story's accuracy, making the date and time of the shot the first details to be misreported. Journalists on the ground in Europe wrote in terms of "yesterday" and "last night," but the censors' process delayed the story a few days. Thus initial reports credited the date as October 27, 1917.[4] Many newspapers also confused minutes and seconds, publishing the time as 6:10, although the *Buffalo Enquirer* published it as 6:30.[5]

The identity of the sergeant became the next disputed detail. South Bend, reportedly the sergeant's home, became ground zero for the news coverage. On October 31, 1917, the *South Bend Tribune* reported: "First Shell is Fired by Red Headed Gunner from South Bend"; its source was an Associated Press correspondent on-site with the troops.[6] Two days later, the *Tribune* issued a public call: "If you think your friend has the honor of being the most distinguished artillery sergeant in the world, send in his name."[7]

Motivated by pride and patriotism—and in the absence of facts—people nationwide suggested their son, friend, or neighbor. Everyone seemed to know a soldier with at least one of the attributes listed, and names flew into newspapers from coast to coast. Frederick Wadell had red hair but was still in the States. W. Eaton was an artillery sergeant but wasn't red-headed.[8]

Reporters desperate for the name attempted to impress upon Secretary of War Newton Baker Jr. that this was a matter of historic importance. Baker remained unmoved, claiming he didn't know: "I don't believe the matter is that important."[9] On November 19, almost a month after the fact, a North Carolina newspaper cited the International News Service: "SOUTH BEND, Ind., Nov. 19—The red-headed sergeant who fired America's first shot against Germany in France, has been identified almost to a certainty as John H. Pittman, who enlisted last February."[10] The *South Bend News-Times* agreed, printing a large photo of Pittman with the caption, "Here's Sergeant Who Fired First Shot."[11]

Corporate pride proved as powerful a motivator as personal pride. The *News-Times* eagerly pointed out that Pittman had worked as one of their paper boys. Even as other contenders continued to emerge, The Oliver Chilled Plow Works of South Bend published Pittman's photo in their December *Bulletin* and proudly noted: "John Howard Pittman was a resident of South Bend and an employee of the Oliver Chilled Plow Works."[12]

South Bend's pride in its hometown hero, despite the mystery of his identity, was also on display. The sergeant's reported reply that he hailed from "South Bend, and Proud of It!" was taken up by many local leaders and businessmen. In its November 1917 issue, *South Bend Today*, a publication of the local Chamber of Commerce, called for the phrase to become the city's new catchphrase. In the December issue, an article titled "New Slogan for South Bend" pointed out that the phrase was now being widely adopted, including by the local *News-Times*. [13]

Profit became another factor in reporting the story. Although each wanted an exclusive scoop, newspapers happily sensationalized the mystery to sell papers; as competing claimants emerged, editors accused each other of altering the facts for their own gain. Every time a new contender emerged—by December, the list included local boys F. E. Logan and Leo Bauer, Berkley native Stanley F. Bryan, and Chicagoan Aloysius Hede—papers could publish new articles and sell more copies.

On January 8, the *Indianapolis News* dropped a bombshell: "Alex Arch is Believed to be gunner who fired first shot: only South Bend man in American battery which officers report was first to go into action against Germans somewhere in France."[14] The story was reported from a Washington source, likely Louis Ludlow, a Hoosier congressman and reporter, who was positioned to get to the heart of the matter. He had followed a simple set of evidence: The man had said he was from South Bend; it was confirmed that the 6th Field Artillery had fired the shot; Arch was the only South Bend native in that unit.

In a January 11 article, the *South Bend News-Times* editors reported "an open contest" between their man Pittman and the new contender. They noted that Arch had a father and sister on the home front, neither of whom had heard such a claim. Pittman was described as "a modest chap, not much given to boasting about himself or his doings."[15]

On the same day, the *Chicago Tribune* added another detail in Arch's favor, "a letter written by Arch to his fiancee, Miss Volma [Velma, Wilma] Szabo."[16] Alex had written to her on November 25th with a few details of the event, including the claim that he had fired the first shot: "I'm up on the firing line now and sent the first shot over to the Germans."[17] The letter was censored, did not arrive until December 15, and Miss Szabo had been unwilling to reveal her

HERE'S SERGEANT WHO FIRED FIRST SHOT

John Howard Pittman, this city's red headed sergeant who fired the first American gun at the Germans on the western front in France. Pittman was a former News-Times carrier and the son of Mrs. Albert Cole, 418 N. Walnut st. He enlisted at the local recruiting office last February. He was stationed at Fort Bliss, Tex., for a short time and was among the first contingent of United States soldiers that was sent to France. He is a member of the field artillery.

Figure 1.1 Speculation about the identity of the soldier who fired the first American shot led to several misidentifications. After South Bend, Indiana, newspapers carried the story that a redheaded sergeant from their city was the unidentified man, competing papers put forth different candidates. The *South Bend News-Times* promoted John Howard Pittman, identified as "a former News-Times carrier." Reprinted from *South Bend News-Times*, November 19, 1917.

private correspondence until stories broke with Arch's name in the headline in early January.

At this point, newspapers had correctly identified and credited Alex Arch, but those at the very highest levels of the military and government—General John J. Pershing and the Committee for Public Information (CPI)—pushed the narrative of the "First Shot" and the public's attention in a different direction.

General Pershing, commander of the American Expeditionary Forces, was more than just a military tactician. As his war diary shows, he was heavily invested in managing the public perception of the war. While in Europe, he regularly met with reporters, and his decision-making was often directly influenced by how he thought the American public would react.[18] Pershing was also involved in the financing of the war through the sale of war bonds. The first several attempts at bond sales, called Liberty Loans, were privately run and not very successful. Early in the war, the public was not committed to getting involved in European affairs in the first place, let alone funding the effort. Recognizing the need for a government entity to centralize information dispersal, promote the Liberty Loans, and generally influence public opinion to support the war effort, President Woodrow Wilson created the Committee for Public Information. Under the direction of journalist George Creel, the CPI enlisted the best talent for its departments of News, Films, Advertising and Pictorial Publicity. It issued a daily *Bulletin*, filled with "official" versions of events, and it acted as a clearinghouse for most of the media coverage of the war. Historian Alan Axelrod notes that "the Committee's Picture Division became virtually the only source of war photographs seen by the American people. These were fed to newspapers and magazines at the rate of some seven hundred different images a day."[19]

In early 1918, Pershing visited a group of convalescing soldiers. One soldier impressed the general when he said that "he hoped the war was not entirely finished for him, as he still might render service as a press censor or something." This inspired Pershing, who decided that recuperating soldiers could be useful in promoting the Liberty Loans.[20] Fifty men, intended to represent a broad cross-section of the military, were interviewed and chosen to go on tour in the U.S.: "In this Liberty Loan contingent were artillerymen, infantrymen, machine gunners and signal corps men, representing every section of the United States from New York to San Francisco."[21] They were also chosen for their compelling stories, such as that of Sergeant Eugene McNiff and Corporal Milo Plant, who participated in a daring raid into German territory.[22] Another member of the group was a young corporal, Osborne De Varila, who had played a small role on the first firing crew. It is unclear whether his importance was self-inflated or invented by the CPI, but the prospect of being sent home acted as a strong incentive to dramatize his story.[23] He would later state, "I was picked to go because I had fired the First Shot for Uncle Sam in the war."[24] Before the ship left Europe—with the goal of promoting Liberty Loans—the Committee was promoting De Varila across the United States as the man who had fired the "First Shot," making him an instant celebrity.

At this point, the story of the first shot became a tool of the military and government. When De Varila and the wounded soldiers arrived in Philadelphia on April 29, 1918, the frenzy began: "Hysterical women tried to kiss him; strong men . . . grasped him by the hand, and for fully half an hour after his comrades had left for their hotel he was hemmed in by a crowd, frenzied by enthusiasm that would only be satisfied with a touch of his hand, a smile from his ruddy, blushing face."[25]

De Varila was booked to appear at events from coast to coast, since "Creel believed that there was no substitute for a live presentation" and De Varila generated interest (and sold bonds) wherever he went.[26] Creel later detailed the Committee's work selling Liberty Loans in his book, *How We Advertised America.*[27]

The Committee produced ghost-written first-person accounts in De Varila's name and used their extensive network to place them in papers nationwide, including the *South Bend News-Times*, which had a vested interest in offering an alternative to the *Tribune*'s champion Alex Arch. The first installment, entitled "I Join the Colors," appeared in late June; the series reeked of professional writing, with lines like, "Fritz didn't like that kind of sauerkraut," or De Varila saying, after being gassed, "I don't take mustard with my meat anymore."[28] The twenty-plus serials were ultimately compiled as a book, which went on sale in the summer of 1918: *The First Shot for Liberty*, published by Philadelphia printer John C. Winston Co.

Who was the real voice of *The First Shot for Liberty*? One possible author was Raymond G. Carroll, who worked for the Philadelphia *Public Ledger*, the newspaper that ran one of the first stories, and who had been in Europe with De Varila's division. He had written other popular articles in series form, and his writing was full of the ethnic slurs and sensationalized descriptions present in De Varila's account.[29] He had even written a magazine article entitled "Our First Shot of the War," which had appeared earlier in the year.[30] We do not know how De Varila felt about being given credit for something he had not done, but at public appearances, he seemed to relish being turned into a hero, and the public ate it up.

De Varila may have been riding high, but his claim riled the members of his former battery, who knew the stories were inaccurate. In September,

Capt. McLendon, De Varila's commanding officer, wrote the Associated Press specifically to clear up any confusion: Alex Arch was the man who had fired the first shot. McLendon referred to De Varila as "the Corporal with the Spanish name" who was "sound asleep in the dug-out when the first shot was dispatched."[31] Sergeant Louis Dominick, who had cut the fuse before the "First Shot," threatened, "If I could only see that guy, it would be hard to tell what I would do with him."[32] Private Joseph B. Napieralski wrote that "it was no red-headed Irishman, but a Hungarian, Arch, my sergeant."[33]

In June, Alex Arch was seriously wounded and, like De Varila, was brought back to the U.S. to recuperate—and sell bonds. De Varila, recovered and now embarrassingly in the way, was sent back to the front in September.[34] As De Varila sailed for Europe, Alex Arch participated in the 4th Liberty Loan campaign, billed as the soldier who "Fired the First Shot" by the same agency that had recently been promoting De Varila. Photographs featuring Arch and Capt. McLendon in front of the cannon, clearly taken nine months earlier at the time of the event, began appearing in the press. Later, photos of Arch restaged in early 1918 appeared as well. The CPI would have been aware of these photographs, distributed by their own Picture Division, but would have suppressed them throughout their De Varila promotional campaign. They had no photos taken at the time of De Varila, of course, because he was not the man responsible.

By necessity, the CPI generated publicity with a different focus for Arch. There was little likelihood of Hungarian-born Alex Arch making charged statements of the kind that had been credited to De Varila. The CPI produced no book and scheduled fewer speaking engagements, possibly because Arch had been more seriously wounded. It would, however, have been awkward booking Arch into the same towns that had heard De Varila only a few months before. It also cannot be overlooked that Arch likely had a significant accent, which would have made him a less appealing speaker. Instead, the CPI mostly relied on large print ads, many featuring his image, including one series billed as the "Alex Arch Victory Drive." "Alex Arch, the South Bend boy who fired the first shot—and the other St. Joseph County boys in service—will want to know how we backed them."[35]

Alex Arch's claim continued to find corroboration over time. In 1918, Floyd Gibbons, one of the reporters embedded with the troops at the time the shot was fired, published his personal account, detailing the name and role of every member of the battery.[36] U.S. Army correspondence, today a matter of public record, indicates the location, date, time, and unit responsible.[37] Capt. McLendon himself published an account, years after the fact, in an article for

The First Shot for Liberty

By Corporal Osborne de Varila
Above all an American Book by an American

Corporal de Varila, the red-headed Irish-American who fired the FIRST SHOT FOR AMERICA in the World War, comes from a heroic family that participated in all our wars from the Revolution down. His book is a human document of a lad who left a preparatory school to be among the first to serve his country and has done so. With many thrills and with frequent flashes of humor, he tells the story from the time of his enlistment in PERSHING'S ARMY to his going aboard ship, of the passage across, with its dangers; the tear-bringing reception by the French people, life in the trenches and daring deeds of our boys on the firing line; the experience of being gassed and life in the hospitals. It is the experience that others of our boys may expect to find.

Cloth.
Illustrated.
252 pages.

Price $1.25 net.
At all booksellers.

THE JOHN C. WINSTON CO.
Publishers
Philadelphia

Figure 1.2 By early 1918, the federal Committee for Public Information had identified Corporal Osborne de Varila as the American soldier who fired the first shot. In April, when he arrived in New York City with other wounded soldiers, the War Department sent him out on an enormously successful war bond tour and ghostwrote newspaper articles and a book bearing his name. Reprinted from *New York Tribune*, June 29, 1918.

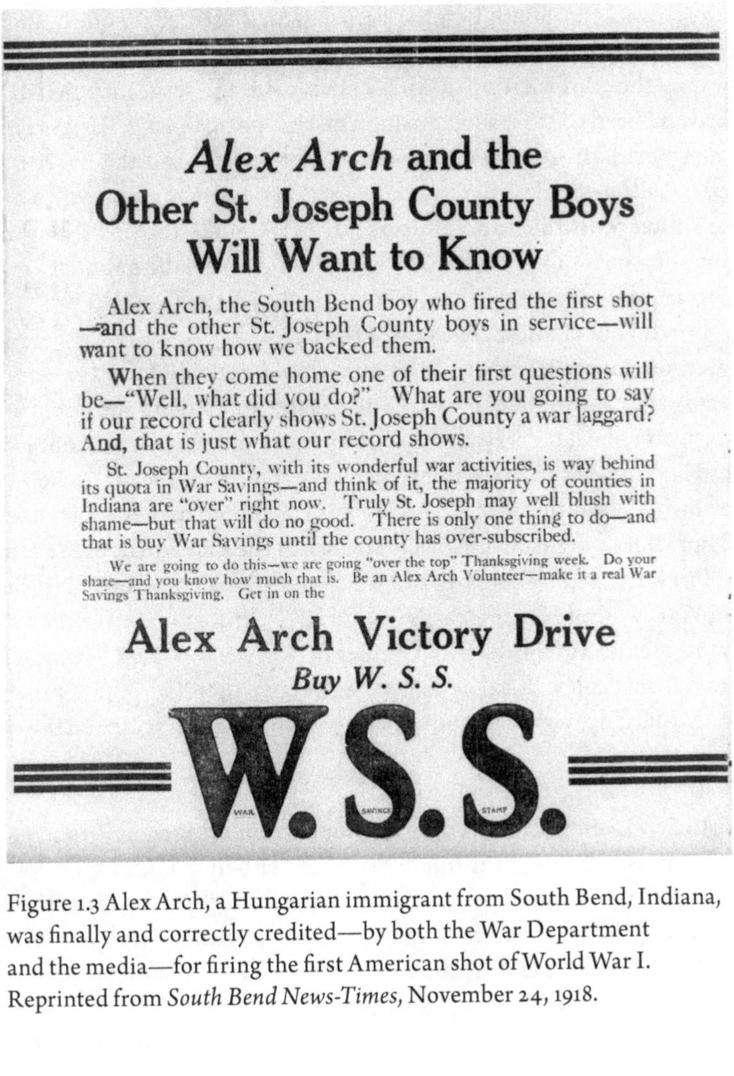

Alex Arch and the Other St. Joseph County Boys Will Want to Know

Alex Arch, the South Bend boy who fired the first shot —and the other St. Joseph County boys in service—will want to know how we backed them.

When they come home one of their first questions will be—"Well, what did you do?" What are you going to say if our record clearly shows St. Joseph County a war laggard? And, that is just what our record shows.

St. Joseph County, with its wonderful war activities, is way behind its quota in War Savings—and think of it, the majority of counties in Indiana are "over" right now. Truly St. Joseph may well blush with shame—but that will do no good. There is only one thing to do—and that is buy War Savings until the county has over-subscribed.

We are going to do this—we are going "over the top" Thanksgiving week. Do your share—and you know how much that is. Be an Alex Arch Volunteer—make it a real War Savings Thanksgiving. Get in on the

Alex Arch Victory Drive

Buy W. S. S.

W.S.S.

Figure 1.3 Alex Arch, a Hungarian immigrant from South Bend, Indiana, was finally and correctly credited—by both the War Department and the media—for firing the first American shot of World War I. Reprinted from *South Bend News-Times*, November 24, 1918.

the American Legion.[38] Notably, Gibbons's account includes De Varila, but McLendon omits his name. The artillery piece became a testament. The gun, on display today in the West Point Large Weapons Gallery, includes writing on its shield: "First Shot at Hun," "Sgt. Arch, Chief of Section," and "Cpl. Braley, Gunner."

Arch ultimately got the recognition he deserved. He received one of the first shell casings, still kept by the family today. At the end of the war, he marched in a ticker-tape parade alongside his gun and shook the hands of cabinet members and congressmen.[39] South Bend, Indiana, named a street after him, and he appears as a celebrity in local history books.

Despite the confirmation of Arch's position as the sergeant who pulled the lanyard and fired the first shot, misinformation persisted. De Varila's *First Shot for Liberty* had already been distributed nationwide, and the publisher continued to sell the book. Even today, researchers cite it as a source.[40] De Varila himself, after returning to action, was quickly wounded again by mustard gas. He died in a hospital in 1920, and his death did not make national news. His hometown obituary stated that he "personally set the fuse that fired the first shot," but did not claim that he pulled the lanyard.[41]

Later, one other member of the unit would contribute to the confusion. Robert Braley was immediately credited as the gunner, but the public was not always aware of what every member of a battery did. As one account clarified, Braley "laid the piece," but artillerymen accept that it is the man who pulls the lanyard who "Fires the Shot."[42] Braley was celebrated for his actual role at the time, but later in life enjoyed local publicity in the Cincinnati area as the man who "Fired the First Shot." As the *Cincinnati Enquirer* wrote, "He 'Started' World War . . . And Never Heard Last Of It!"[43] Unfortunately, as late as 1976, upon the occasion of the death of Gunner Braley, the *New York Times* picked up the story from Braley's local newspaper and stated that "Corporal Braley jerked the lanyard." Once again, the power of a good news story trumped the truth.[44]

Historical truth always needs to answer to competing agendas and points of view as it passes through the filter of time. After being processed through the demands of censorship, pride, patriotism, profit, and propaganda, the simple facts of the "First Shot," perhaps unexpectedly, eventually won out. Alex Arch is widely celebrated today as the hero who fired the "First American Shot of World War I."[45] As we contemplate a modern era of "fake news," it is important to remember that the struggle to reveal the truth behind a story has always been fraught with obstacles.

GRETA A. FISHER, BA, MFA, is a local and family history librarian at the St. Joseph County Library in South Bend, Indiana. She specializes in Central European immigrants to the Midwest. She is particularly interested in placing family stories in their historical context.

LAUREN E. KUNTZMAN, MA, MLIS, is the director of the Family History & Learning Center at Medina County District Library in Ohio. Her research interests include French genealogy, tracking criminal ancestors, and exploring the past through historic newspapers.

NOTES

This article appeared in volume 115, no. 1 (March 2019).

1. Idus R. McLendon, "The First Shot," *American Legion Monthly*, October 1931, p. 59.

2. "South Bend Boy Fires First Shot: Red Headed Sergeant Pulled Lanyard Which Sent Shell Into Germans," *South Bend News-Times*, October 31, 1917, p. 4.

3. "South Bend, Ind. and Proud of It!" *South Bend News-Times*, November 25, 1917, p. 12.

4. Floyd Gibbons, "U.S. Guns Bombard Enemy, Shells Now Fall About Foe Trenches: Gibbons Tells of Beginning of Real War," *Chicago Sunday Tribune*, October 28, 1917, p. 1.

5. Raymond G. Carroll, "America's First Shot Against the Hun in War for World Freedom; This Document Tells What Happened at 6:30 a.m., Oct. 23, 1917," *Buffalo Enquirer*, January 5, 1918, p. 5.

6. "Americans in Trenches are Fighting Mud," *South Bend Tribune*, October 31, 1917, p. 1.

7. "Who Is Sergeant? Friends of Two Men Fail to Establish His Identity," *South Bend Tribune*, November 2, 1917, p. 6.

8. Ibid.

9. "Baker Does Not Know Firer of First Cannon: Identity of Red Haired Gunner from South Bend Unrevealed," *South Bend Tribune*, January 9, 1918, p. 2.

10. "A Red-Headed Sergeant Fired the First Shell," *Gastonia* (North Carolina) *Gazette*, November 19, 1917, p. 2.

11. "Here's Sergeant Who Fired First Shot," *South Bend News-Times*, November 19, 1917, p. 1.

12. "An Oliver Man Fired the First Shot," *The Oliver Bulletin*, December 1917, p. 14, St. Joseph County Public Library, South Bend, Indiana.

13. *South Bend Today* continued to feature the phrase on its cover, its title page, or at the bottom of interior pages throughout 1918 and into 1919, after the war had ended.

14. "Alex Arch is Believed to be Gunner Who Fired First Shot," *Indianapolis News*, January 8, 1918, p. 11.

15. "Who Fired That First Shot in France Anyway? Now Comes Alex Arch Claiming the Honor," *South Bend News-Times*, January 11, 1918.

16. "Fired First Shot," *Chicago Tribune*, January 11, 1918.

17. "Sergt. Alex L. Arch Fires First U.S. Shot," *South Bend Tribune*, January 10, 1918, p. 1.

18. John L. Pershing, John J. Pershing Papers: Diaries, Notebooks, and Address Books, 1882–1925; Diaries; Set 1; 1917, May 7–1918, Sept. 1, Manuscript/ Mixed Material, Library of Congress, online at https://www.loc.gov/item /mss35949003.

19. Alan Axelrod, *Selling the Great War: The Making of American Propaganda* (New York, 2009), 147.

20. Pershing's diaries indicate that he made hospital visits on only four dates in the first half of 1918. The entry of March 6, from the hospital at Baccarat, mentioning Lieut. Merrill's statement, is the single instance in the diary where he mentions a soldier below the command level. Pershing notes that Merrill had lost his leg. Osborne De Varila also mentions a soldier he met at the hospital who had lost his leg and swore he would get back in the fight.

21. Osborne De Varila, *The First Shot for Liberty: The Story of an American Who Went Over with the First Expeditionary Force and Served his Country at the Front* (Philadelphia, Pa., 1918), 212.

22. Ibid., 186.

23. George Creel, *Complete Report of the Chairman of the Committee on Public Information* (Washington, D.C., 1920). The CPI invested heavily in managing this story, and George Creel proudly mentions the "Pershing Veterans" as one of the Speaking Division's most successful tours.

24. De Varila, *The First Shot for Liberty*, 213.

25. "American Heroes Appeal to Citizens to Buy More Bonds," *Philadelphia Inquirer*, April 30, 1918, p. 1.

26. Axelrod, *Selling the Great War*, 157.

27. George Creel, *How We Advertised America: The First Telling of the Amazing Story of the Committee on Public Information that Carried the Gospel of Americanism to Every Corner of the Globe* (New York, 1920).

28. "Grants Pass Boy Describes First Shot at Boche," *Oregon Daily Journal*, June 30, 1918, p. 15.

29. In 1917, the Ledger advertised Carroll's series "The Big Hike," in which he recounted his experiences with the troops as they went from the Mexican border to France.

30. "First Shot of the War" advertisement, *Evening* (Pennsylvania) *Public Ledger*, January 5, 1918, p. 7.

31. "An Austro-Hungarian Fired First Yank Shot," *Macon* (Missouri) *Republican*, October 11, 1918, p. 3.

32. "Soldier Boy from Helena Among First in the Firing," *Newberry* (South Carolina) *Weekly Herald*, February 14, 1919, p. 5.

33. Ultimately, the red-headed discrepancy would be cleared up. U.S. Artillerymen wore a red hat cord, and red-headed was a slang term in use by the soldiers. It had never referred to the color of his hair. "Hoosier Gunner Who

Fired First Shot Wounded: Sergt. Alex L. Arch, South Bend Hero, Sent Opening U.S. Shell Against Huns," *Indianapolis Star*, June 10, 1918, p. 1.

34. "U.S., Army Transport Service, Passenger Lists, 1910–1939," s.v. "Osborne De Varila," image 166, digital image available online at www.ancestry.com.

35. *South Bend News-Times*, November 24, 1918, p. 10.

36. Floyd Gibbons, *And They Thought We Wouldn't Fight* (New York, 1918), 156–57.

37. Report of John R. Starkey, Major, 6th Field Artillery, Oct. 23, 1917, 1st Division War Diary, 1st Battalion, 6th Field Artillery, A.E.F., *United States Army in the World War, 1917–1919*, vol. 3, *Training and Use of American Units with the British and French* (Washington, D.C., 1948), 451.

38. McLendon, "The First Shot," p. 18.

39. *New York Tribune*, September 14, 1919, p. 3.

40. See, for example, David R. Woodward, *The American Army and the First World War* (Cambridge, U.K., 2013).

41. "American That Fired First Shot in War Dead," *Red Bluff* (California) *Daily News*, June 9, 1920, p. 4.

42. Gibbons, *And They Thought We Wouldn't Fight*, 157.

43. *Cincinnati Enquirer*, October 24, 1957, p. 15.

44. "Robert Braley, 80, Credited With First U.S. Shot in 1917," *New York Times*, March 22, 1976.

45. "America's 'First Shot' in the War," Library of Congress: Echoes of the Great War, May 11, 2018, https://www.loc.gov/exhibitions/world-war-i-american -experiences/about-this-exhibition/over-there/industrialized-warfare/americas -first-shot-in-the-war/.

TWO

On Convoy Duty in World War I

The Diary of Hoosier Guy Connor

EDITED BY JEFFREY L. PATRICK

DURING WORLD WAR I THE United States Navy's primary role was the safe transport of troops and supplies to the war in Europe rather than classic engagements with enemy ships on the high seas. This vital mission guaranteed the arrival of over two million American troops to the front lines, along with tons of supplies to support them, in the short nineteen-month period of active United States involvement in the war. The navy could proudly claim that no American troop transport was lost to enemy submarines while eastbound to Europe. "For this splendid record," wrote one report, "the Navy, which armed, manned, and convoyed the troop transports, deserves the highest commendation."[1]

Some 503,000 enlisted men and 32,000 officers were serving in the American Navy at the time of the November 1918 armistice.[2] One of these enlisted sailors who helped protect the flow of American troops and supplies to the Allies was Guy Burrell Connor, a resident of Cromwell, Indiana.[3] His diary, written during the last year of the war, reflects the daily life, concerns, and observations of an average battleship sailor risking his life escorting ships in these Atlantic crossings. Connor wrote of two convoy missions he participated in, noting the daily happenings on board his ships, his brief stop in the Azores with descriptions of the people and scenery, and the persistent concerns of sailors, such as mail, liberty, and pay. Although much has been written about the combat experiences of American soldiers in France during the war, the navy has received far less attention due to its less glamorous but indispensable role in the conflict. Connor's diary is a brief but enlightening glimpse into the life of the American sailor during the "Great War."

What follows are the surviving entries of Connor's diary.[4] Some passages have been deleted, such as Connor's careful detailing of his ship's coordinates while at sea. Apparently several pages are missing, so the entries begin abruptly in July 1918, and quickly move to the start of his first convoy duty in September of that year.

JULY, 1918[5]

Got back to the Pennsylvania[6] at the Brooklyn Navy Yard July 17th after having the best leave and I certainly did hate to get back. Everything is in terrible shape and things are being rushed so as to get through before time is up. Have been trying to get transferred to a landwire job but guess it won't go through. Theres too many men in the radio force on the Pennsy and I want to get where I can have more of an opportunity to do something. Left Navy Yard July 15th and landed at Base Two the next day.[7] All we do is stay at this place and I wish I could get somewhere. We passed a ship on the trip down that was torpedoed shortly after.

SEPT. 6TH -

At 8:30 AM I was transferred to the New Hampshire[8] with W.W. Walsh and glad to get away from the Pennsy.[9] The N.H. is going into some sort of active service for they are getting a new Radio Gunner two chiefs and myself and Walsh. We left Yorktown for New York at 4 pm Sept 6th not knowing if our final destination was Russia, Japan or just out on convoy duty. We have stores enough for several months and coal for a month so I guess we are going somewhere. Some of the crews living compartments are filled with coal.[10] At 4 pm Sunday Sept 15 we left New York Harbor and when outside we picked up a convoy of seven transports. The cruiser "Pueblo" destroyers "St Louis" Stribling and Stringham are also in the escort.[11] After proceeding on a south by southeast course we met a detachment from Hampton Roads and now we have eleven transports, one cruiser, two destroyers and a battleship with us. The St. Louis left shortly after delivering the Hampton Roads detachment. The transports are the = Pocahontas, Martha Washington, Powhatan, Aeolus, Finland, Henderson, Koenigen Der Nederlanden, Calamares, French SS Patria, British SS Ulna and British (Anglo-Russian) Kursk.[12] Theres about twenty thousand or more men in this bunch. We have been traveling just a week now, taking a course direct toward the Azores Islands and at the present time (Sept 22nd) we are just entering the war zone. Here is a schedule of our position and time, which shows what course and speed we are making. The time is Greenwich Mean Time.

Figure 2.1 The USS *New Hampshire*, a Connecticut-class battleship launched in 1906. In September 1918, Indiana native Guy Burrell Connor transferred on board to serve as one of the ship's radio operators during its troop convoy missions. Courtesy Library of Congress Prints and Photographs Division.

SEPT. 21ST 1918. . . .

Last night I picked up all of Washingtons arc and spark schedules but they were very weak. I have been standing my watches on the bridge until some of the new men missed a few messages and now I'm in the main radio but I'd rather be on the bridge where theres plenty of air. In the day the uniform is white pants and undershirts and at night blues and watch caps. We are routed out about four a.m. to man our general quarter stations for thats the time the subs like to attack. About two days out, the Finland broke down and had to drop behind while she repaired her port and starboard engines. We called the St Louis to stay with them and we continued. They caught us about thirty hours later. A couple days later the Henderson and Stribling dropped back to fuel the destroyer but they decided to wait until dark. After midnight one night we saw five big transports going back to the U.S.

A submarine stood back a couple miles one day and took a shot at the convoy in hopes of getting at least one ship. We saw the wake of the torpedo headed for the Henderson in time to save them.[13] The Stringham came alongside us three days ago and received sealed orders from the Captain. They left at once and returned last night about nine o'clock. . . .

SEPT. 22ND 1918 . . .

SEPTEMBER 23RD

. . . Have the 4 to 8 am watch this morning.

SEPT. 24–1918.

Have the 8–12 am watch now . . .

Worked hard all day yesterday fixing the buzzer system and putting in a Key Reactance. They have been setting the clocks ahead so much lately that a person has to hurry to keep up with the time. When we start back it will be the other way. I have been picking up lots of stations over here among them are Madrid, Eiffel tower, Horsea, and Nanen, Germany. Also some Italian station.[14] This morning I heard Darein working San Diego (6000 arc).

. . . some Spanish station sending on spark comes in on 2400 and 6000 covering Washingtons schedule completely. We called our naval station in the Azores five times without any results. Also Broadcasted msg. to them on "J" and "M".

SEPT 25TH 1918

Heard stations in Morrocco Spain, England and Germany working last night and also heard British warships working. We are very near the coast of Europe. Last night instead of copying Washington press, I went on arc and copied English press from Horsea and Carnarvon. They send it about twenty eight or thirty per minute and I got four pages in less than forty five minutes. We have been having abandon ship drills today and I also went aloft to fix the antenna. I heard that in the entire convoy there was only seven or eight deaths since we started. One Marine Captain on the Henderson died.[15] Most of the sickness and death is due to Spanish Influenza which is spreading some now. . . .

Reports came down from foretop just now of firing heard off port bow. Four distinct shots heard. I just sent a message to Sigourney and rec'd one from him. He used commercial procedure, I used U.S.N. procedure. Covered 600 on black receiver all during 12–4 pm watch. Heard Cape Finisterre Spain, Alfonso XII and Reina Maria Cristina working all afternoon. About six o'clock p.m. a bunch of destroyers met us and the Pueblo and Stribling started back. We remain with the convoy until we reach longitude 15°. Theres about a dozen destroyers with us now.[16]

SEPTEMBER 26TH

Have the Midwatch . . .

Unable to hear Washn spark this am Lat 4451 Long 1713. Azores too weak to copy. Heard Casablanca (Morrocco) sending war warnings. Copied Italian press from Roma (S. Paolo).

At 12 noon we left our convoy and started back for the United States making 17 knots per hour. As soon as we started back we headed into heavy seas and the ship is sure rolling and pitching now. Was unable to hear any of Washingtons spark schedule account too far away and heavy static. . . .

SEPT 27TH 1918

Last night our port engine broke down and we are making only ten knots with starboard Engine. We would sure be a good target for a torpedo now for we couldn't get out of its way. Scrubbed hammocks today.[17]

SEPT 28TH 1918

Last night we sent a message to Commander US Naval Forces in Azores to be sent to Washington by cable. Both our engines are going badly and we are headed for the Azores to either get coal or get repairs. Just sent another message to Azores. Wasn't able to copy Washington Spark today but by tomorrow I think they will come in better. "Shorty" [Yeakll?] is handing out the dope on the Azores now. Bananas, wheat corn uncivilized and civilized. We may not get back to the states for a long time now. . . .

The "Stribling" Came to us today and is convoying us to the Azores. We only make about ten or eleven knots but should reach the Azores some time tomorrow. I got busy this afternoon scrubbed my hammock a jumper and some underclothes. Have orders from Gunner Recksiek to help Chief Weeden make a few jumper connections tomorrow. Will work at it in the Morning only for I have the twelve to four watch tomorrow . . . Copied Monsanto a Portugese station and ponta Del Gada just a few minutes ago. First picked up Washington Spark to copy at 11 pm tonight Lat 3945 Long 2504W. Must get some press for the crew now. . . .

SEPT 29TH 1918

Arrived at Ponta Del Gada this morning about ten o'clock and the Islands are the most beautiful sight I ever saw. They are like mountains, or rather they are mountains sticking up out of the ocean and far into the clouds. They are green at this time of year and the fields are laid off in even plots that seem plastered on the side of the mountain. Here and there white houses with red roofs dot the country, and the towns are built more compact than ours. The houses are similar to those of the Mexicans and the people are mostly Portugese. Ponta Del Gada has about 25,000 population. I imagine I would like to live here for a while at least and if I did it would be up on the mountain where everything is green and nice. The fields are all fenced off with hedges. In some places theres also a stone wall along the roads with broken glass on top to keep out trespassers. Admiral Dunn is our naval officer here and he is also the power over the people of the city.[18] The "Tonahpaw"[19] an old monitor flys his flag and theres three subs of the K Type here, a couple of our gun boats and a few French sub chasers. The "Marietta" and "Arethusa"[20] are also here. When we moored here there was a big Portugese troop ship in which had been chased in here by subs. It sailed from Africa for Portugal and theres all kinds of people aboard with every kind of a uniform on also a few women. We are a curiosity here for the people hire bum boats and row around the ship to look us over. Some of the natives come out and dive for money in the water. One fellow threw five pennies in and one of the divers got them all before he came up again. I cant say how long we will be here but I can't see why we should stay here for theres no place to get fixed up. All we can do is overhaul our engines. Its wonderful to know that we were about three days in the submarine zone with crippled engines and then got through without hitting a submarine. We copied one SOS today and one Allo. The "Henry George" was gunned and wanted immediate assistance.[21]

SEPTEMBER 30TH 1918.

Still at Ponta Del Gada eating lots of pineapples. Natives come alongside with bumboats full of pineapples and other kinds of fruit to sell. Only one tenth of the crew gets liberty here each day and its only for six hours. Theres plenty to drink here. Every other store has wines and liquors to sell and things are very cheap. They all advertize their wines, private rooms and women. The women of the older families on the island wear a peculiar cape and hood or bonnet. Both are black, the cape reaching their shoe tops and the hood is narrow, long and high, standing up like the comb on a chicken. 'Tis said that in years past the spaniards used to come over here and pick all the pretty girls and take them back to Spain so they got the idea of disguising the girls to make them appear older. Some of the older men wear these costumes also.

Figure 2.2 During World War I, Portugal allowed the United States to establish naval bases in the Azores. For Connor and other radio operators, establishing contact with the station on the islands was crucial to communications.
The port of Ponta Del Gada and its surrounding countryside also provided much-needed shore leave for sailors. Postcard photo, c. 1918.

OCTOBER 1ST 1918.[22]

Still at Ponta Delgada. We coal ship tomorrow and will no doubt leave in a day or so. All the fellows are getting money to keep for souvenirs. Would like to take some things back but theres nothing but cheap novelties to be had. The sidewalks here are very narrow and inlaid with fancy stones. When a person gets on one street here you have to go to the end for theres no cross streets or alleys. Wish I could get some mail from home. Will be glad when I can hear from Alice again for its been almost a month since I had a letter from her.

OCT 2ND 1918.

Still at Ponta Delgada. We have four corpses from the Chicago to take back to the U.S.[23] We are coaling ship today and will leave tomorrow for the U.S. I worked all day putting jumpers on the antennas and it was some job.

OCTOBER 3RD 1918.

"Field Day" today getting cleaned up after coaling. We left Ponta Delgada at four thirty making fifteen knots all the way unless our engines go back on us. Will be glad to reach home once more so I can draw some money, get a haircut, decent bath and get all squared away again.

OCTOBER 4TH 1918

We had to slow down during the night on account of one of our engines going on the bum but we are again making 15 knots. Had another field Day and I finished the antennas. . . .

Wrote a letter to Alice and read a book until Midnight, as though I didn't need the sleep, but I also had some wet clothes in the 7 inch passageway drying. Took them out and went up on the main deck and flopped on a couple hammocks until general quarters.

OCTOBER 5TH 1918.

Today is payday but instead we get captains inspection. I guess I'll have some big roll coming when we finally do get paid. We wont be in for several days yet—possibly a week and I guess we get paid the very day we get in. One of our engines is on the bum again and we are making only about ten knots again. If we get back without getting torpedoed we are some lucky. . . . Saw a big school of whales today and they caused quite a little excitement for theres very few that ever saw any whales. We are making 16 knots now but can't tell how long the engines will hold up under that speed. Got Washington Spark fine tonight . . .

OCTOBER 6TH 1918.

Enroute to USA from Azores making good time. Quiet Sunday Nothing of importance happened. . . .

OCTOBER 7TH 1918.

Still enroute home from Azores. Heard we would get in on next Saturday. Hope I get some liberty then for I need lots of things. . . .

OCT 8TH 1918.

Still several days out from U S A. About 970 miles to go yet. Guess we wont get in until about Saturday. I shifted a rat tail today and worked hard all day too.... Unable to hear Ponta Delgada at 10 pm . . .

OCT 9TH 1918—

Woke up about 4 am this morning sick. Stomach all out of order and legs give out. Standing watch but don't feel very well. We are only making about 10 knots and are still about three or four days out. . . .

OCT 10TH 1918.

We are still bound for U.S.A. and should be in inside 48 hours. The pay list was posted today and we get paid tomorrow. I just copied our first orders since we left New York. They were from C in C and no doubt about what we will do. Also picked up Norfolk so could copy but he had none for us. . . .

OCT 11TH 1918.

About one fifty miles to go yet and making 16 Knots speed. Will get in tomorrow morning some time.

Got paid today, drew $86.[24] Now I want mail and liberty so I can get cleaned up. Worked hard all day today with Chief Canning.

OCT 12TH 1918.

Had general quarters at 2 am this morn acct three torpedoes fired at us. We started zig zagging and made about 20 knots getting away from them. Had the 4 to 8 am watch and sighted land at 6 am. First time we have seen U.S. in month. Arrived in Yorktown about ten thirty am. I got ready for the recreation grounds but they were delayed so I went and scrubbed clothes and took a bath. No mail today but one hundred bags tomorrow.[25]

SUNDAY OCT 13TH 1918.

Worked all forenoon on same [alnavs?] and on the main rattail and had the 12 to 4 watch in the afternoon. Mail started coming in in the afternoon and

I got thirteen letters up until time to turn in. Only got one Cromwell paper so far.

OCTOBER 14TH 1918.

Mail still rolls in and I have about twenty letters now and three Cromwell papers only one Journal Gazette.[26] The new captain inspected this forenoon and we had inspection general quarters, fire drill, collision drill, torpedoe defence and abandon ship. In the afternoon Gunner Reiksiek, Sharp, [Meltvid?] Ammerman and I went over to the Pennsy and brought back a wireless telephone set. Saw a bunch of the boys and found that over half the ships company had had the influenza, 500 at one time. Chief Radio Electrician Snyder died with it. I stood watch with him when I first went aboard the Pennsy. Leslie Abell and [Tomy?] Conlon went to the Wisconsin.[27]

OCTOBER 15TH 1918

Coaling ship today and I wrote a couple letters in the forenoon and worked on the wireless telephone in the afternoon. Am pretty dirty right now but theres no use to clean up until after all the dust settles. Am still getting mail. Got seven letters and two papers today.

OCTOBER 16 — 1918

Had the mid watch and we are still coaling ship. Take on about 3,500 tons and then take on stores tomorrow. We leave Friday for New York I understand.[28]

OCTOBER 17 — 1918.

Taking on stores and cleaning up the ship today. In the afternoon I went over to the USS Supply after 300 foot of stranded lead conductor. Took Ware, Fehrman and C D Smith. Was on the supply from four pm until 9 pm.

OCTOBER 18 — 1918.

Still cleaning ship and reading mail.

OCTOBER 19 — 1918.

Captains Inspection Left Yorktown at 3:15 pm bound for New York.

OCTOBER 20—1918

Have the 8 am to 12 noon watch this morning. I certainly had a bad night last night. A new regulation on the water-tight doors keeps them closed only when the watches are being changed. I had the six to eight watch and when I went up to get my hammock it was too dark to see. I couldn't find it so I slept in the tailor shop on deck, in the 4th div'n passageway, on a mess table and finally in the Interfleet. Hughes came in to get a bucket about 6 30 and dropped a big heavy angle iron on my head. I have a nice big bump and gash in my head now. We should reach New York this afternoon sometime and I hope we get some liberty so I can write some letters and send a telegram. We dropped anchor opposite Tompkinsville at 6:30 pm during a drizzling rain. Have been looking at the "Statue of Liberty" and wondering if I will get any liberty. So far things look very doubtful. Word from the Pueblo says they have had no liberty account influenza.

OCT 22ST—1918.

Left New York yesterday at 3 pm for sea without any liberty. Ships present are Cruiser Charleston, destroyers Talbot and Preble and transports Pocahontas, Comfort and Sobral (Brazilian).[29]

OCT 23RD—1918.

"Field Day" today. Three transports and two destroyers with a cruiser joined us about three pm. The cruiser and one destroyer turned back. We now have six transports two destroyers and a cruiser. The hospital ship "Comfort" is with us this trip. I read a lot of stuff about the U.S. intentions to send the Comfort over with a complete civilian crew but I guess they changed their minds. I never thought I would be along when she went over though. . . .

OCTOBER 23RD 1918

The "Sobral" fell back with port engine bad but proceeded at noon. Now we are hanging back with engine trouble. The convoy is out of sight over the horizon. . . . We now have the Aeolus Martha Washington, Duc D Aosta and Mayrant and Radford.[30]

OCTOBER 24—1918

Made 15 knots all night and caught up with the convoy about 8 am. The captain figures on ten days going over and ten coming back. I only hope we pull into New York instead of Yorktown. Copied Bermuda this morning . . . Was on watch today from 7:45 am until 3:15 pm on account of Belmar starting to send a reply to Nanen on one of the peace notes. It was history in radio because it was the first time we have communicated with Germany direct since war was declared.[31] Now I have the eight to twelve pm watch making fifteen hours and thirty minutes on watch today. We are making fifteen knots all the time now and this will be a quick trip if we have no bad luck. . . .

OCT 25—1918.

Very rough today. At daybreak the convoy was about 20 miles ahead but now we have caught up with them. This trip has been enough to get on a persons nerves so far and before we get back I suppose it will be worse. I've aged about five years in the last week. . . .

OCT 26—1918.

Very rough seas today. While on watch this a.m. the receivers audions and everything slid off the shelf on me but I saved them from getting smashed. Waves were coming high enough to pour in the stacks at times. The wind is blowing about 90 miles per hour too. The "Radford" turned back last night with broken steering gear and not enough fuel to make Hampton Roads Va. When daybreak came we could only see three of the whole convoy. We haven't seen the Charleston all day. The Gunner asked me about going up for chief but I told him no. It takes too much money to start in.[32]

OCTOBER 27TH 1918.

Still very rough today. We have all the transports except the "Radford" but the destroyers have turned back. We wont turn back until about next Friday. . . .

OCT 28TH 1918. . . .

The weather is very rough yet and both the main and gun decks are flooded. We have been in this rough weather a week now. Can just hear Washington spark set now. Tried to get Ponta Delgada but something wrong with radiation. Could not get him.

OCTOBER 29TH 1918.

Still trying to get Ponta Delgada this morning. We have heard that the "Kansas" was sunk and some say they met a raider but I don't know how true it is.[33] We are stilling rolling from the heavy seas but the wind has gone down. We meet the destroyers Friday and turn back for the U.S....

OCTOBER 30TH 1918

Last night while I was washing clothes torpedo defense sounded and we fired two shots at a submarine and put on all speed getting away from torpedoes. We were at our stations about an hour.... I was busy all day doing lots of little personal details and am not through yet. We meet the destroyers about tomorrow some time and will turn back soon after that. We will no doubt go back alone and if we have good luck it will be about the 10th of November when we get back. Hope I get leave soon as we get back so I can get to see Alice once more. I'll bet she thinks I'm gone.

OCTOBER 31ST 1918.

We are waiting for some call from our destroyer relief now and they should pick us up some time today....

The destroyers met us about one thirty today and we also passed a ship which resembled a German cruiser but I guess she was one of our own ships. Have been hearing nearly all the stations over here working.[34]

NOVEMBER 1ST 1918....

Fixed the field set so it would work last night. When I got up it was very foggy and raining. Good weather for subs and we are right where they are thickest. We left the convoy at 130 pm today and headed for the U.S. against a nor'wester.

NOVEMBER 2ND 1918....

Still encountering heavy seas and not making such good time. We are due in the states Nov 12th and I hope we get there. Nearly half the crew has Spanish

Influenza and its a surprise to me that they haven't something else the way we are crowded up and the things we have had to contend with this trip.[35]

NOVEMBER 3RD 1918.

About 40 go into the sick bay each day with the "flu" and only four or five coming out. We have 7 or 8 from the radio bunch in there now. We are proceeding very slowly now and wont be in the U.S. for about ten days. . . .[36]

NOVEMBER 4TH 1918.

Making very slow time acount short of coal.

NOVEMBER 5TH 1918.

Still loafing along slow. The big storm is about over now. . . .

NOVEMBER 6TH 1918.

We headed into a hurricane this morning and have been bucking it all day. At least a week yet before we reach the states and more if we continue to run into these storms. We have had only about one day of good weather during the entire trip. . . .[37]

NOVEMBER 7TH 1918.

Payday today—drew $26. Two men died aboard ship today. Things are in an awful state due to crowded quarters. . . .[38]

NOVEMBER 8TH 1918. . . .

Cape Race came in very good this morning. Was told by Mr. Mathis that I would teach theory to the radio men beginning Monday. We had general quarters and all kinds of drills today.[39]

NOVEMBER 9TH 1918. . . .

We were turned out for torpedo defense about two am. this morning. Its getting cold and very rough also raining. Three men have died with influenza. We are making very slow time. Too slow for me.[40]

NOVEMBER 10TH 1918—

Last night I copied the USNavy press telling of the Kaisers abdication and now everyone is talking peace and a chance to get back home. Theres where I want to be right away. The sea is smooth today and I passed a very lonesome Sunday. Sure wish I was home where I belong. . . .

NOVEMBER 11TH 1918.

Hostilities ceased at 11 am today and everyone on the ship is highly elated. The band marched around the gun deck with about half the ships company behind in single file singing and playing different pieces. Everyone is talking of going home but there will be some that wont get home until the full enlistment is served. If peace is declared I will sure make every effort to get out for I only came in on account of the war. It will be at least six months before any one gets home though and it will take time to get settled.

NOVEMBER 12TH 1918

Swinging ship all day to check up compass etc. We get in tomorrow forenoon.

NOVEMBER 13TH 1918.

Arrived at Yorktown at 10 a.m. Now I want some mail and then liberty. A piece of press copied last night says the men in the army and navy will be let out according to occupation. If this is so I should get out acct being telegrapher. We have been underway 24 days without a stop. Everyone is glad to get back even to this dead place.[41]

Connor's later life is unknown. But his contribution to the Allied war effort probably afforded him great pride in the years following the conflict. He could certainly look to none other than Rear Admiral William Sowden Sims, commander of the American naval forces in European waters during World War I, who wrote this testimonial to the men under his command:

> Too much praise cannot be given to the commanders of our troop convoys . . . as well as the commanders of the cruisers and battleships that escorted them from America to the western edge of the submarine zone . . . these commanding officers had the loyal and enthusiastic support of the admirable

petty officers and men whose initiative, energy and devotion throughout the war enabled us to accomplish results ... On the whole, the safeguarding of American soldiers on the ocean was an achievement of the American navy ... And in performing this great feat the American navy fulfilled its ultimate duty in the war. The transporting of these American troops brought the great struggle to an end.[42]

JEFFREY L. PATRICK holds an MA in history from Purdue University and is the librarian at Wilson's Creek National Battlefield in Republic, Missouri.

NOTES

This article appeared in volume 89, no. 4 (December 1993).

1. Leonard P. Ayres, *The War with Germany—A Statistical Summary* (Washington, 1919), 47.

2. *Ibid.*, 37–48.

3. Guy Burrell Connor was born in Cromwell, Indiana, on July 19, 1894. He enlisted in the United States Navy on June 15, 1917, in Indianapolis, Indiana, for the duration of the war. Connor gave his occupation as telegrapher, with his nearest relative as Mrs. Mollie Longnecker, his mother, also in Cromwell. Physically, Connor was listed as 5 feet 3/4 inches tall, weighing 120 pounds (14 pounds underweight), with blue eyes, black hair, and ruddy complexion. National Personnel Records Center, St. Louis, letter to author, September 10, 1992.

4. The diary is currently in the editor's possession.

5. In an effort to provide the most authentic reproduction possible, Guy Connor's account is presented here much as it originally appeared. Connor provided an immensely detailed account of his duties during World War I; his position as telegrapher allowed Connor to record precisely the ship's latitude and longitude. Ellipses have been used where Connor listed hourly latitudinal and longitudinal readings. Bracketed text with a question mark indicates places where Connor's handwriting was not fully decipherable. Connor's original spelling and punctuation have been used in this transcription; in cases where it was impossible to distinguish whether Connor had used upper or lower case, modern usage has been followed. Location and spacing of dates have been standardized and set in bold type.

6. The battleship USS *Pennsylvania* (BB-38), launched in 1915 and commissioned the following year. Department of the Navy, Naval History Division, *Dictionary of American Naval Fighting Ships* (9 vols., Washington, 1959–1991), V, 250–54. This work is hereafter cited as *DANFS*, followed by volume and page number. Connor served on the *Pennsylvania* from December, 1917, following

his graduation from Naval Radio School, until his transfer to the USS *New Hampshire* in September, 1918. National Personnel Records Center, St. Louis, letter to author, September 10, 1992.

7. Connor probably meant August 15 rather than July 15.

8. The USS *New Hampshire* (BB-25) was a Connecticut class battleship launched in 1906. The ship had a relatively uneventful history before World War I, consisting of cruises to Europe and support operations for U.S. troops intervening in Central America and the Caribbean. Once war broke out, the ship served as a training vessel for a year and a half until it began the convoy mission described by Connor. The ship continued in active service until decommissioned in 1921. Her complement was 850 men. *DANFS*, V, 56–57. Detailed information regarding the *New Hampshire*'s armament, engines, personnel, and other features can be found in Department of the Navy, *Ships' Data—U.S. Naval Vessels, January 1, 1916* (Washington, 1916), 14–23; Naval History Division, *The Battleship in the United States Navy* (Washington, 1970), 44–45; and Department of the Navy, *Register of the Commissioned and Warrant Officers of the United States Navy and Marine Corps, January 1, 1917* (Washington, 1917), 282, 344.

9. The *New Hampshire*'s deck log for September 6, 1918, reported that Electrician 1st class G.B. Connor, USNR, and W.W. Walsh, Electrician 2nd class reported on board from the USS *Pennsylvania*. *Deck Log* of the USS *New Hampshire*, Record Group 24, National Archives, p. 699. Hereafter referred to as *Deck Log*.

10. The *New Hampshire* anchored off Tompkinsville, New York, on September 7, at 5:45 P.M. *Deck Log*, p. 703.

11. The ships Connor refers to are: the USS *Pueblo* (originally named *Colorado*), armored cruiser number 7, launched in 1903 and commissioned in 1905, *DANFS*, V, 400, II, 145; the USS *St. Louis* (cruiser No. 20), launched 1905, commissioned 1906, *DANFS*, VI, 245–46; the USS *Stribling* (destroyer No. 96), launched and commissioned in 1918, *DANFS*, VI, 653; and USS *Stringham* (destroyer No. 83), also launched and commissioned in 1918, *DANFS*, VI, 655.

12. Connor noted the following ships: the USS *Pocahontas* (SP 3044), a ship seized from Germany at the start of the war, converted to a troop transport, and commissioned in 1917, *DANFS*, V, 333; the USS *Martha Washington* (SP 3019), launched in 1908, seized from the Austrians in 1917, and commissioned as a troop transport in 1918, *DANFS*, IV, 252; the USS *Powhatan* (SP 3013), built in 1899, seized from the Germans, converted into a troop transport and commissioned in 1917, *DANFS*, V, 365; the USS *Aeolus* (ID 3005), launched 1899, another converted troop transport originally seized from Germany, commissioned in 1917, *DANFS*, I, part A, 81–82; the USS *Finland*, a troop transport launched in 1902 and commissioned in 1918, *DANFS*, II, 406; the USS *Henderson* (AP-1), also

a transport, launched in 1916 and commissioned the following year, *DANFS*, III, 295; the *Koeningen der Nederlanden*, launched in 1911, a converted troop transport seized from the Dutch and commissioned in 1918, *DANFS*, III, 675; and the USS *Calamares* (AP 3662), a troop transport and refrigeration ship built in 1913 and commissioned in 1918, *DANFS*, II, 10. The exact identities of the *Patria, Ulnaland*, and *Kursk* are unknown.

13. According to high-ranking American naval officers, a U-Boat would be very fortunate to acquire any "kills" on transport ships by this point in the war for several reasons, including "the comparative scarcity of troop transports, the width of the 'lane' in which they travelled (1400 miles), the high speed which they maintained, and their constant zigzagging." Rear Admiral William Sowden Sims, *The Victory at Sea* (New York, 1920), 361–63.

14. Nanen was the largest German radio transmitting station, located outside Berlin. For a detailed account of the U.S. Navy's radio communications network and its enemy competition, see Josephus Daniels, *Our Navy at War* (New York, 1922), 250–55. Horsea was a British Admiralty station, exact location unknown, in operation as early as 1912. Department of the Navy, *Wireless Telegraph Stations of the World, including Shore Stations, Merchant Vessels, Revenue Cutters and Vessels of the United States Navy* (Washington, 1912), 26. For an account of the training of U.S. Navy radiomen during World War I, see C. H. Claudy, "Training Radio Men," Sea Power, V (October, 1918), 257–87. For a detailed account of U.S. Navy communications equipment of the World War I period, see Captain L. S. Howeth, *History of Communications-Electronics in the United States Navy* (Washington, 1963).

15. Probably Captain William Workman, who died on the *Henderson* on September 24, 1918. Department of the Navy, *Register of the Commissioned and Warrant Officers of the United States Navy and Marine Corps, January 1, 1919* (Washington, 1919), 897.

16. According to American Rear Admiral William S. Sims, this would be an insufficient number of escorts for a convoy of this size. He wrote that "A convoy of four or five large troopships would be surrounded by as many as ten or a dozen destroyers." Sims, *The Victory at Sea*, 361.

17. Connor's fear of submarine attack due to the *New Hampshire*'s slow speed was not without foundation. As Rear Admiral Sims wrote, "Ships which made less than 12 knots an hour were not deemed safe" for transporting troops, as "one of the greatest protections which a ship possesses against submarine attack is unquestionably high speed." *Ibid.*, 360.

18. Rear Admiral Herbert Omar Dunn, born in Rhode Island on May 29, 1857, and appointed to the U.S. Naval Academy on June 9, 1873. After graduation, he advanced through the ranks until promoted to rear admiral on August 6, 1915.

He was placed in command of the Azores Detachment, Atlantic Fleet on November 22, 1915. Department of the Navy, *Register of the Commissioned and Warrant Officers of the United States Navy, January 1, 1919* (Washington, 1919), 10–11.

19. Connor means the USS *Tonopah*, a double turreted monitor originally named the *Nevada*, launched in 1900 and commissioned three years later. *DANFS*, VII, 234, V, 51–52.

20. The USS *Marietta* (PG-15), a patrol gunboat launched and commissioned in 1897 which served as an escort on convoy duty. *DANFS*, IV, 238–39. The USS *Arethusa* was a cargo ship built in 1893 and commissioned in 1898 which carried fuel oil from the United States to the Azores. *DANFS*, I, part A, 360–61.

21. Connor refers to the USS *George G. Henry* (ID-1560), a tanker built in 1917 which entered navy service the following year. It was attacked by a German submarine on September 29, 1918. Although damaged, the ship managed to fight off the U-Boat. *DANFS*, III, 77.

22. The *New Hampshire* was honored on October 1 with a visit from the rear admiral commanding Portuguese naval forces in the area, who came aboard for twenty minutes. *Deck Log*, p. 757.

23. The USS *Chicago*, a protected cruiser and flagship of the submarine force, Atlantic, launched in 1885 and commissioned in 1889. *DANFS*, II, 102. The *New Hampshire's* log reported only two caskets from the *Chicago*, with two others from unnamed ships. *Deck Log*, p. 759.

24. Detailed information regarding Navy pay can be found in the Department of the Navy. *Register of the Commissioned and Warrant Officers of the United States Navy and Marine Corps, January 1, 1919, 1011*; and Archibald Owen, Jr., *Navy Yearbook*, Senate Document No. 418, 65th Congress, 3rd Session, 1918–1919 (Washington, 1919), 871–72.

25. Connor failed to note that two officers of the Brazilian Navy reported aboard for instruction. *Deck Log*, p. 785.

26. Connor refers here to the Fort Wayne, Indiana, *Journal-Gazette*.

27. At 2:35 p.m., a general muster was held in which Captain L. H. Chandler turned over command to Captain Ridley McLean. At 5:00 p.m., the log noted that one wireless telephone set was received from USS *Pennsylvania*. *Deck Log*, p. 793.

28. To further explain the enormity of the coaling procedure, the operation took almost twelve hours on both October 15 and 16. On the 15th alone, 900 tons of coal were taken on board. *Deck Log*, pp. 795–97.

29. The ships Connor noted are the following: the USS *Charleston* (C-22), a protected cruiser, launched in 1904 and commissioned the following year, *DANFS*, II, 82–83; the USS *Talbot* (Destroyer No. 114), launched and commissioned in 1918, *DANFS*, VII, 16–17; the USS *Preble* (Torpedo Boat Destroyer No. 12), launched in 1901 and commissioned in 1903, DANFS, V,

368–69; the *Pocahontas*, referred to in note 12; and the USS *Comfort* (AH-3), a hospital ship built in 1906 and commissioned in 1918 which joined the Cruiser and Transport Force, Atlantic Fleet, to return American wounded from France, *DANFS*, II, 152–53. The *Sobral's* identity is unknown.

30. The ships Connor refers to which have not been previously identified are the USS *Mayrant* (Torpedo Boat Destroyer No. 31), launched in 1910 and commissioned the following year, *DANFS*, IV, 283–84, and the USS *Radford* (Destroyer No. 120), launched and commissioned in 1918, *DANFS*, VI, 12. The identity of the *Duc D'Aosta* is unknown.

31. Connor refers to the U.S. Navy radio receiving station at Belmar, New Jersey. Daniels, *Our Navy at War*, 250–55. The text of the note to Germany can be found in Arthur S. Link, ed., *The Papers of Woodrow Wilson* (65 vols., Princeton, 1966–1992), LI, 417–19. Further information regarding armistice negotiations and the role of the U.S. Navy can be found in Howeth, *History of Communications-Electronics in the United States Navy*, 295.

32. Connor not only suffered misfortune due to rough seas, but the heavy seas also "washed out temporary bulkheads and from 15 to 20 tons of coal were washed overboard." *Deck Log*, p. 817.

33. The rumor was not true. The battleship USS *Kansas* (BB-21) was launched in 1905 and commissioned in 1907. It was not attacked by German forces during World War I. *DANFS*, III, 597–98.

34. The *New Hampshire* encountered several ships on this day. At 2:50 p.m. a ship was sighted heading toward the *New Hampshire*, so at 3:07 p.m. General Quarters was sounded. Only a few minutes later, however, at 3:35 p.m., the ship secured, undoubtedly realizing the mystery ship was not German. At 4:10 p.m., two steamers were sighted, along with a third at 4:20 p.m. *Deck Log*, p. 827.

35. The *New Hampshire's* log recorded frequent squalls from 4:00 a.m. until 8:00 a.m. To make matters worse, on November 1 the log admitted that "Influenza took on an epidemic form aboard this ship October 30," so bad that general quarters was omitted on the recommendation of the medical officer, with an "overflow of cots on port side main deck aft." On November 2, 1918, 112 cases of influenza remained aboard, with 137 cases occurring since September 18. *Deck Log*, pp. 825–35.

36. Connor was correct in his estimation of the seriousness of the influenza epidemic aboard his ship. The ship's log for November 3, 1918, noted 152 influenza cases on board. *Deck Log*, p. 837.

37. The ship's log recorded that from 8:00 a.m. until noon the wind increased, and the sea became moderately heavy. At 1:00 p.m. the *New Hampshire* encountered "a gale from the southward which lasted for an hour." *Deck Log*, p. 843.

38. The ship's log stated that one man died of pneumonia at 9:35 a.m. *Deck Log*, p. 845.

39. "Mr. Mathis" was Ensign A.J. Matthes, who arrived aboard the *New Hampshire* on June 10, 1918. *Deck Log*, List of Officers Nov. 1–30, 1918. Connor was correct about the drilling. From 8:00 a.m. to noon the ship held torpedo defense drill, general quarters, battle drill, etc. *Deck Log*, pp. 846–47.

40. The *New Hampshire*'s log noted that torpedo defense was sounded at 1:32 a.m., but the ship was secured at 2:00 a.m. The sea was recorded as choppy, with rain squalls. At 5:30 p.m. the ship went to Torpedo Defense stations, held searchlight drill, and secured at 5:56 p.m. *Deck Log*, p. 849.

41. The *New Hampshire* dropped anchor at Base #2, Yorktown, Virginia, at 9:25 a.m., November 13, 1918. *Deck Log*, p. 863. Connor continued to serve on the *New Hampshire* until his discharge on July 28, 1919 at the U.S. Navy Demobilization Station in Pittsburgh, Pennsylvania. National Personnel Records Center, St. Louis, letter to author, September 10, 1992.

42. Sims, *The Victory at Sea*, 366.

THREE

A Hoosier Nurse in France

The World War I Diary of Maude Frances Essig

ALMA S. WOOLLEY

MAUDE FRANCES ESSIG WAS BORN November 29, 1884, on a farm west of Elkhart, Indiana. She died in September, 1981, in the Veterans Administration Center in Dayton, Ohio, at the age of ninety-six, after being a resident of the home for twenty-nine years. After Essig's death a nephew found among her possessions a handwritten sixty-eight-page paper entitled

> My Trip Abroad with Uncle Sam—1917:1919
> American Expeditionary Forces in France—
>   Reserve Army Nurse Corp—
>   American Red Cross Nurse #4411
> How We Won World War I
>   By *Maude Frances Essig*—
> Superintendent—Elkhart General Hospital 1915–1920
> Elkhart, Indiana

The cover page also stated that Essig had compiled the account during the summer of 1919 from letters she had written to her mother, from her own diary, and from memory. There is no evidence that she ever attempted to publish or circulate it. The paper was sent to one of Essig's former students, who brought it to the Illinois Wesleyan University School of Nursing in the belief that its contents would be of interest to the school in whose evolution Essig had played a prominent part. The paper's script is similar to printing and not difficult to read. The handwriting is identical to that of a book of committee minutes owned by the IWU School of Nursing, each signed by Maude F. Essig. It is also identical to that on letters, notes, and cards sent to former students living in the area of Bloomington, Illinois. The second title, "How We Won World War I," must have been added, however, after another world war gave the numeral "I" to what had formerly been known only as the Great War.

Essig's manuscript, in the form of a diary, begins with a brief entry dated August 15, 1915, documenting transfer of her Red Cross membership from the Chicago to the Indianapolis chapter and ends on March 22, 1919, with her return from France to Elkhart, Indiana. Nursing duties are described as they directly influence the narrative, and from them it is possible to glean a picture of the nurse's role in two crucial phases of military operations during World War I, the army's base and evacuation hospitals.

There were five levels of care for American soldiers wounded in battle in Europe during World War I. Women were involved in only two of them. The system was designed for the type of war being fought, the distance from hospitals in the United States, and the kind of transportation available. In the field itself members of the regimental medical detachment applied first-aid dressings and carried or assisted the wounded to *aid stations*. Here other regimental medical officers applied dressings and splints and prepared the wounded for transport. Enlisted men and litter bearers took them to collecting stations and ambulances. The *field hospitals*, about five miles back of the front lines, were similar to present-day Mobile Army Surgical Hospital (MASH) units. They received the wounded from ambulances and triaged them, performed emergency surgery, redressed wounds, relieved pain, provided nourishment, and treated shock. *Evacuation hospitals* were set up from twelve to twenty miles or more back of the lines on railroad sidings. Women army nurses worked in these evacuation units. Here patients received more thorough care before they were taken by train to the *base hospitals*. Gathered hurriedly but carefully by government and civilian effort, the base hospitals were sent in thousands of pieces to be assembled in Europe to care for American wounded. With them, also hurriedly assembled, went groups of civilian doctors, nurses, technicians, and supporting staff, who, for the war's duration, were absorbed under the aegis and direction of the military.[1] Essig was among those who answered the appeal of the popular Red Cross recruiting poster, "What are you doing to help?" by joining one of these base hospital staffs.

Essig served during the war on the staff of Base Hospital 32, a unit organized by the Indianapolis chapter of the American Red Cross. Although official involvement of the United States in World War I did not begin until early April, 1917, planning for the Indianapolis-sponsored hospital began in February of that year. A large part of its financing was provided by Eli Lilly and Company, a pharmaceutical firm, as a memorial to its founder. The initial donation of $25,000 in February, 1917, was followed by $15,000 from the Lilly family, and

the rest was raised by the people of Indianapolis.[2] Staff members of the Indianapolis City Hospital, later known as Marion County General Hospital and
then as Wishard Memorial, organized the unit. The personnel were to include
twenty-two physicians and surgeons, two dentists, sixty-five graduate nurses,
six to ten civil employees, and 153 enlisted men; approximately that number
sailed with the unit to France. The Indianapolis chapter of the American Red
Cross gave each nurse who enlisted a rubber blanket and fifty dollars in gold as
a parting gift. The people of Indianapolis continued to support Base Hospital
32 throughout the war. Socks, afghans, pillows, quilts, and supplies of all kinds
were made, assembled, and shipped to the unit. Especially welcomed were
candy, cigarettes, and apples—all luxuries in war-torn France.[3]

After a number of staff changes Dr. Edmund D. Clark, an Indianapolis
surgeon, assumed the directorship of Base Hospital 32 and organized it for
overseas duty. Clark's staff included a chief nurse, Florence J. Martin, superintendent of nurses of the Indianapolis City Hospital, whose task it was to recruit
and organize the graduate nurses for the staff.[4] It was she who wrote to Essig,
her counterpart at Elkhart General Hospital, on June 28, 1917, inviting Essig to
join the staff, since membership was by invitation only.

In October, 1918, during Essig's tenure at Base Hospital 32, the unit had an
emergency capacity of 2,400 beds. During the hospital's entire period of foreign service it admitted 9,698 patients, which was slightly more than 4 percent
of the total number of United States wounded. Over 98 percent of these were
transferred to other hospitals or returned to duty. The total death rate was only
1.22 percent. Of the sixty nurses in the unit, most of whom were from Indiana,
three became ill and returned home before the unit left for France, where the
hospital was established. One became ill during the voyage and died at the
naval hospital in Brest, and six returned to the United States because of sickness while in France. Twenty-four nurses from Iowa were added to the unit at
a later date.[5]

Base Hospital 32 contributed toward the medical progress that is one of the
small compensations for the suffering of war. There, as in all hospitals, research
was done on wound inflammation, the use of x-ray and fluoroscopy in locating
foreign bodies, and the treatment of shock. Sixty percent of the patients who
reached Lilly Base Hospital were gas cases. The most severely affected died immediately or en route to the hospital. Exposure to mustard and phosgene gas
caused severe damage to the respiratory system and pulmonary edema. Burned
membranes in the throat, bronchi, and lungs necrosed and caused obstruction
and respiratory failure. Even hospital attendants were frequently burned by
contact with clothing and blankets which had been exposed to the gas.[6]

No satisfactory treatment had been developed for gas inhalation, so the hospital was free to use whatever seemed to provide relief. The English treated these cases with oxygen and benzoin steam inhalations, but an otolaryngologist at Base Hospital 32, Major Lafayette Page, rejected this treatment. He believed that the oxygen was unnecessary and that the steam merely soaked the tissues. He realized that in order for recovery and healing to take place it was necessary for the injured tissue debris to be removed from the lungs, primarily through the natural cough reflex. He therefore devised a mixture of guiacol, camphor, menthol, and oil of thyme and eucalyptus that was introduced into the trachea through a syringe. When it reached the bronchi, it caused coughing to expel the products of inflammation and suppuration. The patient received immediate relief, breathing was facilitated, pain reduced, and healing begun. This treatment was widely copied in other American as well as English hospitals and became the standard treatment for this injury. Of the six thousand gas cases treated at Base Hospital 32, only two died of gas inhalation.[7] In addition, Major Harry Byrnes, an ophthalmologist at the hospital, showed that the open treatment of eyes exposed to poison gas was more beneficial than the common practice of bandaging.[8] Essig noted: "It is remarkable to see how the burned eyes respond to treatment."

Base Hospital 32 also made other medical advances during the war. A combination of ether and chloroform under a closed hood reduced induction time for anesthesia from twenty minutes to one to two minutes. Another innovation was the use of a nasopharyngeal tube for anesthesia, particularly for head surgery. Because the hospital staff recognized that spinal injuries, especially those resulting in severed cords, had a poor prognosis, patients with these injuries were sent home as soon as possible in an attempt to secure the best care for them. And a warning was issued against eating the "beautiful blue grapes" that grew in the French mountains when it was discovered that a particular type of "mania" was the result of belladonna berry poisoning.[9]

Essig comments infrequently concerning the nursing treatments that were administered to patients at Base Hospital 32. She focuses instead on the day-to-day lives of the nurses, who often worked impossible hours under nearly impossible conditions. Essig and her colleagues among the volunteer base hospital nursing staff bore their trials not without complaint but with determination and pride in their obvious importance to the war effort and to other Americans.

Like Essig, the great majority of nurses who served in the war were recruited by the American Red Cross. At first they were assigned directly to the base hospitals, as Essig was, later directly to the army or navy. Need for medical and nursing care soon became great in the army camps within the United States. Thousands of men died of pneumonia and meningitis without ever leaving the country. Many of the nurses waiting to be assigned to hospitals overseas were sent instead to the camps to work, and several lost their own lives as a result. In the fall of 1918, while Allied forces were gaining victories in Belgium, army nurses in camps at home dealt with the Spanish influenza epidemic under crowded and difficult conditions. They joined public health workers to detect, isolate, and care for victims of typhoid, meningitis, and other contagious diseases.[10]

During the war the Red Cross also sent nurses to French army hospitals to help care for American wounded. A famous recruiting slogan for the Red Cross was "American nurses for American men." The importance of this practice becomes clear from the many letters written home by soldiers describing their relief at waking up in a hospital and hearing an American nurse speaking English.[11] Essig saw the problem in reverse. She dealt with Hindu, German, English, and French patients as well as American wounded and found it difficult to communicate with them.

Despite the dangers that Essig must have realized were involved in wartime nursing,[12] she records in her diary no period of hesitation, no qualms, no obstacles to her decision to accept Florence Martin's invitation to join the staff of Base Hospital 32. She considered it an honor. A somewhat proper but very human young woman, she did not disdain creature comforts, but her personal and professional ideals enabled her to forgo them for a cause in which she believed. In July, 1917, she "reported in person to Miss Martin for personal interview," then returned to Elkhart to await her summons. The telegram arrived on September 6 with directions to "report to Miss Martin, City Hospital, Indianapolis—on Sept. 7, 11 A.M. to be sworn in—" A busy day and night ensued; in an emergency board meeting her responsibilities as superintendent were turned over to an assistant, and she tried to put her "house in order." Leaving Elkhart at 5:30 on the morning of September 7, Essig arrived in Indianapolis in time to take the oath of office. The standard military operating procedure of "hurry up and wait" went into effect, and after two nights and one gloomy day in a hotel a group of sixty nurses left Indianapolis by special Pullman on September 9 and arrived in Penn Station in New York City on Monday, September 10, at 8:00 a.m. In her diary Essig describes the arrival:

We lined up alphabetically—as we did later for endless experiences— marched by twos and followed the flag! ... We waited ages and finally were taken to Grand Central Station where after more waiting we were finally taken to U.S. Army Hospital No 1 at Bainbridge Ave and Gunhill Road [in the Bronx]. Arrived in time for a late lunch and there began our taste of Army life.[13]

The Bronx barracks served as a mobilizing station for nurses, as did Ellis Island in New York Harbor. The nurses from Indiana joined 250 others who were already there, assigned twenty-five to a "ward," each with a bed and chair, three dressers to a group. On September 13 Essig wrote: "My duties for the day were to sweep the ward and line up the beds, dressers and chairs. Every one makes his own bed & dusts—We all had drill in a near by field—learned to salute and to 'suck in your belly'—We all returned mighty weary and sore of foot."

On September 20, "Our uniforms arrived—Classy! . . . Gala occasion Endless chatter, trying on, fixing marking and picture taking—"

After another week of "drill and duties," the group moved again, this time to St. Mary's Hospital in Hoboken, New Jersey, where the Catholic nursing sisters were responsible for housing the waiting nurses. Essig was "one of eleven crowded into one room over the laundry—formerly 'Helps' quarter—one narrow cot, a chair and 1 ft. of space each—" Thursday, October 4, Red Cross and Army Parade Day, was the highlight of this waiting period. Ten thousand women, including more than two thousand nurses, paraded down New York's Fifth Avenue from 79th Street to Washington Arch to demonstrate their active support of the fighting men.[14] The nurses quartered in Hoboken joined their hospital units to march "69 blocks—16 abreast."

> The nurses for overseas duty followed the chief dignitaries and Sousa's Band—each unit in different parade dress—ie—some in slickers, some in white uniform & cap—some in blue dress uniform—some with capes all blue—some with corner of cape thrown back to show red lining, many variations Our unit wore blue dress uniform—(no wrap) and dress hat—It was a gorgeous sight . . . It took 6 hours for the parade to pass any one point—The most wonderful sight I ever hope to see. . . .

Three more weeks passed. The nurses spent their time after duties being entertained by friends at Overlook Hospital in Summit, New Jersey, and going on lunch and theater trips to New York. Activities were somewhat constrained by the fact that no one had yet been paid.

On October 19 Essig's group left Hoboken and was "nicely deposited on Ellis Island—one step nearer 'Over-There'"—with the rest of the personnel from Base Hospital 32. Essig reported: "This is a beautiful spot The air is grand—a wonderful view of the Statue of Liberty It is a view worth fighting for—" More visiting, dining, and sightseeing, with much partying and sharing of boxes of food from home, resulted in the lament, "Beautiful weather, good eats and I am getting *Fat*—" The monotony was somewhat relieved by daily French classes, which Essig described on November 3 as "progressing and leaving me in the rear." Later she wrote: "For class, two of the nurses hid under their beds—two staid in the bath room and others just disappeared—Out of a class of 19, 8 were present—Class is more unpopular than scrubbing—" On November 5 she commented: "Fine weather but we are sick of all this waiting and of being of no use to any one—and broke—I have just 24¢ The pay master's money ran out before he reached our unit—which means we will have to sign another pay roll—"

By the end of November, 1917, Christmas boxes from home began to arrive, and "In trying to eat everything, I broke off a front tooth, which means I must see a dentist—I look a sight—" Another period of Thanksgiving and birthday feasting, as well as several dental appointments, ended abruptly with orders for departure on December 3. Baggage space was limited, so extra clothing was hurriedly given away, mailed home, or worn in layers. "One of the nurses dumped a lot of nuts sent to me in her umbrella and we were glad to have them later when food was at a premium—"

The ship assigned to carry the personnel of Base Hospital 32 was the *George Washington*, an American transport that had recently been taken from the Germans and that carried approximately seven thousand passengers. Twenty days later the ship arrived safely at Brest in France, but the voyage was extremely rough. Essig and many others were seasick: "I fed the fishes all day and all night—I really wanted to die but lived to tell this tale . . . Nothing anyone can do—I must endure—Every one is most kind, but all I desire is to be left alone, and, if possible just pass out . . . Oh for our Hospital—Good Old E.G.H." Just as Essig began to recover enough to return to activity, the ship entered the Bay of Biscay and encountered a tremendous storm. Several lifeboats and crew members were reportedly washed overboard, and everyone was confined to cabins. Captain Carleton B. McCulloch, M.D., adjutant of the unit, later wrote a nine-stanza poem entitled "Lines Dedicated to the Bay of Biscay." His general sentiments were summed up in the last stanza:

When the struggle is concluded and the victory is sure,
The foe must take some punishment most grievous to endure;
I'll offer this suggestion when the councillors convene—
They be made to cross old Biscay in some Fall like Seventeen.[15]

On December 18 Essig wrote in her diary that she had been successful in bribing a porter with twenty-five cents to get her a sour pickle. "It was what I craved and needed and worth a dollar—" Her electrolyte balance was undoubtedly at least partially restored! The coast of Brittany was sighted on December 20, and the ship anchored in the Bay of Brest. Hospital personnel remained on board until December 24 while the thousands of troops disembarked.

An afternoon of sightseeing—at an old chateau in Brest—was followed by a two-day rail trip across northern France. Four nurses were locked into each compartment and given rations for the trip. "Attending to nature's wants was a serious problem—Jam and Tomato Cans served our need—" Christmas Day brought a stop in a town where sandwiches could be purchased to supplement rations. Members of Base Hospital 32 communicated with each other "by sticking our heads out of the little window in our little doors—" The train ride ended in Contrexéville la Vosges at 3:00 a.m. on December 26. An unheated building recently vacated by French soldiers, with all toilets frozen, was the group's lodging for the next two days. Essig wrote: "I slept all night in my sleeping-bag under my down comforter which had been brought all the way from home (not such a crazy idea as some had thought—)."

On December 28 the group moved up the hill to the buildings which would house Base Hospital 32. The town of Contrexéville, about forty miles southwest of Nancy, was a summer resort with a spa whose healing waters were shipped in bottles throughout France. The resort had three parks, tennis courts, and a casino with a theater, gaming rooms, and a salon. Hotels, villas, and small hostelries, as well as a location fifty miles behind the front lines and near a railway, made the town suitable for a military hospital site. The French had been using some of the larger buildings as hospitals but had recently evacuated them for American use. Five of the buildings were assigned to Base Hospital 32. Two hotels were designated as surgical units and three as medical. Their planned capacity of five hundred was eventually increased to 1,250 beds. Some of the other buildings were assigned to Base Hospital 31 from Youngstown, Ohio. It took until March to organize and equip the buildings. Certain sections of the buildings and cellars were sealed for storage of what were believed to be art objects, wines, and other items for future peacetime use.[16]

Hospital equipment had arrived prior to personnel and was stored at a medical supply depot. The first task for the unit attached to Base Hospital 32 was to clean the buildings, recently abandoned by the French "in an extremely unsanitary condition." Refuse had to be removed; floors, windows, and woodwork washed; and plumbing, electrical work, and carpentry done before the buildings could be used as hospitals. Special lighting and wiring were needed for surgery and x-ray, and sterilizing equipment, as well as additional sinks and drains, had to be installed. This work was done during January by the enlisted men.[17]

Essig and three other nurses were assigned to a room on the eighth floor of a hotel at the top of a hill. She wrote: "In peace time I am sure we would pay a handsome price for our room—especially the view—" Having once more unpacked, she and a small group were notified at 3:00 p.m. on December 29 that they would form a temporary relief detachment to go to Base Hospital 15, the Roosevelt Hospital unit from New York, then in Chaumont, France.

At 4:30 the next morning, the group of thirty repacked their belongings and left by truck for the train. Chief Nurse Florence Martin gave Essig the travel orders and placed her in charge of the detachment. Another difficult trip ensued.

We boarded the train at 7:00 Changed trains at Nuilly and again at Longres [Langres]—Some of the nurses obstinate—two refused to change at Longres and I had to grab their baggage off the train and they followed their baggage . . . We waited in Longres from 11:30 until 6:00 P.M.—Terribly cold and damp—no heat . . . Some of girls climbed the steep hill from station to village—City sets on a high hill surrounded with a wall built by Ceasar . . . I tried to make the hill but something went hay wire inside me—terribly nauseated and pain in left side—We finally arrived at Chaumont—[General John J.] Pershing's Headquarters—at 7:00 P.M. very weary Sore and Cold. Total distance from Contrexville—as the CROW flies—35 miles—I thought we traveled at least 10 times that—

In the nurses' quarters at Base Hospital 15 Essig and another nurse shared a six-bed ward with four of the Roosevelt nurses. "After our satisfying repast Miss Francis, Chief Nurse, talked with us, giving a list of dos and donts—She delegated me to be in charge of the nurses while here—which responsibility I do not want, and which a few of the nurses I feel would enjoy having. . . ." Work began the next morning, December 31. The hospital was overcrowded and had little equipment, and the new nurses were assigned to various pavilions to relieve and do cleaning. Essig commented:

The place looks hopeless—No conveniences—Very little equipment and so many patients—everything so dirty—made me think of Florence Nightingale and her experiences at Crimea! . . . The present rush of work is due to a tragic hike—ordered by some commanding officer—for members of the 42nd Div. across France—Boys were unduly exposed to freezing weather—pneumonia, frozen feet, bad ears (mastoiditis), meningitis etc.— not to mention the very common cold—[18]

Since it was New Year's Eve,

> The regular nurses—mostly Roosevelt Hospital graduates gave a dance for the
> officers of Base #15—Base #32 nurses were invited to *not* attend—Miss Francis
> was afraid there would be too many women for the men who had been
> invited—Later—however—about 10 P.M. some of the nurses followed by
> Miss Francis came to our nurses insisting they attend since they had more
> men than women Our nurses went to bed instead—at least most of them
> did. The affair lasted most of the night and from our quarters sounded pretty
> wild—A great way to welcome in a New Year especially in such a terrible
> time—The music was good—provided by 101st Regimental Band—Too much
> drinking and smoking—None of our nurses smoke and of course are looked
> upon as old foggies from the wild and wooly west!

January, 1918, began cold and damp. Essig found herself in an uncomfortable position between sick and complaining nurses and the chief nurse of Base
Hospital 15. On January 2 she reported:

> Many of our group have colds and are feeling badly Much griping ... Unable
> to get a doctor to see the sick ones and no medications—I know they hold
> me responsible for all that goes wrong ... [on January 3] I listened to endless
> complaints and reported sick nurses to *Miss Charles*—asst chief nurse—I
> made rounds later with *Dr. Martin* and tried to secure medications ...
> *Miss* [Nellie M.] *Birch* furious after her first night on duty. Says sanitary
> conditions are terrible—no precautions possible against infection—She
> knows this will be the end for all of us. I feel helpless—I think Miss Francis
> holds me responsible for so much complaining—I wish I could care for
> patients

The next weeks were occupied with trying to keep warm, do laundry, get medicine for the sick nurses, and keep the group functioning. On January 8 Essig
wrote: "Snowing and much colder. Everyone sick and complaining I feel disgusted and discouraged—We are surely not much Help to anyone here. I want
to go on duty but Miss Francis insists I am her assistant and in charge of B.H.
32 nurses The nurses do not agree with her ..." On January 9 she continued: "I
pleaded with Miss Francis to put me on regular duty—just anything—she said
she would—Food not so good the cook is sick!" Essig's request was granted on
January 10 when she was assigned to duty in the sick officers' pavilion. Several
nurses had measles and one had mumps, but these were apparently confined
and did not spread. By January 15 more friction had developed between the
Roosevelt unit and the nurses from Base Hospital 32.

Miserable day—raining ice-water—Only three patients now. One of Roosevelt nurses . . . thinks it is a disgrace to their nurses to have to work under me and does not lose an opportunity to insult me. She refuses to carry out any order that I may post—(She thinks Indians still roam the middle west and Chicago has only racketeers—ignorance is prevalent)

The January rain produced mud, but off-duty hours were used for sightseeing, laundry, purchase of souvenirs, and visits to a dentist. Essig was still dealing with the front tooth that she had broken just before leaving New York and was attempting to have root canal work done whenever she could get away for appointments. Visits to the hot baths in the town were not frequent but were greatly enjoyed. On January 28 she commented: "I was told I am supervisor of Officer's Bldg—Miss [name deleted] went to the Commanding Officer with her troubles—and in return he had her transferred to the worst Bldg on the grounds—on night duty—I am surely sorry this unpleasantness had to happen because of me—" By January 31 she was forecasting the end of her stay in Chaumont.

> Ten orthopedic nurses arrived today for regular duty. The[y] are a fine group—have been on duty in Paris. Also five of Roosevelt nurses returned from Military Hospital #3 in Paris where they have been on detached service. B.H.#15 family is increasing, so we think our days here are numbered. Miss Francis has asked me to ask for transfer to B.H. #15 and stay on—How I would love to do just that but it doesn't seem to be the right thing to do.

On February 4, with no warning, Essig's group was ordered off duty to pack for the return to Contrexéville. They arrived in that town at 9:00 p.m.; but no one seemed to be expecting them, and accommodations were again sparse.

> Our room is as bare as a barn in "Hotel Jeanne Pierre," third floor front—We each have a miserable French cot, a chair and that is all—we must buy pillows we have nothing but a straw bolster—and I refuse to put my head on that—It seems strange that some units are well provided for and we have nothing—I almost wish I had staid in Chaumont.

On February 6 she reported:

> I have a boil on my neck which is not pleasant . . . The utility room (?) opens into Mary Housers and my room—It is the only place where the 24 Nurses living on our floor can congregate around a little stove (usually heatless) to take baths, wash, visit and such—It is like a continuous "coffee clotch" It takes an expert to keep even a semblance of a fire in the peanut of a

stove—No rest in our room—but we do have some fun swaping yarns—A
sheet strung across one comer of the room provides the bathing facility! The
cord occassionally breaks and furnishs amusement for all but the bather.

After two more weeks of cleaning five hotels, including the frozen toilets, "Miss Martin ordered that nurses were no longer to scrub floors or wash
wood-work—" Essig continued to visit a dentist for root canal work: "how it
did hurt—no Pain Killer in the army—" The monotony was relieved by occasional packages from home with sweets and such amenities as bath soap and
toothpaste. Essig was then assigned to the second floor of the Cosmopolitan
Hotel, the main surgical building, which could accommodate a total of five
hundred patients. The weather continued wet and cold, and she wrote: "The
rain continues—Our Bldgs are so very cold and damp—Water drips from the
walls—especially bad in our patients room . . . I went to church at 10:30 Very
fine talk on Faith and we surely need it—"

March brought some relief from the weather, and spirits rose. Short excur-
sions to local sights to buy souvenirs helped pass the time. "Little rivers (?)
of stench flow down each side of the Roads Sanitation is awful—not up to
U.S.A. Standards." Patients in the hospital were still mainly sick personnel.
Finally, on March 23, she reported: "We received our first real convoy about
300 All 42nd Div.—Rainbow Div. I received 68 on my floor mostly mustard
gas burns—Terrific suffering—"

On March 24 she continued:

> What a change from last week. 82 patients on my floor—About 20 doctors
> assigned to my floor All want something, every place—Stat—We do not
> have supplies nor equipment to meet their demands This type of burn is
> terrible and nothing seems to give relief—Eye and genitalia burns are most
> painful—Terrible situation—The patients are good scouts—and most
> appreciative—So happy to be in the hands of U.S.A. They came to us from a
> French Evacuation Hospital and they say nothing was done for them and only
> thin soup was given to drink—Most of the boys are from Iowa, New York and
> Wisconsin—

By the end of March there were ninety-one patients on the floor. As charge
nurse, Essig's chief duty was to "secure endless supplies and keep records ad-
equately." She lamented: "I would so love to do more for the boys but others are
responsible for nursing care—Two meals a day are all Ive been getting—I am
dead tired—the corridors are so long and the walk from Nurses' Quarters to
"Cosmo" is uphill all the way and much too long—" On Easter Day the nurses

Figure 3.1 Staff of Hospital A, Base Hospital 32, Contrexéville, France. Five buildings in the resort town became part of the base hospital; two large hotels, including the Hotel de la Providence, were used as surgical units. Courtesy Library of Congress.

were awakened at 5:45 a.m. by Easter hymns being played on four horns. "It sounded Heavenly." But working conditions were still difficult:

> We use endless surgical supplies and at this rate I dont see how we can keep going—We have no water in our building (frozen or turned off for the winter) Every drop we use must be carried from outside—We try to keep one bath Tub filled—heat what little we can on sterno stove, using denatured alcohol . . . The orderlies have to work terribly hard—beside carr[y]ing the water up four flights of stairs they have to carry up all the food and the fuel for our fire place—Convalescents help as they can—but so far we have had few convalescents.

On April 4 Essig wrote that she was "very much upset" because she had been transferred to a convalescent floor at the top of the Cosmopolitan and had eight flights of stairs to climb. "*I dont like it*—I worked so hard to get things organized and clean on 2nd Eme—now I will have the same on this floor—Miss Martin *said* the change was made, because I had worked so much harder than other nurses and she felt I should take it easier for awhile—I doubt her reason, however—" Shortly after the transfer Essig herself became a patient and was isolated with erysipelas, a streptococcal infection with localized inflammation of skin and subcutaneous tissues, as well as systemic symptoms. Her "very *sore face*" was treated with "Continuous Mag. Sulp [magnesium sulphate] dressing heated on Sterno—Painful ordeal—and lonely—" Five days later she returned to duty and the eye, ear, nose, and throat specialist said that she had not had erysipelas, but "Furunculosis of Nose."

At the beginning of May a United States Commissary opened, and Essig commented: "we can buy many things we do not need—candy and cigarettes top the desires—me for candy—our nurses do not smoke cigarettes—(with two exceptions)—" May passed with few patients being admitted. Mother's Day, Joan of Arc Day, and opening of the resort theater by the Red Cross were all celebrated. Memorial Day was the most elaborate since two American soldiers had been buried in the Contrexéville cemetery.

After the German drive on the Marne in the spring of 1918, wounded of all nationalities arrived in trainloads. The admitting corpsmen took them to the bathhouse, a convenient conversion of the spa, and scraped off the mud from the trenches. Each patient was given a Red Cross bag for his personal belongings, as well as pajamas, bathrobe, slippers, towel, and washcloth. Clothes were sent to a sterilizer to get rid of germs and the ever-present lice. Wounds were redressed and x-rayed for shrapnel, and surgery was done if necessary. Patients were either sent back to the lines or transferred to convalescent hospitals, so that beds at the base hospital could be kept open for new convoys. Many stories were written home of the confusion and humorous incidents that resulted from dealing with multilingual patients and their unfamiliarity with American determination to disinfect everything possible.[19]

In early June Base Hospital 32 received two convoys of French and English wounded. Most had gunshot and shrapnel wounds, but some had been gassed or were shell-shocked. Essig's difficulty in communicating with the French soldiers motivated her to resume studying French. She admitted: "I am not an apt pupil."

When evacuation hospitals in the area became filled early in June, the designation of Base Hospital 32 was changed to Evacuation, which meant that the wounded were received directly from the field hospitals and the dressing stations at the front lines. On June 19 a list of nurses who were "to be ready to leave on one hour's notice for service at the front" was posted. Essig wrote: "I wish I might be on the list but I am not." On June 25 a large convoy of wounded arrived, and the German prisoners were put on Essig's floor.

I was allowed to care for them—Twelve Boche—under guard . . . The
Germans are in bad shape—and require much care—All have high
temperatures—all very young—they seem to be afraid of me—One who
talks English says they have been told repeatedly that if they landed in a U.S.
Hospital they would be poisoned . . . One of the prisoners needs considerable
care—His face most of it was shot away and feeding is a problem—He is
most grateful and is improving—

At last, in July, Essig's tooth was fixed; the gold cost $5.00. She did not enjoy
the teasing that ensued. Further problems required a wisdom tooth extraction
shortly thereafter. On the seventeenth she reported standing in line for a bath
at the Red Cross bathhouse with Mrs. Belmont Tiffany, a New York society matron who became a Red Cross leader abroad. Essig felt "almost like somebody
to be in such distinguished . . . [company]—War is truly a leveling influence."
    As a result of the fighting around Château-Thierry in June of 1918, the num-
ber of seriously wounded soldiers arriving directly from the front steadily increased, and some busy weeks ensued. Many were evacuated after treatment,
but many required surgery and intensive care before being moved. On July 24
Essig wrote:

We are very busy All beds are filled and every staff member is working the
limit. The stretcher bearers are working very hard—They have to carry the
patients up the 8 flights of stairs, then down 7 flights to operating rooms and
back up the 7 flights to bed—I surely pity them . . . Our census today is 130
on my floor—I shudder when I have time to think of what they have been
through—The patients are all cheerful and so glad to have such a "swell
place"—many are lying on straw ticks on the floor—Much better than lying
out on the battlefield waiting for some one to rescue them—they say—Last
night 14 of my patients went to surgery—three surgical teams worked all
night—My patients were all back from surgery by 11 P.M. and it meant a busy
night for me and my one orderly—All patients had eaten red beans for supper,
and had ether anesthesia on full stomach—so we had some really sick boys
until the red beans were eliminated—When awake they gave no trouble and
were wanting to help—One fellow with a T. of 104.6 at mid night I watched
carefully—he slept finally and at 5 A.M. I found him sitting on the edge of his
bed eating a chocolate bar left on his bed by a Red Cross worker—Later he
got up on his own power and went to the toilet—His back was riddled with
shrapnel and surgery had made two long incisions the length and breadth
of his back—and had inserted several Dakin tubes which I irrigated every
two hours—I was unable to comprehend their endurance—Several were of
this fellows caliber—Another badly wounded fellow, who had been lying

on the floor before surgery, I thought should have a bed after surgery and made a switch with a less serious patient—but—when the poor sick fellow returned, he absolutely refused to keep the bed *and* when he awakened, I had to make another switch and let him rest in peace on his *own straw-tick on the floor*—Dakin tubes and all—He slept after the move until morning and never roused even when I irrigated the tubes—Such guts!

Convoys of wounded continued to arrive. On July 29 Essig commented:

Our census increases day by day. We receive and evacuate every other day. More arrive than are sent away—My floor is fairly quiet after mid night—Most of the patients sleep through Dakin irrigations, yet when they are awake they fuss considerably about treatments—Last Thursday we received a large convoy at an early morning hour—and we staid on duty until noon—17 hr. stretch—off duty until after our evening meal—That evening 16 of our patients went to surgery—no operating done after 11 P.M. These are busy nights and busier days. Miss [Mary L.] Elder, charge nurse is anxious for me to get off night duty and relieve her—Says she cant take it—Our patients are coming directly from *The Front* and they say it is terrible—lying there waiting for help to come—All come in awful condition—no previous care has been given to their wounds—It takes a lot of soaking to clean their wounds, dried blood, filth and dirt and lice—The bath-house is not able to cope with the situation and neither can our limited staff and walking patients—Four of our nurses left for the front—Conditions are worse there—We do have a roof, a floor and everyone is fed after a fashion. No one works less than 12 hrs. in 24 and most of us do more—I see no one these days but my patients—I am happier than any time since in France—I feel I am really needed. No deaths yet.

By the end of July the number of patients on the floor was 140, and all leaves were cancelled. Everyone's nerves were frayed. "Miss Elder said she never knew things could be so bad. It is sad that some nurses refuse to take orders from her—and say to her as they did to me—'You dont *rate* any more than I, and Ill take no orders from you'—Thank God that type are a minority, but they make our work most difficult—"

By August the numbers of wounded decreased enough to allow for leaves and time for attention to personal needs. Essig had her hair shampooed and wondered at the ability of the French to get even long hair clean with only two quarts of water. A week of sightseeing in southern France at the end of August included plenty of sleep, food, and shopping. In the resort village of Chamonix Essig watched the full moon rise over Mont Blanc, and was "so over come

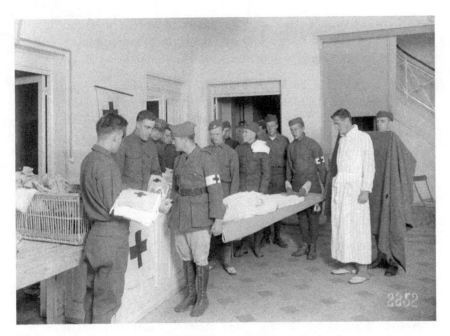

Figure 3.2 In June 1918, as Allied casualties mounted, Hospital 32 became an evacuation facility, where soldiers arrived directly from the front. Trains carrying the wounded stopped at the resort town's thermal baths, where soldiers who had been lying in fields and trenches were bathed. Courtesy American Red Cross Collection, Library of Congress.

I could not sleep—The nearest Heaven I ever hope to be in this world—" The trip culminated with a weekend in Paris and a whirlwind tour of the major attractions, as well as a trip to Versailles. Essig observed: "French women are surely temptresses and it is small wonder if our boys go wrong—in Paris—Soldiers— U.S.A—are not given passes to Paris but they get there AWOL."

September was quiet and cold. Essig relieved a night supervisor on leave and was in charge of the five buildings comprising Base Hospital 32. She refused the permanent assignment, as she did not like either night duty or the supervisory responsibility. There was a celebration to commemorate the first anniversary of their taking the Oath of Allegiance.

The end of September was the beginning of the "Big Drive." The Meuse-Argonne campaign lasted six weeks and involved over one million American troops. They were successful in penetrating the Argonne forest held by the German army and in reaching the railway bringing troops and supplies to the enemy. American losses were approximately 117,000 dead or wounded.[20] The number of patients on Essig's floor rose to 175, and another frantic period of caring for many seriously wounded ensued. On September 30 she wrote:

> Our men are winning but the price is to high . . . One is never equipped nor prepared for such Hellishness—Never thought I could work so hard—Many of our staff are off duty sick and for a couple of days I thought I could not take it but am up and at it . . . We have 175 patients on our floor—all have been wounded and most require dressing daily—beside serving meals and the innumerable things that should be done . . . I am responsible for a lot of clerical work and for keeping up supplies—For the first time we did get a few baths given today—The patients are so patient and so grateful for the little they receive They say "This is so much better than the trenches"

Florence Martin and many other observers also told of the relief and gratitude of the wounded American soldiers when they found themselves in the care of American nurses. Martin wrote:

> Ever since we have been here we have had letters and letters telling us what wonderful, unselfish work we are doing. We all have heard this until we are ashamed . . . we are getting what I wish many at home who are working quite as hard as we, could have, and that is the privilege of being right here in the midst of things.[21]

October brought many more wounded to Base Hospital 32. On October 4, 1918, Essig commented:

> The rush continues only more of it—Miss Martin drives us off duty at 8 P.M.—but our hours of duty are without end—We are never finished—We recieve [sic] new patients and discharge all that we can—The *Bath-House* is a Godsend—The boys are *usually* taken to the B.H.—shed their *lousy* uniforms are given Baths and clean pajamas & bath robes—before coming to us—Their uniforms are sterilized to kill the cooties and when discharged they leave in some awful shrunken outfits—To be free of cooties even for a short time is heavenly the boys say—A bath, clean clothes, wounds dressed and a few square meals—make new men of them—I never saw hungry men—Food is carried up 8 flights of stairs in huge garbage cans and served on the men's mess kit—the servings are a mess but the men dont seem to mind—Anderson starts at the front end of the corridor and ends up at the rear where he turns over all the food left to the German prisoners—They fare well-and in return have to wash the cans to be returned to the kitchen—They wouldnt think of running away—haven't had it so good in a long time in spite of some of the awful injuries—

On October 7, 1918, she continued:

> We have 160 patients and 40 have Flu beside their wounds. The odors
> are bad. Even the Dakin's Sol. on wounds cannot overcome the odors of
> pus—sweat and lysol—The latter is our only way of sterilizing equipment
> and instruments—no *boiling* facilities We are working 12–14 hrs—and it is
> impossible to walk down 8 flights and 1/2 mile to nurses Quarters *for meals*
> with the thought of having to walk back up the hills, up 8 flights of stairs
> again—We eat as we work—grab what we can—Some of our personnel
> are very sick—

The hospital's capacity was further taxed by the influenza epidemic that affected both patients and staff. Many other diseases complicated the task of caring for the sick and wounded, including diphtheria, malaria, mumps, rheumatic
fever, tuberculosis, arthritis, tonsillitis, bronchitis, pneumonia, and enteritis.
Encephalitis was common, as was trench fever, a viral infection transmitted by
lice, and trench foot which brought pain, burning, redness, and then cyanosis
of the feet and was caused by prolonged exposure to wet and cold.[22]

The press of patients continued, with rumors of peace to encourage everyone. Near the end of October Essig herself was feeling "rotten" but took quinine
and aspirin, did not tell anyone, and kept working. "I am not satisfied with any
of the care we are able to give—but everyone is doing his best and the patients
are grand—Weather is cold and rainy—" On November 10 she saw a soldier
from home: "Frank Anderson—an Elkhart fellow—arrived on our floor yesterday I tried to do everything possible for him and gave him the afghan sent
me by the Shiloh Field Post—He was most appreciative—It was good to see
someone from home—Much talk of *Peace.*"

The Armistice ending the war was signed in November, but the work, the
cold, the frozen pipes, and the eight-flight climb continued. Sick and wounded
from what was now called the Army of Occupation kept the patient count steady.
On December 6 the remaining forty patients were discharged, and the floor
prepared for closing. On December 8, 103 new patients were admitted. "None
of the patients is very sick but all had to have beds, pajamas, bath robes, towels,
blankets and all had to be fed—as usual they were straved [*sic*]—I had one nurse
to help me—I did the ordering and dressed wounds as necessary." The cold,
the rain, and the mud also continued; but Christmas boxes arrived, and festivi-
ties of the season began. The prisoners were still in residence. "The German
patients—now on 2nd Floor had a big celebration—Beautiful decorations—a
crèche and everything—The[y] sang carols and seemed happier than anyone
else!—The nurses gave them Amer Cigarettes and they were delighted—"

By the middle of January, 1919, all patients had been discharged, and another period of waiting, of rumors, and of moving in bits and pieces began. On February 6, 1919, Essig wrote: "The Hospitals have all been closed and equipment has been shipped. There are only the various details, ie; coal, ashes, water and food to supply our needs—The days seem so very long and—cold—Every thing is frozen up except one Toilet!"

At last, on February 20, the remaining personnel received orders to move. Several train trips and cold nights later they arrived in Brest to begin the long voyage home on the *America* on March 3, 1919. On February 23 Essig reported hearing that Jane A. Delano, chairman of the Red Cross Nursing Service, had been operated on for mastoiditis at Savenay, where "she had been making a personal survey of the nursing situation in France prior to being stricken—" Essig later added to the diary that Delano had died at Savenay on April 15, 1919.[23]

The homeward voyage was as uncomfortable as the voyage to France. There were twenty-seven nurses assigned to one stateroom. The ship also carried one thousand patients as well as the 104th Field Artillery of the 28th Division. This was the first combat division to return from France, and New York City was preparing to give them an enthusiastic welcome.

> I left Brest feeling on top of the world but not for long—Why should any one with a cast iron stomach ordinarily get so desperately sick and want to die and end it all. . . .
>
> I have been sick, sicker, sickest off and on—Have existed on sour pickles, salty crackers mostly some grapefruit and orange—Have kept to my bunk. So long as I lie flat on my back all is well . . . —

On March 13, 1919, the ship docked at Hoboken. "What a grand and glorious sight the *Statue of Liberty*! I was out on deck and missed nothing of our entry into the Harbor—All so wonderful—What an experience for little M.E.!"

The next few days were spent eating, resting, shopping, and renewing friendships. The transition time was apparently not free of difficulty. A cryptic diary entry for March 15 summarized: "It was not the happiest of days—our first Sunday back in U.S.A. but we expected too much—We are all human . . ."

On March 18, 1919, Essig lamented:

> We had our Physicals and hope to leave soon—We had to turn in our Red Cross belongings—It broke my heart to turn in my precious cape—Some simply said they were "lost in action" but I could not say that—much as I wanted to keep it—History was all wrapped up in that cape—with all the holes

burnt into the lower edge where it flipped against our little stoves—Never a day that it had not been on duty with me—my faithful friend—

After final clearing of physicals, Essig left New York and arrived in Elkhart, Indiana, at 4:15 p.m. on March 22, 1919. The diary ends: "Such an exciting time—I felt over whelmed—Everyone seemed glad to see me back and needless to say *I am DELighted to Be Back Home*[.]

Fini"

EPILOG

Following the war Essig, like many of her wartime compatriots, turned to administrative and teaching duties in the nursing field.[24] From 1920 to 1922 Essig resumed her position as director of nursing at Elkhart General Hospital. Then, in 1924, she became director of the Brokaw Hospital School of Nursing in Normal, Illinois; director of nursing at the hospital; then administrator of the hospital from 1930 to 1940. During World War II she moved to Passavant Memorial Hospital in Chicago as assistant director of nursing.[25] She retired from Passavant in 1948, and in 1952 she went to live at the Veterans Administration Center in Dayton, Ohio, a retirement home for persons with military service. She remained there until her death in September, 1981. Essig was buried in the National Military Cemetery adjoining the center as she had requested.

ALMA S. WOOLLEY was the Caroline F. Rupert Professor of Nursing and Director of the School of Nursing, Illinois Wesleyan University, and Dean of the Georgetown University School of Nursing and Health Studies. She died in December 2005.

NOTES

This article appeared in volume 82, no. 1 (March 1986).

1. Percy M. Ashburn, *A History of the Medical Department of the United States Army* (Boston, 1929), 340–43.

2. Marie Cecile Chomel and Anselm Chomel, *A Red Cross Chapter at Work* (Indianapolis, 1920), 234, 236.

3. Benjamin D. Hitz, comp. and ed., *The History of Base Hospital 32* ... (Indianapolis, 1922), 3, 22; Chomel and Chomel, *Red Cross Chapter at Work*, 241, 245–46.

4. Hitz, *History of Base Hospital 32*, pp. 3, 5; Chomel and Chomel, *Red Cross Chapter at Work*, 240.

5. Chomel and Chomel, *Red Cross Chapter at Work*, 237–42.

6. *Ibid.*, 251–55; Hitz, *History of Base Hospital 32*, pp. 132–35.

7. Chomel and Chomel, *Red Cross Chapter at Work*, 255–56; Hitz, *History of Base Hospital 32*, pp. 135–36.

8. Chomel and Chomel, *Red Cross Chapter at Work*, 251–53.

9. Hitz, *History of Base Hospital 32*, pp. 142–43, 156–58.

10. Ashburn, *History of the Medical Department of the United States Army*, 307–30. The United States surgeon general's report for 1919 indicated that while 52,423 men had died in battle, at sea, and as a result of wounds during 1917 and 1918, another 50,714 had died of disease. *Ibid.*, 318. See also Henry P. Davison, *The American Red Cross in the Great War* (New York, 1919), 84–89.

11. Chomel and Chomel, *Red Cross Chapter at Work*, 247, 249; Davison, *American Red Cross in the Great War*, 89–90.

12. Between 1917 and 1920, 197 nurses gave their lives in the course of their military service. Most died from disease or accidents. Many were decorated for valor, and several were awarded the Distinguished Service Cross. Davison, *American Red Cross in the Great War*, 92.

13. With the following exceptions all excerpts from Essig's diary have been transcribed as nearly like the original as possible. Essig's script is similar to printing, and she always used a capital "R" regardless of the location of the letter in a word. These have been lowercased unless a capital was grammatically correct. In a number of instances decisions concerning initial capitalization were arbitrary. Misspellings have been retained, as has Essig's practice of using dashes instead of other forms of punctuation, even at the ends of sentences. If no punctuation was placed at the end of a sentence, a double space is used to indicate a break in thought. Explanatory material, complete names of individuals, omitted letters, or correct spellings of places have sometimes been inserted in brackets.

14. Hitz, *History of Base Hospital 32*, p. 23. The number of women who marched is reported as fifteen thousand by Davison in *American Red Cross in the Great War*, opposite 86. In Essig's diary the Red Cross Parade is erroneously cited as having occurred on Thursday, October 3. The dates for the entire week are mismatched with the days of the week.

15. Quoted in Hitz, *History of Base Hospital 32*, p. 26.

16. *Ibid.*, 45–48.

17. *Ibid.*, 50–52.

18. For information concerning the 42nd "Rainbow" Division and concerning battles and wartime strategy during World War I, see Robert H. Ferrell, *Woodrow Wilson and World War I, 1917–1921* (New York, 1985), 56–57, 71–73, 81–83, *passim*.

19. Chomel and Chomel, *Red Cross Chapter at Work*, 250–51; Hitz, *History of Base Hospital 32*, p. 78–79.

20. Ferrell, *Woodrow Wilson and World War I*, 81–83.

21. Quoted in Chomel and Chomel, *Red Cross Chapter at Work*, 247.

22. Hitz, *History of Base Hospital 32*, p. 111–29; Ashburn, *History of the Medical Department of the United States Army*, 352–55.

23. Jane A. Delano was superintendent of the Army Nurse Corps from 1909 to 1912. She resigned this position in 1912 to become chairman of the Red Cross Nursing Service. When the United States entered World War I, eight thousand nurses had already been prepared to serve. During the war Delano helped supply twenty thousand nurses for service. Buried at Savenay and later reinterred at Arlington National Cemetery, Delano was admitted into the Hall of Fame of the American Nurses' Association in 1982. American Nurses' Association, *Nursing Hall of Fame* (Kansas City, Mo., 1982), 5. See also Davison, *American Red Cross in the Great War*, 92.

24. Throughout World War I leaders in the nursing profession in the United States challenged colleagues to use their experiences in Europe to enhance and upgrade the nursing profession. By proving the usefulness of their formal education during the war, nurses could ensure increases not only in the nursing ranks but also in the money needed to improve schools of nursing. Discharged nurses were urged to put their wartime training to use in administrative and teaching positions in nursing schools and in public health work. Especially important in promoting these ideas were Delano and Isabel Stewart, head of the Department of Nursing Education at Columbia University. See Isabel Stewart, "Testing the Nursing Spirit," *American Journal of Nursing*, XVII (May, 1917), 707–11; Stewart, "Recruiting the New Nursing Army," *ibid.*, XVII (September, 1918), 1199–1203; Jane A Delano, "How American Nurses Helped Win the War," *Modern Hospital*, XII (1919), 7–9. Although the nursing profession did make great strides as a result of World War I, nurses, who were neither officers nor enlisted personnel and who were thus hampered in giving direction and instruction, were refused military rank. Not until 1947, after World War II, was permanent commissioned officer status achieved. Philip A. Kalisch, "How Army Nurses Became Officers," *Nursing Research*, XXV (May–June, 1976), 164–77.

25. Essig's move to Passavant was in the nature of a return. After attending the public schools in Elkhart, Essig had received her nursing education at Passavant Memorial Hospital School of Nursing and the Illinois Training School for Nurses in affiliation with Cook County Hospital in Chicago. Graduating in 1907, she had worked for the Chicago Visiting Nurse Association as a school nurse, infant welfare nurse, tuberculosis nurse, and industrial nurse before going to Elkhart General Hospital and Nursing School as superintendent, thence to France.

FOUR

"Oatmeal and Coffee"

Memoirs of a Hoosier Soldier in World War I

KENNETH GEARHART BAKER

EDITED AND INTRODUCED BY ROBERT H. FERRELL,

TRANSCRIPTION AND POSTSCRIPT BY BETTY BAKER RINKER

KENNETH GEARHART BAKER (1896–1988), BORN in Rochester, Indiana, was a veteran of the two world wars of the century that has just ended, and in his last years, in the 1980s, he remembered the earlier one better than he did the later. By then removed to a retirement apartment in Florida, he began in 1984 to write his memories of the war of 1917–1918 and of the occupation of Germany in the early months of 1919. He wrote with a pencil on a yellow paper tablet, while sitting (so his daughter, Betty Baker Rinker, remembers) in the easy chair of his living room. By the time he finished he had completed virtually a small book. He died in 1988, and his daughter arranged in 1993 for his manuscript to be typed. She deposited a copy in the archives of the U.S. Army Military History Institute, a part of the Army War College in Carlisle Barracks, Pennsylvania, and it was there that the present editor found it.

The author of "Oatmeal and Coffee" was the second son of Hoosier farmer Charles Baker and his wife, Mary. After the family, including a younger sister, moved in 1901 to a farm southwest of Wolcott, Kenneth Baker attended country schools in White County until 1912, when the family moved to Monticello, the county seat, where Kenneth graduated from high school around 1915.

When the United States entered World War I, Baker and his friend Henry Brucker were enrolled in a technical training course for electricians at the Milwaukee College of Engineering. On May 8, 1917, they enlisted in the 1st Wisconsin Field Signal Battalion of the Wisconsin National Guard, which when taken into federal service became part of the Thirty-second (Michigan/Wisconsin) Division. This was the division with which Baker spent the remainder of his army service, except for five months in England when, having been hospitalized and left behind when his division moved on, he became a "casual," i.e., a soldier not regularly attached to a unit.

After the war Baker returned to Indiana. He entered Purdue University in the autumn of 1919 and graduated with a degree in electrical engineering. He married his Purdue sweetheart, Bertha Walton, in 1921 and was employed for the rest of his life as a sales engineer with the Wagner Electric Company in Indianapolis, except for another stint in the army during World War II. Pearl Harbor brought him back into the military; he applied for a commission in the U.S. Army Air Forces and served as a base supply officer and an executive officer.

There is of course something nostalgic about reading Baker's account today, in a new century with World War I far in the past, beyond memory of most Indiana residents, and with only a small remnant of its veterans still alive—at last count the state's surviving vets numbered sixteen out of the tens of thousands of Hoosiers who took part in that war and who for so many years were leaders in the state, and, some of them, the nation. The entire generation that included Kenneth Baker and his contemporaries, those born in the 1890s, is nearly gone. American Legion parades of yesteryear, so familiar to later generations, are now far in the past. The toy trains with cars marked "40 & 8," representing the freight cars in France in which forty soldiers or eight horses were transported to the front, which appeared in the parades on Memorial Day, the Fourth of July, and Armistice Day, are no longer to be seen. Indeed Armistice Day, a staple celebration of some of us Hoosiers older than average, has now been translated into Veterans Day. If someone asked the average Indianan what day is or was the real Armistice Day, he or she would respond, probably, with surprise and almost surely without being able to relate the long-ago and for a while so-well-remembered date of what seemed established for eternity as the most important event in national and world history—the armistice declared in the eleventh minute of the eleventh hour of the eleventh day of the eleventh month in 1918.

World War I, begun in Europe in 1914, changed the history of Europe, America, and for that matter all nations and peoples of the world. In 1917 Americans hastily approved going to war. They had been shocked by the way in which imperial Germany had not merely plunged Europe into war two and one-half years earlier but had behaved so wantonly in sinking the great liner *Lusitania* in 1915 and then almost two years later defying the government of the United States by resuming the unrestricted use of submarines, an act that brought the American declaration of war.

All this was a prelude to the enlistment in the U.S. Army or acceptance of the draft by Kenneth Baker and so many other Americans, in hope of Germany's defeat and the survival, as they put it, of civilization itself.

How does Baker's memoir fit into the literature of American participation in World War I? Libraries now contain shelf upon shelf of accounts, and how important is his?

Its sources are difficult to detail. It is unclear how Baker managed to hold his experiences in 1917–1919 in his mind for nearly seventy years. Like so many soldiers of his time he kept a diary, which was contrary to regulations. Unfortunately, his daughter reports, after he brought it home his horrified mother read it and destroyed it. But it is clear that, even without his diary, he did remember what, after all, may well have been the most impressive experience of his life. Until he reached nearly the end of his narrative he kept the chronology straight. (At the close he was apparently losing the ability to concentrate; he died not long after finishing it.) In seeking to end the account he also, one suspects, departed from chronology in order to include all sorts of miscellaneous experiences. His memory was no doubt aided by his copy of his division's history, published in 1920.[1] A post-World War II trip to England may have included France.

In one way Baker was not typical of American soldiers during World War I; while many of them found it intensely difficult to record their experiences, this soldier from Rochester somehow had learned to write in a straightforward way. He managed, with ease, to achieve a tight literary style. And he could introduce humor, in contrast to so many of the accounts of World War I that were sober to a fault.

In other ways he was typical of men of his time. He was a private all the way and never forgot that fact. He deeply resented the privileges of officers and especially the belief of so many officers that the men were too stupid to understand almost anything. Although he was an officer himself in World War II, Baker could not forget that he had been treated as though he were incompetent twenty-five years before. On occasion his narrative is bitter, and time after time he recites how he and his fellow "bucks"—buck privates—feigned stupidity, often to excellent effect. He also was typical in remembering the old saw that there is a right way to do something, a wrong way, and the army way. The procedures of the army struck him, as they did so many of his fellow soldiers, as peculiar to the point of idiocy. And he was immensely proud of how, when the action came, turning from warm to hot, the procedures of RHIP (rank has its privileges) dropped off, the bucks took over, and their judgment and heroism won the war—not the army's way.

Baker was justly proud of the Thirty-second Division. When the army expanded in World War I from a virtual constabulary of a little over one hundred thousand officers and men to a massive force of four million within a year and a half, West Pointers and other regulars continued to believe that they were the men who counted, the saving remnant. Feeling between regulars and National Guard officers and men ran high, and the more so because almost without exception senior guard officers lost their commands to regulars once troops arrived in France. Army talk was always of what the First and Second divisions had done or could do, and it was said that National Guard divisions, such as the Thirty-second, were not as good. In fact the Thirty-second saw a great deal of action and performed very well, and they should have proved—the lesson was available but forgotten between the world wars—that the nonprofessionals were as good as the regulars.

The soldier memoirs of World War I are not easy to measure because there are so many of them. But it is difficult to find memoirs any better than Baker's. For Indiana the only comparable accounts are those of Elmer W. Sherwood, published as a narrative in 1919 and as a diary ten years later. Sherwood's books were announced as remarkable both by Booth Tarkington and in 1929 by General Charles P. Summerall, former commander of V Corps and by then chief of staff of the U.S. Army, although Sherwood's diary was bowdlerized so badly that it is in need of republication. The diary of Indiana's Elmer Frank Straub also stands high on any list of World War I books, although it begins slowly and takes on flair only toward the end. Among the several hundred unpublished memoirs and diaries now in the Military History Institute at Carlisle Barracks, Baker's clearly is superior.[2]

—⟶⟶—

Editor's Note: The diary is reproduced essentially as it was written. The transcriber has silently corrected some spelling errors and replaced some commas with periods.

If anyone is interested, I was born in Rochester, Indiana, the second child of Charles and Mary Baker, August 5, 1896. My older brother, Walker Willis was born in Wolcott, Indiana on December 3, 1894, and my sister Madge at Otterbein, Indiana, 1900.

In 1901 we moved to a farm 8 miles southwest of Wolcott. Here I started to school in the fall of 1902. A small country school having three of us in the first grade. I went to this school until December, when we moved to another farm a mile and a quarter southwest of Wolcott and I was transferred to what to us was a very large school, having eight rooms in a two story building. No inside plumbing however, that was to come later when we moved to Monticello in 1912, county seat of White County, Indiana.

As fate ordained, I was born just at the right time to get into the first World War. I will never know whether I was born just at the right time to get into it, or whether it was started just at the right time to get me, but either way, we got together. Like most kids of the correct age, [I] just couldn't wait. At the beginning of the war, "Hank" and I were in school in a city some distance from our hometown, and as was usual at the time, were interested in this war as a rather distant excitement. Our heroes were the fliers, so when the war came we immediately decided that we wanted to be fliers, but being very naive, thought that all we had to do was go to some recruiting station and the army would jump at the chance of getting us to fly one of their 'aeroplanes.' Well, we soon found out that it was not that simple. If we were to get to fly one of their planes we had to know somebody, say like a governor or a senator or at least a judge, to endorse us. Then, if we passed the physical and moral examinations, they might consider us. We were crestfallen and disgusted and ready to pass the army up and let them fight their war without us, when the recruiting sergeant gave us a bit of what he must have thought was sage advice. Since the flying part of the army was a branch of the Signal Corps, we should consider joining the Signal Corps, and then transferring to the flying section. We went home and talked this idea over, and decided this might not be a bad idea, since we both had decided we did not want to be in the infantry. After mulling the idea over a while we decided to give the Signal Corps a try, so we went looking for a recruiting station for the Signal Corps. We found it in the form of a National Guard recruiting station, who assured us they could sign us in the signal battalion and that we could put in an application to transfer to the flying section after we had been in a short time. That recruiting sergeant would tell you anything just to get your name on the dotted line. We signed, and the atmosphere changed at once. Now we were in, we were told, not asked. We were told we could go home and stay there until we were called, which would be in about a month, and that we should be ready to leave on orders so we were to be ready at all times, and were not to leave on any extended trips so as not to be readily contacted.

We went home and in due time received notice to report at such and such a place at such and such a time.

Well, it was a little sooner than we had expected. But since the war was moving along maybe they had had to speed things up a bit so we decided to accommodate them, even though it had interfered with a fishing trip of a few days.

Upon arrival at the armory where we had been ordered to report, we were introduced to an old army custom, hurry up and wait, stand in line and wait. After standing around most of the day we were told we could sleep in the armory on a cot or go out to a hotel, or home, just so we were back by seven o'clock in the morning. We chose a hotel. Most of the men lived in the city so went home. Next morning we arrived on time and after waiting around for two or three

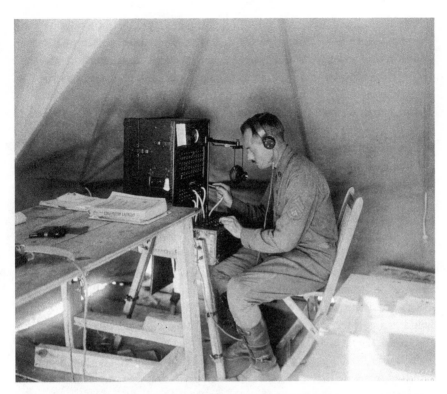

Figure 4.1 A signalman at a field switchboard. Soldiers in the Army
Signal Corps were responsible for establishing and maintaining
telephone and telegraph lines and staffing switchboards for essential field
communications. Courtesy American Unofficial Collection of World
War I Photographs, National Archives and Records Administration.

more hours got on a train and started for our camp site, some 70 miles from the
city. We arrived at camp in the evening, were lined up again and marched to our
tents. Fortunately some one had already set them up, otherwise we would probably slept in the open that night. After having been in camp all of half an hour
we were lined up again and my name was called and I was advised that I was on
guard duty. That was what you got for having a name that started with a letter at
the first of the alphabet, B for instance. Later we decided the reason for this was
that most sergeants had never learned their "letters" in school beyond C, so each
day in making up details they always started with A and rarely got beyond C.

    With 5 or 6 other would-be soldiers who knew about as much as I did about it,
we were marched off to the guard tent to join other unlucky souls. At the guard

tent we were lined up again and assigned the hourly shifts we would be actually walking on duty. I drew, or rather was assigned, hours 10:00 to 12:00 pm
and 2:00 to 4:00 am, told to stay at the guard tent and be ready at our assigned
hours. I had a bunk in the guard tent, but sleeping was impossible. I had no idea
what I was in for.

Punctually at 10 minutes before 10:00 we were lined up and marched off to
duty, the four in my group went to the back of the camp ground and were told
we were to guard the camp at the side we were covering and were to prevent any
intruders from entering or insiders from leaving. In my ignorance I asked the
corporal in charge of us how we were to stop anyone who wished to come in or
leave, he looked at me in a very superior manner and said, why you challenge
them—you say "Stop! Who goes there? Advance and be recognized." Then, in
my ignorance, I blurted out "But what if they don't stop?" That stumped the
corporal, for in his book all challenged people stop. Then finding himself, since
he did not want to be shown up by a common "buck" private with one day's
experience, he said "you call the Corporal of the Guard." Well, that sounded
OK to me. I was willing to pass the buck and responsibility on to him. But I
wondered how far the ones we were trying to stop would be gone by the time
the corporal got there, but decided that was his worry, not mine.

This was a sad night, walking back and forth over a given course about two
hundred feet long through eight inch high grass that was wet with dew when
you started and got wetter by the minute. By the end of term I was soggy wet
up to my knees, and remember, was still in civilian clothes—still wearing light
oxfords.

We were relieved at twelve and marched back to the guard tent to rest till
2:00 am when we were to go back for some more. I took off my shoes and
socks—wrung the socks out and hung them up to dry. At two o'clock they
were back and we went back to the same spot, and went through the same
agony all over again. At four o'clock we were relieved again and told to stay at
the guard tent until six, at which time we were dismissed and advised that we
had the day off to rest.

My first day in the army was to be remembered but not looked back upon as
a day to be fondly remembered.

True to their word, I was not molested all of my second day however at
chow time I learned what the mess call on the bugle sounded like and was
introduced to the army main stay in the food department, "slum." It is made,
as far as I can remember, as follows. Take a 35 or 40 gallon GI can, fill it about
1/3 full of water, preferably clean, and heat to boil. Into this put about 40 or
50 lbs of chopped up beef in chunks about bite size, to some as big as your fist,

about half a bushel of potatoes, (this is the amount left over from a bushel after a KP has peeled a bushel), these are cut into bite sizes also. Then carrots and onions and any other vegetables that may be lying around. You boil this mess until a potato feels more or less soft. Then you take a large iron skillet, put in a good supply of lard, melt it and get it hot, then add a goodly supply of flour to the grease and heat over a hot fire, stirring vigorously until the flour is brown and dump into the boiling mess in this GI can. The result is a brown gooey mess that will stick to your ribs, mess plate, clothes or anything else it happens to touch. Particularly tight to your mess kit when you try to wash it out in the lukewarm water supplied in the GI can for that purpose after the meal. Even I could believe that the whole mess was not too sanitary.[3]

On the third day we were all lined up in front of our tents early in the morning, so we may be counted and answer to our names, alphabetically of course. I guess this was to see that no one had gotten disgusted and taken off the night before.

Here again my name got me in bad, starting with Ba I was first in line and sure enough, first name called for detail, rations detail. What that was I had no idea, neither did the three others, but we soon found out that we were to get in a wagon and ride over to the rations dump and draw the rations for the battalion for that day. Now the rations dump was about a mile from our camp site, on a railroad spur along which a platform had been built.

On to this platform provisions were unloaded and then divided up for the various organizations of the division. Our battalion had a small sign over the area assigned to it. When we arrived the sergeant in command of our detail reported [to] the QM sergeant[4] in charge of the rations distribution and checked our list, pointed to the pile of groceries and said there it is, take it away, so we loaded it on our wagon, which was none too clean, and the bread was unwrapped, but never the less we piled it in the wagon and went back to the camp. Here we delivered it to the company kitchens, in quantities equal to their size. It may be well here to tell you how our battalion was made up.

There were four companies. First was the Headquarters Company. It was small consisting of about fifteen to twenty men. Next there were three service companies, Co. A, which had approximately 150 men in it, Co. B about the same number, but Co. C had about 300 men in it. I was in Headquarters Company. I presume my name had something to do with that also, starting as it did with a B.

When we got back to the company after the groceries were delivered, the sergeant called me into the headquarters tent and said, do you think you could deliver the rations, and I said I thought I could, and he said you are on permanent rations detail. I said "all by myself?" and he said no, each morning at

7:00 AM a wagon and driver will be here for you and three other men to help. You are responsible to see that the rations are delivered. That was all the instructions. There was that fatal name again, beginning with a B. How else could you explain it otherwise.

It didn't turn out to be so bad however, because being on permanent detail I was excused from all other details. I would not have to walk guard, stand reveille, take exercise in the wet cold grass in the morning, or do any of the routine training exercises. Life was sweeter.

Things went along for a week or two. The operation of rations delivery rather smoothed out, except a wrangle every day with the mess sergeants each of which seemed to think he was being short changed, which of course was not the case, at least as far as we were concerned. The mess sergeants were particularly touchy about the meat, sugar and syrup. As it was set up, A and B companies each got a quarter of beef each day and C company got two quarters. This worked out so that A and B company got a front quarter on alternate days and of course C got a front and hind quarter each day.

Each company mess sergeant was after me to get him more sugar, canned milk, cookies. There was nothing I could do about it, or at least so I thought, until we four rations flunkies began to get army wise. We soon learned that by being very helpful at the dock like helping the QM "bucks" in distributing the various groceries and unloading the refrigerator cars we could accidentally put certain things in our truck instead of where they were supposed to be. These things usually turned out to be a hind quarter of beef instead of a front, or a 50 pound bag of sugar or a gallon of syrup, a case of milk or jelly or jams.

I will have to admit that we probably favored A Company a bit with these goodies since that is where we ate, and that it also paid back in kind every once in a while as the mess sergeant got me into the back end of the cook tent every once in a while where we enjoyed a steak or other goodies never enjoyed by the buck privates and on a par with any officer in the field. My first lesson in the army—don't be too particular and a little back scratching usually pays off.

After being in camp a week or ten days we were issued a uniform. As usual, lined up and marched over to QM tent in which the "cottons" as they were called, were piled presumably in sizes, shirts, pants, leggings, and socks and shoes. As we marched by they threw a shirt, hat, pants and leggings and socks at you; when they got down to shoes, they did give you credit for knowing what size you wore, and then gave you the next half size larger. They didn't give you any underwear. Whether they assumed you didn't wear it or that you had your own I will never know.

About half an hour after the issue was over I think one of the largest exchanges of clothing ever existed started and went on for the next twenty-four hours. Being a more or less standard size, I made out very well on the whole.

Things went on rather smoothly for a week or two when one day we got orders to strip for physical and shots. It turned out that the physical was to be given in a small farm house on the camp grounds about a mile from our tent site. Here we were all lined up in front of our tents ready to go when some bright officer discovered that the sandy rocky field between us and the farm house was also covered with sand spurs which were hell on bare feet, so we were permitted to get our shoes. After another half hour delay we got on our way to the farm house, by this time the sun was well up and hot, so 500 of us strung out over a field, naked as jay birds, headed for a small house, capable of holding no more that fifteen or twenty, with the examining crew with equipment, inside at one time. The rest stood out in the sun getting redder by the minute. This was some very poor planning by someone in charge, but this we were soon to learn was par for the course.

Upon entering the house we were given a battery of orders, such as bend over, spread your buttocks, stand straight on one leg, on the other, open your mouth, say aah, raise your arms, take a full breath, let it out, raise your right arm, wham—a needle in it, raise your left arm, another needle, scratch till it bled—a dab of vaccine, and advice not to wipe that arm. All this in a constant walk between two rows of medicos, out the front door of the house, and no orders as to whether that was all or where to go. So we stood around in the hot sun and after about two minutes one keeled over, "dead out" from strain and heat, soon another, then another, and altogether there must have been close to seventy-five or eighty on the ground. We drug them over and put them in the shade of a couple of trees in front of the house. After a while each would come to, sit up and look foolish. After a short time some officer came out and said we were to go back to our tents. This was unusual to give a bunch of enlisted men credit for enough intelligence to find their way back home. I guess the officers felt fairly secure in turning a bunch of buck privates loose alone to find their way home a mile across a field in plain sight, and especially since they had no clothes. We were to all report back in one week to check on our vaccination; mine didn't take so I had to go through the whole business again in a week.

Life rather settled in for a time except the camp was overrun by visiting friends, relatives and girl friends. This kind of curtailed our activities as far as dressing and trips to the latrine was concerned when under normal circumstances certain clothing was considered unnecessary.

Time passed, all types of rumors were always flying around, but finally one began to emerge as a dominant theme. We were going to move about every place in the U.S. but it finally settled down to some place in the south, but to every place from Florida to California. Things were quite confused, but as time passed the weather got colder where we were, and when ice began to form on our water bucket at night we were ready to move. But no one seemed to know where. Finally one day an order came. Pack to move, nothing but army issue was to be taken. Now over the period of time that we had been in this camp a lot of junk had accumulated in the way of sweaters, mufflers, gloves, socks etc., from doting mothers and girl friends. The pile of junk was astounding, and could no way be hid in a standard army back pack.

At last we were lined up and marched over to the train. It looked good, made up of Pullman cars which would indicate a long ride. Also there were to be only three men to a compartment, two to the lower bunk and one in the upper with the excess equipment, such as back packs, etc. Actually the two in the lower had the best, but as we got shaken into place quite comfortable. Intervals in the train were interspaced baggage cars equipped as kitchens.

After three or four days and nights of riding we finally arrived at our destination, and we were not real sure where we were then, but had deduced from the information gleaned from casual conversation with locals at the rail stations along the way that we must be some place in Texas. Why all the secrecy we didn't know, but information was scarce. At least for us.

We were shunted on to a siding at the camp, unloaded and marched to our tents. It turned out that they were an improvement over the last camp, the tents even had board floors in them and one electric light, about twenty-five watts.[5]

When everything you own is either on your back in a pack or you are wearing it, it usually does not take long to move in. We were all settled in about forty-five minutes, with old rumors taking up just where they left off when we left the old camp.

One rumor that persisted was that we were going to be mounted. Why, no one seemed to have the slightest idea, and wondered why. Imagine riding a horse around a front line filled with trenches, and fox holes. Even the officers couldn't be that dumb—even the higher up ones. But in a couple of weeks we got horses, and a picket line and the whole mess that goes with them. It turned out, however, there were not horses for everyone, just enough for the officers to ride and the dog-robbers to take care of.[6]

Things moved along more or less smoothly for two or three weeks, then lightning struck as far as I was concerned—the sergeant came to me one morning and said "You have a horse." And I said "Me? I can't have a horse, I am just a buck private. No buck private has a horse. Besides, I don't want a horse. I already have four mules and a wagon to take care of, and that is all I need or want." Sarg just says, "You don't have to take care of them, you got a helper and now you got a horse whether you want one or not." And I said "What officer owned the horse, and why can't his dog-robber take care of his horse like all the rest do?" Sarg just said it does not belong to anyone, so now it is yours. "What is the matter with it?" I asked. "Nothing as far as I know," said Sarg, "except it needs cleaning up and a little feed. It is tied up in the stall down by the equipment shed at the end of the company street, better go down and get acquainted."

I went down to see what had been foisted off on me and why. A buck private with a horse just couldn't be—there had to be a catch some place, and there was.

This horse turned out to be the meanest looking horse I had ever laid eyes on. I mean he had an evil eye, and when I got close to him he took a bite at me. He missed, but not far and I heard his teeth snap. This horse was no animal to get careless with. I circled around him and he took a kick at me. After carefully scrutinizing him, I decided he must have been dreadfully mistreated and was fighting back. He was always on the defensive, he had had no care and known no gentle treatment.

First he had to be cleaned up, the army would insist on that. I went back up to company headquarters and asked Sarg who was mad at me. No one that he knows of, but I had grown up on a farm and they had thought I might know about horses. (How wrong they were).

I sat around and thought about it for a while, then went over to the kitchen and wrangled an apple away from Cookie and took it down to "Pinto." I decided to call him "Pint" [sic] for lack of anything better. He was wary of any gesture of kindness, but hunger won out and he actually took the apple from my hand, and not my hand with it. He even let me touch his nose, but little. I hung around him for a time and then fed him a bucket of oats in his manger feed box and put some hay in his manger, and brought him a bucket of water. He drank it as if he hadn't seen water for a week, so I gave him a second bucket and left him for the night.

Next morning he didn't seem quite so hostile, another apple helped. I decided it was time to try to curry him and give him a good cleaning up, however remembering my first meeting, decided not to trust too far. I tied his head solidly to the manger so he couldn't bite, second maneuvered around the stall side, reached through and got a rope tied around his front leg and jerked it out from under him and tied it up so he only had three legs to stand on. It seems as though a horse has trouble trying to kick standing on three legs, he loses his balance trying to stand on two legs and kick at the same time. He also has trouble trying to kick sideways, so if you want to get struck by a horse or kicked, you must get in front of him or in back.

After spending the larger part of two months in Texas, camp rumors began to circulate about a move overseas, also about losing our horses. It seems the generals in Washington had finally decided that horses would not be such a good idea in trench warfare even if they were indispensable during the Civil War. This was a new war with telephone communication. As I had anticipated, one day Sarge had me come into his tent to tell me that Pint would be taken away. They did, but they got a lot different horse than had been brought to me. All I could hope for was that he got a good home.

As rumors usually did, they materialized eventually, so in the first week of December we were marched over to a train again, loaded into Pullmans and headed generally in a northeasterly direction, but not a word was said as to where we were going.

After seven days on the train we were unloaded and marched to a two story barracks building heated by a big furnace in the middle of the first floor with heating pipes going to the second story. We needed that heat, it was really cold. We heard we were in Hoboken, N.J.[7] We were around the barracks for two days and I mean around it, we were not permitted to go outside. No one wanted to, it was just too cold.

Two days later we were loaded on to a ship—a big ship. By rumor grapevine we were on the White Star liner, *Baltic*, English. You knew it wasn't American the minute one stepped on. We were marched to our stateroom. I think they marched us there to see we did not desert when we saw our so called stateroom. This room was one floor below what appeared to be the first open deck, the room itself was six feet wide, eight feet long and about six and one half feet high. Into this space six of us with all our gear were packed. Two bunks on either side, two across the end. This gave us a dressing space in the middle two feet wide and four feet long. No toilet of course, it was one deck up and a real horror; about twenty feet square, toilets along one side and a urinal trough along the other. Half of the toilet seats were broken or missing entirely, the other toilets were plugged up and over flowing. They could only be used by standing on them, which was being done, or not used at all, just the floor. There was about an inch of water and raw sewage sloshing around on the floor. It was a horror. After being on board about three or four days an officer came around and asked how everything was, he heard, nothing happened.[8]

The night after we boarded the ship we took off and went north to what we heard was Halifax harbor. We did not disembark but were on board for a day or two while a convoy of all sizes of ships was assembled and on the second night we put off, moving slowly since no one could go faster than the slowest ship, which we learned was about 8 knots.[9]

After our first night aboard we were herded to the mess hall, a large room full of mess tables with a serving table at one end. For our first breakfast we got a bowl and a spoon; into the bowl was slapped a gob of cold oatmeal, a small amount of canned milk, two small pieces of bacon so cold it was turning white as the fat congealed, a cup of cold tea with a little bit of sugar, and a slice of bread. Nothing else. For the next 13 or 14 days exactly the same thing. Of course there was plenty of griping by the men but nothing was ever done. The other meals were just as bad; lunch would be fried potatoes, a piece of chicken, which was immediately dubbed sea gull, because it was argued that only a soaring bird would have as large and long a feathers as the feather holes in the bird's wing indicated. It just had to be a sea gull, and not a chicken wing, and besides there were plenty of gulls available. On an occasion or two we got fish, and it never varied while we were on board that ship, not even the cold cup of tea.[10]

After we had been on ship for thirteen days one of the men who had been out on deck just at dusk to get a breath of fresh air before ducking to our stinking stateroom announced that land was visible on both sides of the ship, so we decided that we must be at the narrowest point between Scotland and Ireland. He hadn't been in the room more than a minute or two until we heard a dull heavy thud. We rushed out on deck and someone said the ship just back of us had been torpedoed and that the torpedo had been meant for us being the largest ship in the convoy. All of a sudden there was much activity with small torpedo boats racing around dropping depth charges. They never got the submarine as far as I ever heard, but they were having a lot of activity for a while. Our ship put on speed and soon pulled out of sight of the damaged ship in the fast fading evening light. Next morning we were in Liverpool.

In Liverpool we heard that the torpedoed ship was named the *Tuscania*. It had stayed afloat for over two hours and most of the troops aboard had been saved because of this, and also the closeness of land. Our division had only lost 15 men.[11]

On Liverpool docks we were loaded on trains, a sorry looking mess of soldiers. The English who saw us land must have thought what a sorry looking bunch and they expect to win the war. After a comparatively short ride we were unloaded at Winchester and I immediately went looking for the infirmary. When I had found it a couple of doctors looked and said Ah! and loaded me in an ambulance and off I went to a hospital. There I was put to bed with a mattress on it and clean white sheets. A couple of doctors came to see me, looked at my throat, said Ah! disappeared and shortly were back with syringe needles big enough for a horse and gave me shots on both sides of my stomach and left. Next morning I had water blisters as big as my thumb all over my belly. The doctors came in, looked me over, said Ah! and left. I was warm and sleepy, so the next thing I knew it was next morning, the welts on my belly were gone and the soreness in my throat was better. The doctors came in, looked me over, said Ah! and left. There was another day which didn't make me mad; clean and warm and reasonably good food. Another 24 hours passed and when I awakened the soreness was all gone from my throat, and I felt good. The doctors came in, looked me over and said send him back to his outfit.

This was the beginning of a bad time for me because my outfit had moved on during the two days absence and I was now a casual. In the army a casual is just another way of saying you are going to get the dirty end of a lot of work details, and doubly sure if your name starts with an A, B, or C. So I say again, if you are thinking of joining the army as a buck change your name to start with an X, Y or Z. No sergeant in the army ever got beyond ABC in the alphabet, so all details are made up of bucks whose names start with A, B or C. My name started with B so I was the first to be sent right back out to the hospital, this time as a KP, kitchen police, peeling potatoes. After a week of this a promotion was forthcoming. I got promoted to dish washer. While the army was supposed not to keep a man on constant detail for over 48 hours, they forgot the regulations and kept on all the help they could get, always asking for more. I found out that if you did a reasonably good job you were kept on and on, the way to get gone was to be dumb, undependable, and lazy. But I didn't get smart fast enough.

In the evenings we sat around the kitchen table and played cards. At first not much gambling, as no one had much money. I didn't have a cent. Finally there was a pay day for everyone but me, being a casual, with no known home. The kitchen help feeling sorry for me made a pot of 7 shillings so I could join the game. This game lasted all night, and in the morning my 7 shillings had grown to over $350 as I found out when I took it down to the base post office the next day and sent $300 home to my father to put in the bank for me. The next night a new game started. I went to bed, there were a lot more dishes to be washed the next day.

This went on for weeks. Ever so often I went to the casual office and asked to be sent back to my company, always got the same answer from the sergeant—in a day or two. Time went on, every few days a couple of us would walk into the city and walk around looking the town over, also Winchester Cathedral, a very noteworthy edifice said to have been built in the 1100 hundreds. I was in it a number of times and got to know one of the caretakers who liked to show us around and tell us the history, and of the repairs and changes that had been made over the years. Just at that time they were doing quite extensive repairs, shoring up the foundation. It seems according to the caretaker the original building was built on oak pilings in low marshy land, and in the last two hundred years or so the marsh had dried out so the water was now some ten or twenty feet lower. The tops of the oak pilings supporting the cathedral had dried out and rotted, letting the whole edifice sink approximately four feet. At first running abutments were built along the side to brace up the walls, but this had been deemed inadequate, so now an effort was being made to pour concrete pilings inside the church, which they were in the process of doing. Some 40 years later I visited the cathedral. It was still standing, so the latter method of shoring it up must have been successful.

My social life with the opposite sex had gone to pot, and as I had struck up a "cross the counter" acquaintance with a girl about my age who worked in a tobacco shop which her father owned, but was run by her and her mother. Her father was on duty during nights in the home guards, a sort of police organization, for the duration. All the regular police were in the army. After one consultation with mother it was agreed that I might escort the young lady home after work. We took a short walk in a park along the Itchen River which ran through town, and then cut through the cathedral grounds which were completely enclosed by a high stone wall and heavy iron gates, which were closed and locked at about 10:00 pm at night, a fact I was not aware of. We arrived at her home through some winding narrow streets, all very dark, except for some very well shaded gas street lights about every two blocks. After arriving at her home we sat around and talked about America. They seemed to have some very vague ideas concerning the U.S. Later mother served some tea and cookies, called biscuits by them, and I was off to find the camp the best I could.

I started out to retrace my way to the cathedral gates, but when I got there they were closed, locked and very dark. I decided that if the cathedral wall could be followed eventually I would come out on the other side. Unfortunately this couldn't be done, no street followed the wall, but led off in all directions it seemed to me, so I wandered around trying to go west till I hit High Street which I knew. After wandering around for some time I stopped to get my bearings if possible when a faint sound of heavy diesel engines could be heard sounding as if they were coming from above. Looking up could be seen the silhouette of a German Zeplin heading to the northwest toward the industrial heart of England. There was no interference from the English as the Zeplin was flying above the flying height of the fighter planes of that day. I watched for a time till it went out of sight, then resumed my hunt for High Street which was eventually found and I arrived home about 2:00 o'clock. That was the end of my social life in England.

I was getting tired of England and my job as a KP, boring tedious hard work. I kept a ceaseless bombardment on the casual office where I always got the same answer, in a day or two. One day I happened in and an officer was in the office and he asked how long I had been on special duty away from my outfit. When I told him three months, he said "What!" and turned to the sergeant and said get this man out and the next day notice came for me to report to casual head-quarters. When I arrived the orders were ready for me to report to 107th Aero Squadron maintenance in Scotland. So there was quite an argument while I tried to convince the powers in the office that I did not belong to the 107th Aero Squadron but to the 107th Field Signal Battalion and that it was in France. This finally accomplished I was told to come in the next day.

I went out to the hospital and put my things together, said my goodbys, wished the poor "buck" who had been assigned my beginners job of peeling potatoes good luck, with a little good advice on how to get away unless he liked the job.

Back at the casuals headquarters next morning twelve of us who had been separated from our organizations that had moved on to France were lined up with our packs on our backs with a "90 day wonder" second lieutenant in charge.[12] He did not have to carry a pack. We started to walk, no one ever told us where we were going, how far or anything. We had been given a small package, which turned out to be a sandwich and an apple. We were also told to fill up our canteens. After much map study we finally chose a road and started walking, and kept walking all day. By 4 o'clock in the afternoon our poor lieutenant was pretty well bushed and he didn't even have a pack to carry. Finally we came to a little town in which there was a contingent of U.S. soldiers. We were turned over and the lieutenant disappeared. We twelve casuals were assigned bunks, so after we were fed we went to bed sure the next day we would move on.

Next morning we rousted out early for breakfast, you guessed it, oatmeal and coffee, but it was made in a U.S. GI kitchen and hot. After breakfast, we were called out, front and center, for detail, which was regular routine with "bucks" present, and as usual if your name started with A, B or C you were called first. I was put on guard duty at a double gate which as far as I could see really closed off nothing, was used by everybody that was going that way. I was told to guard the gate, I never did find out who I was to guard it from, or what. On duty, two hours on, two hours off, twenty four hours a day.

This went on for about three weeks, when from sheer exhaustion and des-peration, I went to the guard room, a sergeant and an officer who had never been there before when I had called, wanted to know how long I had been on duty, when I told him he turned to the sergeant and said "Is this true?" The sergeant didn't know how long I had been on duty but he smelled trouble for someone, he knew as well as any "buck" 48 hours was the limit without relief.

Next morning we were lined up again. I had had a full night's sleep the night before for the first time in three weeks. Most of the men who had walked down to this town with me were among this bunch.

Next morning after a breakfast of oatmeal and coffee and a slice of bacon, of all things, we were put on a train, third class of course, and were on our way to Southampton. Why any "buck" private was put on a train to go only a few miles, walking distance of a day, is more than we could figure out, we decided the army must be losing its grip or someone made a mistake. Anyhow, when we got to our destination and into a barracks building, we could not figure out why we were not immediately called out for a potato peeling detail or a dish washing stint, but after a couple of hours laying around it became apparent, we were called out and marched down to a dock, and onto a medium sized ship. Here we went down two decks, both of which were filled with horses and mules. It was easy to figure out who was to be taken care of first in case of trouble with German bombs, which the army thought was more valuable, horses and mules or "buck" privates.

We went down two decks and arrived in what appeared to be a mess hall, at least the large room was partially divided into two rooms, the one we went into had two tables in it. These were picnic type tables, substantially built, with seat boards running full length down either side. In the other half of the room were already arrived our traveling companions, who were as far as we could determine, English army Moroccan soldiers, at least they had on English army uniforms. With that each one wore a turban instead of a regulation English army hat and a sash about his waist in which he carried the most evil looking long curved knife one could imagine. They looked like someone you should be friends with, no hostilities. We started in at once to be friendly even if we could not understand a word they said.[13]

Along about four o'clock in the afternoon we were called out to eat, two decks up and a few feet from our ladder down was a kitchen, and just beyond that was apparently the mess hall, in which was a hastily put together mess facility. The mess we were served was also put together in a hurry, fried greasy potatoes, a piece of meat of some kind, we decided it was horse that had been either starved or worked to death, bread, one slice, and a cup of lukewarm tea. We were in this place for an hour or better and the Moroccans were not with us. If what they got was no better than ours, I would not like the job of serving them after seeing those knives they had.

When we finally left the mess hall we went out on deck and it was dark. As we sauntered back toward our deck ladder I noticed a tall can sitting on the deck outside of the kitchen door. It had apparently been set there to cool the contents. We filed back down our ladders and sat down around a table after taking our packs off and piling them in a corner.

We hadn't been seated very long before we heard a clanking and shuffling of feet. Apparently someone was coming down the ladders in a hurry and carrying an object of some kind. We soon found out—here came one of the "bucks" toting the cooking container that had been outside the kitchen door, and he was yelling, "Hide it quick!" We did, it went under the pile of backpacks we had just piled in the corner. We all sat down at the dining table and began to talk, the Arabs looking on. We did not have to sit long when down the ladder came what must have been the ship's chef, or at least the head cook, looking around and demanding where it was. We of course were all innocence, no one knew anything in true "buck" manner. The guy took one glance at the Moroccans, each with his hand on the handle of his long curved knife, and decided to call it a day as far as he was concerned.

After a short time, and a little reconnoitering above decks, we investigated what we had obtained in our can. It turned out to be a beef stew, still hot and good. We each filled our mess kits, over half was left, so we gave it to the Arabs and they seemed very happy with it. I wondered how they ate it without a fork or spoon, but they seemed to get along OK with three fingers, and we made friends for life.

Shortly after we had finished our dinner the ship began to move, and a bit later we went on deck and we were in the channel. Black, not a light in sight. We went down to our room and got as comfortable for the night as possible. I got a bench to sleep on, not too bad, but not to be recommended either.

Next morning we were in a harbor and docked, awakened, marched off to a camp and breakfast. You guessed it, oatmeal, almost warm, with coffee and a bit of canned milk. Back at the barracks the usual happened, detailed to the kitchen and potatoes to be peeled. Here we had only butcher knives to peel with. Peeling a potato with a butcher knife is not the easiest thing in the world, the potatoes turned out square by the time we were finished. The wonder is that the mess sergeant didn't make us peel the peelings over again.

Next day we were loaded on a train in the third class car, of course, and started off toward Paris. Some time later we arrived at the Paris terminal and ordered out, and taken to the U.S.A. office, told not to leave, but soon felt the need of a rest room. After a little inquiry we found it, but could hardly believe that men and women used the same doors to enter, contrary to American teachings.

Upon entering, we found ourselves in one large room with a T division through the center. Men right women left. Upon getting into the men's half we found the one wall was completely covered by stalls about two and a half to three feet deep, no door in front and the only fixture being a hole in the floor about five inches in diameter, that was all. Later I had an opportunity to look in the other side. The women were no better off than the men as far as accommodations. Not to be cowed by lack of modern toilets, we entered the stall as many others were doing. As might be expected, all had not hit the hole in the floor. It was a filthy place. After having been in the cubbyhole about so long, there appeared at the entrance an old woman with toilet paper for sale, holding out three or four sheets of paper, obviously out of a sales catalogue, and saying one sou. She made no sale to us. Any "buck" with one weeks service had learned to carry his own paper in goodly quantities, it has many uses. It must have been pretty tough on a guy without a sou, but it was obvious how he overcame the dilemma by cleaning his finger on the stall wall, and took pride in who could make his mark the highest. We arrived at the conclusion there must be a lot of tall Frenchmen.

We all collected back at the U.S.A. canteen where you could buy American candy bars, cookies, cigarettes, etc. We got a good supply of all, pockets full, which was a wise move. We never saw a U.S.A. mess hall for two days. We sat around the U.S.A. office for a while when a sergeant took us out into the section of the terminal where you boarded the train to your destination. We were taken way back and put into a third class passenger coach, no one ever heard of a "buck" riding in any other class, and told not to leave it, the car would be picked up later. We sat around the car for a time with all types of cars coming and being picked up. At last a flat car was pushed on to the siding next to us. On this little flat car were loaded wine casks, three large ones first, then two smaller ones, then on the top a cask of about 25 gallons.

After the switch engine and brakeman had left, one of the men in the gang looked out and said, "They have delivered the wine," and got up and went over to the flat car and came back to report that the casks were full. We got a coopers pin somewhere and went back to the wine casks and soon knocked the bung loose in the little cask on top, and brought back a cup of wine, the type we call rouge, sour as vinegar, but wet. We all went over and filled our cups, and sat around drinking it. When we had finished, we decided it would be easier to bring the little cask to our car, than to keep going over to the flat car to fill our cups. With a bit of doing, we got the keg mounted in the back of our 3rd class car.

Later in the afternoon they parked a 1st class passenger car on the track next to us. Of course we looked it over and decided it was superior to ours, cushions on the seats and seat backs, also lace curtains at the windows—luxurious.

It was getting late in the afternoon so we decided since it looked as if we were going to have to spend the night in the 3rd class car we would be much better on the cushions in the first class car than on the hard benches of the 3rd class, so we pushed the first class car over on our switch and the third class over where the first class had been. Cushioned seats make much better beds than plain boards. By this time it was dark so we decided to turn in. Some time during the night we were bumped around and connected to a train and headed out, where we did not know.

Next morning, about 9 AM we were switched onto a side track, after sitting around about an hour a Frenchman came along to ask us where we were going. He could speak a little English, and when we got it through to him we were headed for Alsace, he threw up his hands and said we were almost to Brest, just the opposite direction. After a while some other Frenchmen showed up, and a great palaver took place. It was decided that we had to be sent back to Paris. An American sergeant came out to see us, asked a hundred questions and got no answers. We were at our stupid best, we knew nothing, but asked no questions. We were put on another car, not first class needless to say, and told to stay, but we pleaded we needed a rest room, so we were given permission to go to the rest room, and incidentally use the canteen to replenish our candy, cookies and cigarette supplies. Necessary since we had had nothing to eat but these for at least 24 hours.

Sometime during the night we were moved out and started, someplace we hoped in the right direction, and sometime the next morning we arrived at a small town, which we learned was in Alsace, the area we were supposed to be trying to find. And to make everything fine for me, after sitting around for some time, who should drive up but my old pal Hank Brucker, to haul us back to Division Headquarters. Not necessary for me. I knew where I was going, we soon arrived at Headquarters Battalion and I was home after 5 months of being a casual trying to get there—Army efficiency.

Going back to company Headquarters, was soon back to my own quarters. Assigned to a hay loft in a convenient barn, complete with cows, rats, chickens and cooties. My first encounter with the big lice that were everywhere, and with which I carried on a losing war for the next five months. After being around for several days, being assigned a truck to drive, all my own, everything was just right. I was bunked up in the barn hay loft with the rest of the company men. One night we kept hearing a rat or some other rodent rooting around and snuffling around. Finally Hank got tired listening to it, reached over, got one of his shoes and let fire in the general direction of the noise. The noise stopped, but the next morning, look as we might, we never did find Hank's shoe. Hank had a difficult time trying to explain to the supply sergeant why he only needed one new shoe. It seems that regulations concerning the missing of one shoe, and issuing of one shoe had never been written. Hank had to settle for two shoes.

Things went along for two or three days, when one morning I awoke with a sore throat, and I went over to the sick bay to have it attended to. That was my mistake. The doc took one look, said "ah" and in about two minutes I found myself in an ambulance off to the hospital. The hospital was only three or four miles away, and was a church. The pews had been removed and iron beds had replaced them. It was run by the French.

Hadn't been there 5 minutes till a French doctor came in, looked at my throat, said "ah" and soon came back with a syringe big enough for a horse, and gave me a couple of shots in my belly, covered me up nicely in bed and left. In a few minutes a French nurse came in and explained how she could speak English, which was a good thing or I never would have suspected it. She also had a thermometer, a tongue depressor, a throat swab and iodine bottle. First she handed me the thermometer and as I started to put it in my mouth as I had been taught to do, the nurse grabbed it and started some wild gyrations, a chorus of voices from the G.I.s in the adjacent beds all sang out at once "stick it in your ass." I learned from that that the French have some strange ways.

The next day my throat was better and I was feeling much better, and was introduced to French cooking, that is, army style. You guessed it, oatmeal for breakfast, but with milk and sugar, warm, really not bad. For lunch we had toast and soup, very thin, with a cabbage leaf in it, for dinner we had toast, potato and some kind of meat, usually chicken or rabbit or maybe mutton.

The menu never varied. One day at lunch one of the not so sick men called out "some one is going to catch hell in the kitchen tonight, there are two cabbage leaves in my soup."

Days passed. The same routine every day, the nurse came in, took my temperature, or I did, depressed my tongue, took a swab, painted my throat with iodine, and said "positive." This went on for three weeks, then one day she came in and said the doctors have decided you are a natural carrier. I never did find out what I was a carrier of, but that made no difference, I was sent back to my outfit. When I reported in to my company, the sergeant said, "I am sorry, but we couldn't keep your place open any longer, you are transferred to Company C," and out I went. I said good-by to Hank and out I went.

Now Company C in our battalion was trained to install telephones in the field and to maintain lines of communication on the front, and were farmed out to the infantry battalions or companies to keep the company telephone [in] communication with battalion, other companies and regimental headquarters, and on occasion with division, but not often, mostly between companies and battalion, also outposts. All this so called training was supposed to be taking place while I was in England and in French hospitals trying to get back to my company. I missed it all, but I could hook up a phone and install a switch board, which was all any of them could do. I hadn't been at my new assignment but a day or two when the supply sergeant called me in to see what was needed to get me up to combat supply shape. After giving me a good going over he decided what was needed in my case was a tin kelly, gas mask, pliers, 45 automatic pistol, extra shells, dagger, electricians knife, first aid kit, friction tape, wire, all hooked onto my web belt around my waist, along with my mess kit, cup and canteen.[14] In addition a French made field telephone, in a wooden box, wooden hinged top, and weighing about 25 lbs., carried on a strap over my shoulder. It was awkward and heavy.

For some days rumors had been flying around that we were going to go to the front, and two or three days later we were loaded into Packard three ton trucks and headed in a generally northerly direction, but none of [us knew] where we might be going.

After riding several hours, and getting very well cramped up, I was staring out the back end of the truck, and I noticed a dead American soldier laying in the shallow ditch along the road, and in a moment or two another, then another looking as if they had been dragged off the road not too long ago. I started counting, and counted 252 before we seemed to be entering a fair sized town. We still did not know where. After driving a few more blocks we crossed a stream on a pontoon bridge which appeared to be in the middle of a business district of a fair sized town. Soon after crossing the bridge we made a left hand turn on a street about a hundred feet from the river and in a few blocks were in a residential district, pulled up in front of a nice looking house. As we unloaded the sergeant in charge yelled at us to be careful of "booby traps" since there had not been time to search the houses. The house ten or twelve of us had been assigned to had been a nice home. It was equipped with good furniture, among which was a very ornate grand piano, not too big, but ornate. The "hinies" who had just left the day before had done a good hatchet job, all the pictures had been hacked, glass broken, legs chopped off tables and chairs, the only reason that the piano legs hadn't was because they were too big and hard wood, but they had tried. One of the big "boobies" with us rushed over and threw up the piano top, then just stood there and growled, he looked as if he were paralyzed. I went over to the piano and looked inside, and there on the strings lay a German "potato masher" hand grenade. I didn't have any idea whether it had been triggered or not. Usually after the trigger has been pulled you have three seconds to get rid of it, or it will get rid of you. I dropped to the floor, but nothing happened; big "booby" stood there looking at it and holding up the piano top. Finally I decided the trap had not been triggered, so I gingerly got up to take a look, and told the guy holding up the piano top not to put it down as that might trigger the hand grenade. I got up and looked the grenade over carefully and saw that it had been wired with a very fine wire to a hammer on the piano keyboard. Had someone started to play the piano and hit the right note he would have triggered the grenade, and he and the piano disappeared. After very carefully examining the trap I had the G.I. holding up the piano top brace it up with the regular top brace, and get away, and duck if I yelled duck. Very carefully I reached in with my pliers and snipped the trigger wire in two, it just fell apart and the trigger pin never moved. Very gingerly I reached in and picked up the "potato masher," carried it out the back door, across the lawn, and pulled the trigger in the prescribed manner, and tossed it into the river and ducked down on the bank. In a few moments it went off with a muffled roar and a great deal of roiling water, and only one little fish about an inch and a half came floating to the top. Fish were scarce in that particular spot in the river on that day, August 5, 1918, my birthday.[15]

After that episode, we gave the house a very good looking over indeed, no more traps, so we went down the street for a couple of blocks to the field kitchen for some C rations, bread and a cup of coffee.[16]

Next morning we were routed out early and immediately after breakfast detailed to deliver a quite large reel of phone wire to a company headquarters some place up the field.

We looked that roll of wire over and decided it was too large to carry, so we started to scrounge around looking for something to carry it on. We found an old spring wagon sort of contraption with two hind wheels still intact and a pair of shafts available. We broke the rear two wheels and back axle loose from the damaged body and arranged the coil of wire on the axle, then got the shaft wired to the axle, found an old horse in a barn, hitched him to the two wheels and had a reasonable wire reel cart, and started out to find the company we were supposed to deliver the wire to. After walking and helping the poor old horse pull the reel of wire, for an interminable time, we arrived at a small town on the outskirts of which was a small orchard associated with a farm house. Inside of the fence around the orchard was a fresh grave which had rather been fixed up for an ordinary soldier, but couldn't have been more than a few days old. It had been mounded up with a low stick fence and at one end there was stuck in the ground the long end of a broken airplane propeller, onto which had been tied the shorter end to form a rude cross, and on to this cross piece there had been scratched the name Quentin Roosevelt, son of Theodore Roosevelt.

Our wire was delivered, the poor old nag that had served us so well, if reluctantly, was turned loose to get along the best way he could, and we headed back toward Chateau Thierry and something to eat and a place to sleep. We had covered several miles we were "pooped" out as we were carrying our packs and all field equipment, as we did not know when we would be back, if ever, when we started out that morning.

The next morning we were routed out quite early, had breakfast, and loaded into trucks, and started to a new destination, we knew not where. We were on the trucks two or three hours, when we suddenly turned off the road and into what appeared to be a cave, but actually was a limestone quarry, old and big. It appeared to have about the whole division in it, but of course there were not that many.[17] But there were a lot of men, and a large switch board with at least twelve or fifteen telephone connections. We pulled up a short way inside the entrance, close to the switch board. It was getting dark and we went out looking for a field kitchen. We could smell the coffee. We didn't take long, and were back at our truck in a half hour or so. However in the meantime night had settled and we felt lucky thinking we would be in a good quiet place.

No luck. Hadn't been settled down for a rest more than 15 minutes when a call came for a lineman, and out I went because a circuit was out. I traced it out of the entrance and up over the slight hill over the cave entrance and slightly downward for about half a mile to a company switch board, found a break about 100 feet from the company board, followed the wire on in to the company board and for a while everything seemed OK. The headquarters was located in a dugout built by the Germans, but really not intended for U.S.A. use.

Everything looked serene and protected from an occasional burst of machine gun bullets passing harmlessly overhead, also shells were going overhead and landing a hundred feet or so from the headquarters. It looked good to get a bit of sleep, propped up against the switch board. No luck however. In about an hour word came to me that a line was out, back to battalion headquarters just where I had come from in the cave. So getting myself together I started back to the headquarters board, but soon found that I was following a different line, that made quite a different circuit back, a practice frequently practiced when it was a heavily loaded line, and subject to being knocked out frequently. By this time it was very dark and there seemed to be quite a bit of activity, shells and machine gun fire, and progress slow, and contact with "doughboys" apparently moving toward the front, taking a lot of time, identifying and trying not to get shot by some trigger happy, nervous guy who would shoot and ask questions

Figure 4.2 US and British linemen raising telephone lines in France during
World War I. Courtesy American Unofficial Collection of World War I
Photographs, National Archives and Records Administration.

afterwards. I walked and crawled along for what seemed an interminable time, laying down when star shells came over to lighten up the sky. The Germans seemed to be very interested in that particular part of the front. I don't know what was going on but I had a suspicion that a regiment or division was being moved into the line and "Fritz" was nervous. I was too. After crawling along for some time with the telephone line in my hand I came to a body, and my wire ran under it so I had to feel around it to locate my wire on the other side; then move on for a few feet and run against another, move on; star shells and the place lighted up light as day, and inevitably followed by a burst of machine gun fire and a shell or two coming over. They were all two or three feet high, they did you no harm except make you nervous and slow you way down. It was slow business. Finally I got back to the cave and had a clear board after clearing the break. I was sure glad to get back, since it was beginning to show light in the east. I had been most of the night, was dog tired and plenty dirty. The next morning after having a couple of hours rest I went out to investigate the area I had been over the night before, and counted over 200 dead on the little field I had crawled across the night before.

In front of the cave entrance a road ran. It seemed to be quite an important road from the amount of traffic it carried. In front of the cave entrance and off to one side was dug a small trench about 18 inches wide and 15 feet long. In one end of the trench a post was set in the ground and on top of this post was mounted a German machine gun in such a way as to command the road and particularly, any airplanes that might be strafing the traffic. The Germans must have left in a hurry, because the gun, upon examination, seemed to be in operating condition, even with a belt of ammunition in it. After looking it over and pulling back the cocking lever, pointing it toward the sky, I pulled the trigger and fired three shots before I could get my finger off the trigger.

There was considerable traffic on the road and it wasn't long before a German plane came along strafing the road from about 150 feet up. Whether anyone was seriously hurt I will never know. However, I jumped down in the trench and grabbed the machine and pointed it down the road. Sure enough in a very short time another plane came along strafing. I got the machine gun pointed in his general direction and pulled the trigger and sent a good burst in his general direction. Nothing happened so I must have missed. Later on, one of the German triplane fighters made a run. I was so intent on looking at it, I forgot to shoot. Practically all the ammunition was gone anyhow. That was the only triplane I ever saw. They were so little I don't know how they managed to fly. They must not have been too successful for that is the only one I ever saw.

Out of Soissons the Germans must have made a rather determined stand for we were around there a few days. However I never got to sleep in the cave again. The next I was in the cave it was about all cleaned out, but there had been plenty of activity around where I had been, mostly further and further away from the cave.

One night two or three days later there were three of us wandering around looking for a place to spend the night, when another company lineman came along and gave us a piece of advice. He said that just ahead of us about 50 yards was a narrow gauge railroad and maybe there might be a shed or building near it. We went looking and there sure enough along a narrow gauge railroad was a rather well built log cabin type structure, and the railroad ran up to the only door. No one around, we went inside. There was no one in it and it was clean, and covering over half the floor space were boxes, about two feet square. We decided at once that it would be a wonderful place to put up for the night. There was one little draw back, when you closed the door there was no light. One of the fellows searched through his belongings and came up with a piece of candle. We lit it and set it on one of the boxes, closed the door and bedded down for the night—dry, quiet and a good sleep. Next morning awakened sometime about sunrise, lit our candle, and proceeded to get ready for the day. We were almost ready when the door flew open and a French soldier looked in, took one look, stepped back, said "oiei" and took off on a dead run down the narrow gauge track. I took one look at him and said something tells me we better get the hell out of here. The whole French army will be on us very soon. We got out fast. Down the road about a quarter mile we found a kitchen, and had breakfast. With a little discrete questioning we learned that we had wandered over the line between the French and Americans, and the narrow gauge railroad was put there by the Germans to haul ammunition to the Big Bertha—a big cannon put in to shell Paris, and had actually sent a few shells, but they had quickly dismantled it when they began to retreat and the French and Americans had advanced too quickly. The log hut was an ammunition dump for the guns. They had moved out so fast they had not even got it all moved before they had to leave. Our bed had been powder for the Big Bertha. I am glad none of it had been spilled around on the floor of the log hut or it could have gotten quite warm. That stuff burned rapidly we found out later when we lit a stick and watched it run along the ground.[18]

After leaving Soissons, the war seemed to kind of speed up, never a dull moment and the lines seemed to be always out about the next morning.[19] I was put on an out line and took over the line not going in any good determined direction at all. It seemed to rather be following a road, and it soon became apparent this road had artillery on it, horse drawn 75's, and that they were getting tangled up in my telephone wires in a way they shouldn't, and there was a lot of it. The horses were floundering around and falling over and getting telephone wire under their shoes and around their legs, it was no good trying to clean this mess up in the dark. About two thirty or three o'clock I gave up and sat down by a tree and fell off asleep. When I awoke it was just getting light and the horses and guns were still milling around, the guns more or less pointed in one direction which was over my head. Before long one battery after another went off just over my head. I was partially behind a tree from them, which helped some, but it knocked me out for a while. I finally got my bearings and got up to the road. Here the French were industriously cutting my telephone wires into six inch pieces trying to get it off from under the horses shoes, and around their legs and the 75's axles and other parts. It was easily apparent that that wire would not be used again as a telephone system. I went back to company headquarters and explained why the telephone was out, and apt to stay out for some time. I took another line out in a different direction.

The fighting seemed to be picking up and movement accelerated. The Allies were on the move and all in one direction, which was good. It was becoming quite evident that business at the front was picking up. Days would go by when I would not spend more than a few hours without all my switch boards in various headquarters changing location and I was busy. Would no sooner get one line in and back to headquarters, wherever that might be, when another was out, day and night. One day, or I should say, one night about two in the morning I started out with a line in my hand. We were quite close to the front, for every 5 or 10 minutes a German machine gun let loose and I ducked. It was easy to tell the difference between German guns and ours. When I say ours, I mean French. We had no American machine guns. I never saw an American machine gun on the front until the very last days. I walked a mile to see it—a Browning. The Germans guns had a heavier sound than the French "sho-sho's" we used.[20] Well, the wire I was following took me to a road, and turned and followed this road. Bad practice—too much traffic. In a short distance I came to an American truck stuck along side the road. Being stuck wasn't hard to get in a truck equipped with hard tires. It could be done in a puddle of mud no larger than a campaign hat.[21] Anyway this driver must have gotten himself lost, he had no business being that close to the front with a truck. He apparently found that out, he wasn't around any more. An evil thought came over me. It was misting rain, there was a chill in the air, I was wet, and oh so tired, and the phone wire was repaired. The truck with a canvas top on it looked so dry and besides the truck bed was made of steel with steel sides. That would stop machine gun bullets at that distance if any happened to hit. So I weakened and investigated the inside of the truck. It wasn't empty. There were two men in it, one making groaning noises, the other still—too still. The one groaning asked for a drink. I gave him a long drag out of my canteen of water and sweetened vin rouge—awful stuff, but wet. He said he had been hit in the belly a couple of hours ago by a machine gun and he was cold—could I wrap his blanket about him. The other man also wanted a drink and he was also hit by a machine gun, but in the lung to the right and above his heart. He was also cold and shivering, and wanted his blanket.

It was dark inside, wet and cold outside. I lay down to get a little rest and sleep with my blanket around me, soon was gone. I must have slept for two or three hours, for when I next opened my eyes it was light but still rainy and misty. As I came to, I became aware of my surroundings. I reached out and touched the hand of the man next to me. It was cold and stiff, but he was not feeling it. I looked over at the other man, he was laying very still, not shivering any more. Dead men don't shiver.

I got out of the truck, picked up a wire at the edge of the road, bit into it, found it alive at both ends. One [i.e., headquarters] reported it was just about to move, and would be out in a few minutes, making new connections. So I followed the wire in the opposite direction and soon came to a headquarters of a company, also expecting to move within an hour. I reported the two dead men in the truck, and asked about a kitchen. It was down that way the last they knew, so off I went looking for oatmeal and coffee.

The fighting had been heavy for the last few days, and casualties heavy and replacements were coming in.[22] I took a line back in the direction I had come from the day before and in about an hour or two found myself back where I had started the day before, that is, the same company only in a new headquarters closer to the front. Everything was in working order at the switch board at the moment and it was quiet for the time being. I had just settled down to get a little rest and sleep, never losing an opportunity to rest, when in came the captain with a brand new 90 day wonder of nice fresh new second lieutenant. He was all spit and polish, shined shoes, with a crease in the pants and shiny new Sam Brown belt, polished 45 automatic, probably trained on how to dress a private or enlisted man down and put him in his place if he by any chance forgot to salute an officer, particularly him, and also ready to show everybody how to conduct the war and get it over with.

The captain asked me if I knew where company I was, or if I could find it, and I said I thought I could if it was still on the end of a telephone wire where it had been about an hour ago. The switch board man said he thought it was because he had talked with I only a few minutes ago. Then the captain told me to deliver Lt. So-and-So there at once. I said "Yes, Sir," it was all I could say. I went over to the switch board, asked the operator which was I Company circuit, picked up the wire and said to the Lieutenant "This way," and he said "Sir" in a way to let me know I was to say "Sir" whenever I addressed him. After having proceeded a short time a German shell came over and landed a short distance away. I heard it come and automatically made a slight duck, as you invariably did when shells came over. It landed a safe distance away and the lieutenant said "Why did you duck?" and I said "just from habit, some explode closer, and within range of their shrapnel." The lieutenant asked how I knew it was shrapnel, and I said most of the shells sent over by the Germans on this front at this time were shrapnel because it was more or less open fighting and they were interested in killing infantrymen or wounding them. He then asked how I knew it was a German 77 and shrapnel, and I said, by sound, and didn't elaborate further. I could have said you will learn fast enough, if you live long enough, but then if I had said all of that I would have had to end with a "Sir" and I had about run out of "Sirs" for this guy. We soon arrived at I Company and turned the lieutenant over to the buck private on the board who told the lieutenant that the "Cap" would probably be in in a few minutes if he made it at all. He didn't finish with a "Sir" and the lieutenant didn't say a word. He was catching on it might be better to have these fellows for friends, with so many bullets flying around.

The war carried on for a few days and once again I was on a trip to I Company only a little farther toward the front, once the front had moved a quarter of a mile or more toward Germany. The "buck" on the board asked if I knew where battalion headquarters were and I said yes. He said there was a man here the Captain wanted to go back now. He was not wounded, but had the worst case of shell shock, jitters, nerves he had seen in a long time; he sure was out of it. In a few minutes the Captain came in with the lieutenant, who was the mud-diest, most bedraggled individual I had ever seen; hollow eyed, stooped, gun gone, and shaking like a leaf in the fall breeze. It certainly was the same man I had brought in a few days before, but the strut and cockiness were all gone and when I said to him "follow me" there was no "Sir." This man had learned about war in a few short days.

It was along about this time that I saw the most gruesome sight I had ever encountered. Three of us were following a wire to the company headquarters, the fellows with me to join the company, and me to the board. A few shells came over and we ducked down, not too close to us, we went on a short way when we saw a soldier sitting with his back to a tree, humped over with his head forward on his chest, down in his blouse. One of the fellows with me remarked that maybe the man was hurt, and went over and spoke to him. Getting no reply he nudged him with his foot, and the man's head simply fell off over to the side. He had been hit by a shell sliver that had practically decapitated him and he had been killed instantly. How he had got into that sitting position against the tree I will never know, but all his blood was down inside his blouse. He never heard the shell that got him. There was nothing we could do, so we went on to company headquarters. It struck me a bit, I must confess.

About this time it seemed to me there was a sort of lull in the fighting. I guess we were not pushing so hard, anyway, everything seemed to stand still, the kitchen where I had eaten once or twice stayed put, and I was hanging around for a day or two. The Germans ran up an observation balloon across the small valley from where we were located. Then I was sure the observer who was in it spotted the kitchen at once, and lobbed two or three shells over at us to let us know he knew we were there. The French air force sent fighter planes over one at a time to make a try at shooting the balloon down, usually coming in high and diving down at the balloon. They did not have any success. Of course the balloon was ringed with German machine guns, and they did manage to get one of the French fighters, but they never did shoot the balloon. The Germans did eventually pull the balloon down, but they were a bit late as the ground troops eventually took the sites. Later I was at the balloon site, after it was burned, and saw the truck which was used as its ground base. The truck had a large winch filled with cable which was used to raise and lower the balloon. The truck engine was tied up so as to drive the winches.

It was at this headquarters that I got my first hit with shrapnel. About noon each day the Germans always lobbed three shells over at the kitchen. They seemed not to have the range worked out very well for they always missed by about 100 to 200 feet. The shells always lit over in a little ravine. You could depend on the Germans doing better than this. About the third day they did. A shell came over awfully close to the mark. It was so close there was not enough noise to have any time to duck, but I was trying. Just as I ducked a piece of shrapnel about the size of your hand hit me flat on the hind end. Just like being kicked by a mule with new shoes on. I was protected by my blouse, pants, a roll of telephone wire; never the less it knocked me flat on my face, and I had the sorest fanny for a week you ever saw—black and blue. It is a good thing that shrapnel did not hit edgewise or it would easily have relieved me of half my fanny. It made me more wary of shells. I ducked lower, faster and with more protection if it were available.

Time passed and in the end I got able to walk again without wincing with every step.

It must have been getting along the first of October, anyway, along about this time for some reason, the powers that were decided that we needed a rest.[23] I do not know what brought that on, it had never happened before, as far as I could remember. They must have run out of enemy. We were even loaded into trucks and hauled five or ten miles in some direction, unloaded in a small town that had civilians in it, and not badly shot up. We were advised not to light a light after dark as the Germans patrolled the area with planes at night. It would not have taken very long to find that out on our own. The little town had a road, which looked as it might be of some importance, and a small river running along side. In short time we were billeted in a barn close to the river, and were advised it would be a good time to take a bath in the river and wash our clothes, just as if this wouldn't occur to us. The army never gave a buck private the credit for having enough sense to get in out of the rain, until there was a dirty job to do. Then he was told, go do it.

The next morning I rounded up a bucket, filled it with water from the creek, and had a fire going. Shed my underwear and cooties, my socks and shirt, and had them merrily boiling away in the bucket with a small piece of soap, always available to a buck who had been around for a while. By noon the washing was done and hung out to dry. The day had warmed up to be quite pleasant and we decided it was time to go swimming and get rid of the cooties and cootie eggs that might be hiding away in the folds of our skin. We went down to the stream, which seemed to be quite low, and filled with rocks of all sizes, with a pool of water deeper than elsewhere in the rippling stream. Ideal bath tub, although a bit exposed and chilly in the breeze. I planned to make it as fast as possible, so I stripped off, laid my clothes on a rock on the shore, and proceeded to take a bath, with about fifty other bucks in the immediate vicinity. It wasn't long before I was chilly, ducked into the small pool on the down stream side of my rock and was ready to leave, when I looked up and on the bank was what must have been the entire female population of the village on the bank, located all about the rock where my towel and clothes were piled, laughing and jabbering, enjoying the best show that had been in town for their lifetime. I stood around in my pool of water shivering, getting colder by the minute, hoping they would go away, which they showed no inclination to do. So finally the fellow next to me said, what the hell, and we stood up and headed slowly toward the bank, picking our way carefully among the rocks. The women and kids were all around my clothes, so it was necessary to literally shove them away to get to my clothes. But we finally made it and got dressed, with plenty of close observation to each detail.

By the end of our week, we had only been bombed three times and I was very well de-cootied and could sleep all night without scratching. We were herded back into the trucks and back to the line we went. Not much movement had taken place. We were about where we were when we left. The Germans must have taken advantage to get ready to pull back because in the first few days we were back we appeared to be moving again by the changes made in the various headquarters company stations and outpost positions.[24]

As I was making a run between two switch boards one day, just after I had spliced a wire and got them to talking again, in a little ravine about half way between stations, I came across a couple of stretcher bearers with a wounded man. They were both very well pooped, but one of them, a small guy, was really bushed. He said he could go no further, and would I carry his end of the stretcher a short distance to the aid station. I agreed since the man on the stretcher didn't look as if he had too much time left. He had been struck in the shoulder by shrapnel or machine gun [fire] and had lost a lot of blood. We picked up the stretcher and started for the aid station. It was really rough going and hindered by the fact that the right arm of the man we were carrying kept falling off to one side of the stretcher, which started the bleeding again, and he did not have too much left to lose. Finally I took a piece of telephone wire and passed it around the stretcher a couple of times and bound his arm to his side. In that manner we made it to the aid station. I am sorry to say, however, that our passenger did not. I was somewhat late in getting back to the switch board, but then no one noticed, the lines were still in.

For the next few days we seemed to be making fair progress toward the German lines, but were very busy keeping the lines of telephone communication functioning.[25] One night I went on a call on an out line back to battalion headquarters, finally got it in around about four o'clock in the morning, all bushed, decided to get a little sleep if possible. It was a nice warm balmy night for this late in the fall, so I decided to sneak away about a hundred feet and sleep an hour or two in a little field just a short distance from the exchange. I spread my poncho in what had been an old plow furrow at the end of the little field, wrapped my blanket about me, my shoes for a pillow, and my helmet propped up against my head. I was soon asleep. I do not know how long I had dozed off when there was a roar and I saw all the stars of a constellation and a severe pain in my head and I was out. How long I do not know, but when the shell hit it was dark, and when I began being aware of the world around me again, it was quite light, so I must have been out for at least a couple of hours or more, and I was sick, and had a terrible headache. I lay still for a short time, collecting my thoughts, and getting them together. Finally I began to explore my head to see what damage had been done. My helmet, which had been propped over my head, had taken a beating. It had a large dent in it where a piece of shrapnel had mashed it down far enough to hit my head, and broken a hole in the helmet so that the sharp edge from the break had punctured my skin on my head and dented my skull. However there was little blood on my head, but did it hurt, and when I tried to stand up, it was almost impossible, so I just sat down and stayed there for some time. Finally feeling a bit strange, I got back to the first aid tent at battalion headquarters. They wanted to send me to a hospital, but all my contacts with a hospital had been bad, so they stuck a patch on my head, gave me some aspirin, and a pill for pain, and told me to take it easy for a day or two. That was easy to do for me. In a couple of days I was feeling quite well again, and went back to work, with a very tender head. It gave me something to think about, and more respect for German 77 shrapnel.

After a short time things more or less settled into the old routine. Just one telephone line after another out. No let up. Then one day the news arrived that I had been waiting for the last two months. I got orders to be shipped back to my old place in Headquarters Company back at division headquarters. Just like going home. I was to report back November first. They must have needed a truck driver. I couldn't get away, however, until the top sergeant of the company had his chance to get at least one more days work out of a buck private he was going to lose. He couldn't touch me for a detail so long as I was on the telephone maintenance detail, so I had to peel potatoes again. But I didn't mind, I was going home.

On November first I went back to Division Headquarters and found Company C of the Signal Corps and checked out and reported to Headquarters Company and to the top sergeant, and was immediately assigned a truck—three ton Packard. Moved in with my old buddies, and had a good night's rest, mostly out of range of cannon fire and away off from machine gun fire. Next day I was sent out in my truck on routine runs, and had a good talk with my old buddy Hank, and got a lot of pointers on what to scrounge up to make my truck (tent) habitable, good solid useful information from an expert. Within a couple of days we were on the move again, this time we were supposed to go to a little town not too far away with the name of Dun Sur Meuse. On the way there we passed a sign on the road pointing off to our right, to Verdun. That was the place where there had been a long hard battle before the Germans had finally broken through on their push to Paris, which they had never reached, but had been stopped at Chateau Thierry where we had helped the French stop them, at our first front experience.[26] Upon arriving in Verdun, we could hardly believe how completely a city could be leveled by bombardment. As far as I could see there was not one single building stand-ing, with big shell craters all over the place and trenches. In one place was the notorious trench of bayonets where, along where the trench had been, it was filled, but bayonets were protruding from the ground in an orderly row. It was said that at the end of the bayonet was a man's body, still in an upright position, still with his gun in his hand where he had died when the trench had been filled in by cannon fire, each man stood his post and died rather than retreat. They were French bayonets.

After driving around town we took off for Dun, not too far north. We soon found it. A small French village on the Meuse. The town was mostly intact since it was located in the little valley of the Meuse River. The town had been shielded from the shells because of the rather close, high rise of the valley side just back of the town. Any German shells that cleared the heights just back of the town would also clear the few houses strung along the road, but back closer to the hills, and would land on the road and in the Meuse River or the fields beyond, so the town had been spared.

We were assigned to stay in a stone barn that had lost one corner to a stray shell, because it also had a small barnyard for us to park our trucks in.

We moved in and cleared out a corner of the barn for a place to sleep and built a small fire to warm the place a bit as it was getting chilly after the sun went down. As dark approached we let the fire go down to just a mound of coals and stretched a shelter half over it so as not to be seen from above and keep the heat in. Spent a comfortable night. In a couple of days rumors began to float around the war would be over in a few days. The rumors got more persistent from day to day until a definite date was set. It came and went, but the war was still on.[27] Then the date was moved forward and got stronger and stronger. We had been fooled once, this time we did not swallow the rumor. Then one day an order came through that all firing would stop at 11:00 o'clock. We took this with skepticism, and went on with our business, which was driving trucks here and there, moving various things and men occasionally. About 10:00 o'clock in the morning of the 11th Hank and his truck were sent on a trip down the road. Off he went out of sight, down the road. In about 15 minutes here came a truck down the road wide open, and a shell broke right on it, it appeared to us. In a couple of minutes in came Hank. The whole back end of his truck banged up with what had sure been a near miss of a German shell. Hank said that last one hit right on my tailgate, and those bums up there said the war was over. Had that shell been a couple of seconds sooner it would have hit Hank right on his truck section. It sure would have been tough to get killed within a few minutes of the end of the war.

Within a few minutes of 11 o'clock it seemed as if every outfit in the army was trying to shoot off every piece of ordinance they had. We hid under our trucks. Then at 11:00 everything was quiet, very quiet. We lay there waiting for it to start again, but it didn't, it was for real.

That night we had a real fire in the barn and slept warm. Next day was quiet. We just set around or worked on our trucks and speculated on where we would go and how soon we would start home. This went on for a day or two and the rumor started that we were going up to Germany in the Army of Occupation.[28] In another day this was verified by the fact that we got orders to take our trucks over to the auto dump and get new trucks. We were all elated at the idea of having nice new trucks. Too good to be true. We went over to the dump turned in our trucks and were taken over to a line of old trucks that didn't look as good as the ones we had, and told to pick ourselves out a truck. These old pieces of junk were not nearly as good as the ones we had. I got one which they bragged on a lot, which should have been a warning to me. It was a junker. I barely got it back to our parking lot. The next two days I spent trying to tune up the wreck so it would run. Finally, with a new distributor, new plugs, timing, it ran reasonably well. I also fixed the governor so it did not interfere with the speed, which was strictly against orders, but I could always say that is the way it was when I got it, just be the good old dumb buck.

The next day orders came to me to be ready to take off early since my truck was to be used for the telephone communications truck, and I was to report to a lieutenant so and so, who I did not know[,] did not belong to our battalion, but I was to report to him. The usual army clear, concise orders. If a buck was involved, we were never told anything. As it turned out I did not have to find the lieutenant. He and the sergeant found me in the morning early, asked if I were ready, I said yes "sir," and he said first we have to go get some stuff at headquarters, and we will be off. So off we went to his headquarters, the lieutenant on the seat beside me, the sergeant in the back. The only reason I got to keep my seat was because I had to drive, and I could not do so from the back.

We were off, going south along the Meuse River for a few miles. Then turning off to the left to pick up the Moselle River highway which ran in a general northeast direction. This road was crooked, and up hill and down. Not much time could be made, although it really was not a bad road. We were supposed to get out ahead of the general moving troops, most of who were marching and in horse drawn wagons, slow going. The lieutenant had a map, on which was marked our destination for each day, only about 15 miles per day, and name of small town or wide place in the road where we were to stop and make telephone connections in the local telephone switchboard to Paris, so the General in charge would talk with headquarters in Paris upon his arrival. It seems he held back and traveled with the troops so as to arrive with the kitchen. Of course he was not walking.

I soon found out that it was a good practice to make a call on my old friend the mess sergeant and scrounge food to take along in the truck, just in case. I always managed to keep a supply of bread, C rations, coffee, bacon and jam on hand, which came in handy at times, and made a big hit with the Germans in whose homes we usually stayed.

We had started out on about the third day after the armistice, and were on the road quite a number of days, going slowly for us, but plenty fast for the men who had to walk. I think we advanced roughly 15 miles a day, some days more, some less, easy for me in a truck, but for a man with a full pack, up hill and down, not so easy. I am not real clear on just what day we crossed the Rhine River, it must have been the 12th or 13th of December.[29] We were out in front of the troops a good way when we came to a stretch of a mile or two of straight road, quite good, so I stepped down on the old Packard truck some and made a lot of noise. Pretty soon we could see a big bridge ahead of us and also an MP out in the road frantically warning us to stop. We stopped and the MP wanted to know how we were out so far in front of the main army, and a lot of other questions. I was glad the lieutenant was there, he was in command, I didn't have to say a thing. Just sit there and look as dumb as possible, and finally they decided that we could go ahead, but were not to catch up with the Germans who were a short distance ahead. We drove on to the bridge over the Rhine River, which was located north of Coblenz about 8 miles according to the map the lieutenant had. As we passed the middle of the bridge we could see the tail end of the German army in a column of four about ready to leave the bridge. We drove to within a couple of hundred feet of the hinnies, and slowed down so as not to get any closer, after clearing the bridge.

There was a road leading off to the right, so we took it, and landed in a small town on the river bank, very close to the spot the lieutenant was looking for, the telephone exchange. We pulled up and stopped. He got out and we looked around and lo and behold there was a little restaurant right beside the truck, so the sergeant and I decided it would be a good opportunity to try out German cooking, although it didn't look too prosperous. We went in and the operator and two customers, who apparently just finished a late breakfast or mid-morning snack, eyes popped out. We must have been the first American soldiers they had seen and they apparently had not expected us that day. The two customers left at once. We sat down at a table and ordered three eggs, toast and coffee. The operator looked startled, and said kine eis, bread ersatz un nicht haba fleish—coffee ersatz, nicht gute. I said one minute, and went out front to my hoard in the truck, and came back with a half loaf of badly mashed, white bread, also a chunk of bacon and a glass of jelly. I put them on the counter and said toast, and bacon, also three eggs, and the sergeant echoed, three eggs. We gave him our canteens of coffee and told him to make it hot. In no time we had three eggs, fried strips of bacon and white toast, and a glass of jelly, grape as I remember, a good hot breakfast. And the word must have gotten about as people began to walk past the restaurant to see the American soldiers. In about half an hour the lieutenant came back and said "I see you have already had breakfast," and we said "Yes sir." As we came out the lieutenant said we had to go to Coblenz and look up where the bridge-head command office was to be, so off to Coblenz we went and crossed back to the city which is on the west bank, on a pontoon bridge. There was also another permanent bridge here. How it happened to be spared I will never know.

We found the headquarters and after a time the lieutenant came back and said as soon as we unloaded his material, I could report back to my outfit, which was not far away in Coblenz at present. I took off and soon found them all wondering where I had been.

We were in the city only a few days till we all moved back across the river to a little town where we took up residence in a private house with a barnyard, in which we could park our trucks. This house was fairly large having four rooms in a row on the first floor and four above them. On the first floor a living room in front, then the dining room, then the kitchen and bedroom. The household consisted of a mother and father and two teen aged daughters. There were two of us lodged in the back bedroom on the second floor. The only way we could get there was to go through the daughter's bedroom. It was quite apparent that mamma was quite apprehensive. She needn't have been because there were some very strict orders out concerning our conduct and fraternization.

The company kitchen was about a block away, and my old friend "sarge" was there. We understood from the first that we would not be located here long. During the time we spent in this house along came Christmas and would you believe it we had turkey, dressing, mashed potatoes, green peas, gravy, the whole Christmas dinner. How the army managed that will always be a mystery to me. The German family we were living with could simply not believe it. We brought in heaping mess plates of everything including big cups and canteens of real coffee which the Germans had not seen for a year or two. We divided up and you should have seen them dig into that dinner.

Within a day or two after Christmas the word began to circulate that we would be moving again and sure enough in a few days we got the word. This was not to be a long move, actually not more than ten miles further away from Coblenz, but closer to the perimeter of the occupation. Didn't mean much, we left one morning and were in and established by mid-afternoon. From my view it was a total loss, we ended up being billeted in what had been some kind of school for the feeble minded, at least that was what had been moved in. Our room was what had been a gymnasium, with twelve or fifteen of us sleeping on army cots. Quite a come down from the feather beds we had been sleeping on the last few days, and no women to make them up. There was naturally a lot of squawking. One advantage was, however, all our equipment was in the same building, with our trucks parked in the street on a slight hill, along side the building, which was to cause trouble later.

Things settled down into a routine within a week. I had a daily run with a big Fiat auto which had a body built on the back in which I hauled batteries to the various radio stations located throughout the area which our division occupied.[30] This took about three or four hours a day, and the rest of the time was used up by special missions, or sleeping, hauling stuff here and there, sleeping and reading. One drawback being there was always someone in the room, talking, playing cards, smoking, etc. At least not conducive to sleeping.

I got fed up with this condition before long, and began to figure out how to get a private room in a private home, and was informed that it was possible, if I could find one within a block or so, and I must be in the orderly room during the waking day when not out on duty.

I started looking, and came up with a room in a house about two blocks away and closer to the kitchen than we were now, where my old friend mess sergeant was in charge. The place I found was not a big place, but typical of the houses in the neighborhood. It was situated on a curving street, and sat directly on the street, no yard. The house had two stories in front, two rooms on the first floor and two above. On the back side of the house had been built a sort of T addition one and one half stories in height, about. In the T part on the back down stairs was a dining room, kitchen arrangement, and a stairway going up to the room above, which actually had side walls about four feet high and a gable roof. A stairway led from the kitchen-dining room below. There was no plumbing, although there was a pump in the kitchen sink.

Also attached to the kitchen was the cow barn. By opening a door to the kitchen you could get a close view of a cow facing the other way; convenient for milking. Where would you put her calf?

Also in the back and attached to the house were the chicken coops stacked on top of each other and containing about a dozen hens, also the Chick Sales and a barn or shed containing hay and feed for the cow.[31] There was a regulation by the government that all eggs laid by the hens went to the government for use in the hospitals, and were collected each week.

Light for the house was provided by one drop from the center of each room. I got permission from the sergeant of the Headquarters Company to move out of the gymnasium and offered to put a phone in the sergeants room and headquarters room so he could get ahold of me whenever he needed me. This was the thing that did the business. Before it was all over, we had a regular telephone exchange for the favored few. It took a lot of patching up of old phones to get this system working. Finally everything got worked out. My room had a good bed, with feather comforters above and below. The only trouble being they were too short and had to be laid catty-cornered across the bed to cover me from my chin to my feet. I figured most Germans must be short or they liked to double up in bed. After my room had been fixed up to my liking, it had a comfortable warm bed, a stand along the wall on which were placed an old time bedroom pitcher and wash bowl, along with water at all times, and a mirror for shaving. Along side my bed was a small table on which the local family had placed an electric lamp, after I had run a wire from the ceiling outlet. Where that lamp came from I will never know.

After about two or three weeks, the high brass became concerned about how us poor privates were being housed, so the lieutenants were requested to make a visual inspection of our quarters, and report any irregularities which they came across. The chore fell to the lieutenant in charge of the Headquarters Company. Of course no buck private was told of this inspection, the object being to keep the privates as ignorant as possible about what was going on or what was about to take place.

Well, I was inspected, all out of a clear sky about eight o'clock one morning, my lieutenant burst in upon the people with whom I was living and demanded to see my room. They did not know what to do, except show him the room. He came up and caught me half dressed and shaving and it was well past 8:00 and any buck private was expected to be down to the orderly room and to have had his breakfast of oatmeal and coffee, and be ready for the days assignment. And here I was in my underwear, just shaving, and sitting on the end of the bed was the tray on which my breakfast had been served, and it was only too obvious that breakfast had consisted of two eggs, white toast, jam and coffee served in a china cup, and bacon, two big pieces. The lieutenant took one look and said "Who the Hell do you know"? Well, he knew who I knew, he also knew that I knew there would be just the routine report on my quarters, everything OK. Word came down the next day the lieutenant would like to have a telephone in his room if one could be found. One could be found. I had a better room than he did, more light and more service.

After our inspection, which by the way, was the only one I ever had in Germany, things settled down to more or less a daily routine. I made my daily routine delivering batteries and had lots of loafing on my hands, and since I had a regular delivery run and was on detail I could not theoretically be on two details at the same time, so could not draw KP or guard duty or other details that are always looking around for some poor buck to do them. So I had time to get in a little more trouble. The small courtyard at the school where the company was housed had become a repository for cars and trucks that were not running so well, or not at all. Among this assortment of immobile vehicles was a Harley Davidson motorcycle that was among the casualties. Several guys had had a turn at trying to get it to run, no success, so one day I tried my hand. First had to find out why it wouldn't run. It didn't take long to learn there was no spark getting to the spark plugs. Upon examining the distributor it was obvious the points were not opening and on further inspection the spring to the points were broken, and the points would not open, therefore no spark. After scrounging around for a short time I found a small piece of flat steel that looked as if it may have been out of an old corset or something of the kind. After considerable time and effort, bending and cutting and working on it, it would fit behind the broken copper spring in the distributor so it would open when it should and distribute a spark to the cylinders at the right time, and to my utter astonishment, the engine ran after a fashion.

Well, there was nothing to do but to immediately test it out, no matter the chain was so loose it was practically falling off. I got the cycle on the street, the engine started and off we went. The further we went the better it ran for a mile or two, and we were out in the country in no time, on a very narrow hard top road. The farmers in Germany never miss a bet. The road was just wide enough so that by being careful a couple of vehicles could pass. The farmer had plowed and seeded the normal sides of the road right up to the hard top and the telephone poles sat back in the farmer's field about 8 or 10 feet on either side of the hard top. This area was cultivated and well fertilized with the contents of the honey wagon.

After having gone down the road a couple of miles, I slowed down and turned around and as I slowed the engine began to miss and jump. Anyway, starting back toward home base the engine ran very roughly, missing and bucking. As I gained speed I just aggravated the condition. Finally with a great jerk the drive chain jumped off the sprocket, got mixed up in the rear wheel, off the road we went headed directly toward a telephone pole, which we fortunately missed by about an inch. The cycle fell over. I dived over the handle bars, plowing a nice furrow in the soft, freshly plowed, well fertilized field with my forehead and nose, losing some skin in the process, and collecting some fresh fertilizer, especially too near the road. I lay still for a few minutes taking careful inventory of all my moveable possessions, and decided nothing was missing or broke or lost, and that everything was in working condition. I got up and shoved the motorcycle out to the road, in hopes some one I knew with a truck would come along. I was in luck. Sure enough one of my outfit stopped and asked if he could help. I said yes, help me get this thing in the truck and back home, so we loaded the cycle in the back end. The driver said "Do you look awful! Are you hurt?" and I replied that I guessed not. He climbed in the truck and I walked around to the other side and climbed in, and he said "You stink like Hell. Don't touch anything." We got back to headquarters and drove into the back end of the yard, where we unloaded the cycle and stored it, or rather leaned it against the wall. As far as I know it is still there, but I will bet no one is riding it.

I needed cleaning badly and it took the rest of the day and all of the next day to get reasonably clean and patched up where I had lost skin from my nose and forehead. I laid off motor cycles for life.

—⟳—

POSTSCRIPT

This is the end of the narrative written by Kenneth Baker. He wrote with pencil on a yellow paper tablet while sitting in the easy chair of his Florida retirement apartment. The memoirs were started in August of 1984, 66 years after he had crawled under machine gun fire and ducked shrapnel while mending telephone wires on the battlefields of France. Kenneth Baker was then 88 years old.

He had no diary, no bundle of cherished letters kept by his family, no friends with whom he could reminisce nor questioners to quicken his memory. His only reference was his copy of *32nd Division in the World War* issued by the joint War History Commissions of Michigan and Wisconsin.

The narrative was finished. When I visited my parents in their apartment, I recall reading it to its conclusion with his description of coming home. Unfortunately I did not take the manuscript with me then, and when I did take it for typing the last pages were missing. And Kenneth Baker had grown too tired to write again.

ROBERT H. FERRELL was distinguished professor of history at Indiana University, Bloomington, and author or editor of several books on World War I subjects. Betty Baker Rinker is the daughter of Kenneth Gearhart Baker.

NOTES

This article appeared in volume 97, no. 1 (March 2001).

1. Joint War History Commissions of Michigan and Wisconsin, *The 32nd Division in the World War, 1917–1919* (Milwaukee, Wisc., 1920).

2. See Elmer W. Sherwood, *Rainbow Hoosier* (Indianapolis, 1920?); Sherwood, *Diary of a Rainbow Veteran: Written at the Front by Elmer W. Sherwood* (Terre Haute, Ind., 1929); Elmer Frank Straub, *A Sergeant's Diary in the World War* (Indianapolis, 1923).

3. In World War I slum also was known as slumgullion. By GI can Baker means a government-issue can; the acronym was of World War II vintage. KP is kitchen police, 'police' meaning a detail of any sort.

4. QM is quartermaster, which refers to the corps and officers responsible for providing supplies.

5. The place was Camp MacArthur in Waco, Texas, named for General Arthur MacArthur, father of General Douglas MacArthur. When the army received congressional authority to institute a draft not long after the declaration of war, the military perforce had to arrange construction of housing for the draftees, and the arrangement was for tent camps in the South, wooden barracks in the North. Baker and friends were in one of the new tent camps. The arrangement worked fairly well, save for the tent camps in border states such as Oklahoma, where the Thirty-fifth (Missouri/Kansas) Division was stationed at Camp Doniphan on the reservation of the army's artillery school at Fort Sill. Oklahoma winters were cold, and Doniphan also underwent incessant batterings from sandstorms. Lieutenant Harry S. Truman of the 129th Field Artillery Regiment, a part of the Thirty-fifth's field artillery brigade, which trained over the winter on the Sill ranges, found the tent camp almost unbearable. For Baker's first sight of a barracks camp see page 78.

6. A dog robber was an officer's attendant or personal servant.

7. Until the construction of vast Hudson River piers in the 1920s, with sheds and railroad sidings, the port of the New York area was not Manhattan but Hoboken. Hence the motto of the American Expeditionary Forces (AEF), as troops in France were known, when the time came for return to the United States after the war: "Heaven, Hell, or Hoboken."

8. It is surprising to read Baker's description of the *Baltic* for in May 1917 the liner had carried the AEF's commander, General John J. Pershing, and staff to England. Presumably Pershing did not see such accommodations, nor did officers of his staff. After World War I the officers who accompanied Pershing

established the Baltic Society, annual sessions of which continued into the 1940s, usually with Pershing in attendance.

9. Not long after America entered the war the British admiralty went over to convoys, abandoning all effort—save for ships capable of outsailing enemy submarines—to encourage single sailers. In the spring of 1917 losses to submarines became intolerable and something had to be done. But convoys, though almost 100 percent safe, were inefficient. As Baker related, each ship had to reduce its speed to that of the slowest vessel. Moreover it was necessary to gather ships in port, which was time-consuming. And when a convoy arrived it frequently overwhelmed the facilities of the receiving port.

10. The origin of army entrees was always a source of conversation, especially aboard British ships, and half of the two million troops of the AEF sailed aboard British ships. Sergeant William S. Triplet of the Thirty-fifth Division believed the meat served aboard his ship was Australian jackrabbit. William S. Triplet, *A Youth in the Meuse-Argonne: A Memoir, 1917–1918*, ed. Robert H. Ferrell (Columbia, Mo., 2000), 33. In World War II the present editor found himself stationed for a year in Cairo where local restaurants featured chicken dinners. American troops in the city never saw chickens, but the city contained innumerable vultures.

11. Every soldier who crossed the Atlantic was convinced his ship or another in the convoy was in danger of being attacked by enemy submarines. If he saw wreckage from sinkings, or ordinary flotsam, he identified a periscope. In the case of the *Tuscania*, Baker was approximately correct. That transport was sunk, with loss of thirteen men. Other U.S. ships lost on the eastward trans-Atlantic run were the *Moldavia* and animal transport *Ticonderoga*, with 56 and 215 deaths respectively. On return voyages, the U.S. Navy did not escort ships heavily. Two broad lanes for convoys reached to Europe, with troopships taking a lane different from ships carrying supplies. Troops usually went direct to France, supplies to England. Each lane was two hundred miles wide and difficult for submarines to cover. Supply ships crossed far more frequently (one hundred supply ships to every troopship), and were slower and less protected. Submarine commanders concentrated on them. The Germans also believed that American troops, trained by officers with no experience on the western front, would not affect the fighting.

12. The army commissioned second lieutenants after a training course of three months.

13. Clearly the "Moroccans" were Indian troops.

14. A tin kelly was an army helmet.

15. In the late winter and early spring of 1918 the German high command in the West, principally General Erich Ludendorff and the titular commander Field Marshal Paul von Hindenburg, fixed upon a now-or-never strategy, a series of

massive offensives against the British and French forces in northern France, in hope of breaking their lines and ending the war before the AEF could affect the outcome. At that time, the late winter, the AEF had hardly been in action, only a division or two having served in the line, and then in training, taking part in no offensives or indeed action beyond two box barrages put over by their German opponents in which the Americans essentially were worsted, men killed and taken prisoner. The first of Ludendorff's offensives began on March 21 and initially was a huge success, promising to divide the British and French armies and roll the British forces up to the Channel, meanwhile taking Paris. Eventually it failed, only to be followed by four more lunges against the Allied forces. The last of the offensives began on July 15 and came to a quick end. Three days after its beginning two American divisions, the First and Second, together with a French Moroccan division, jumped off against a salient, a wedge, into Allied lines in the vicinity of Soissons. The counteroffensive, which ended on August 6, forced German withdrawal from the salient, albeit at a large cost on both sides. It was the first major American battle against German troops, and the inexperienced men of the AEF went forward in bunched formations, to be mowed down by artillery and machine guns, sometimes in windrows. After Soissons a series of attacks forced the German army back. On August 8, three days after Baker rode along the body-littered road he here describes, the British moved forward in an offensive that at first stunned the German high command. The truly large U.S. campaigns followed at St. Mihiel (September 12–16) and, by far the larger, the Meuse-Argonne (September 26–November 11).

16. The C-ration was a staple of the World War II menu, and Baker who was a veteran of both wars was writing in its memory; he refers to canned stew of some sort.

17. This must have been the cave at Tartiers.

18. Named by the Americans for the heiress of the Krupp munitions firm, Bertha von Krupp, the rifle also was known as the Paris gun. Emplaced prior to the offensive of March 21 it fired on the capital for weeks and caused panic until Parisians recognized it was an instrument of terror, rather than a preliminary to the capture of the city, and steeled themselves to resist it. The gun caused hundreds of casualties, one of the worst occasions being when it sent a shell into a church during services.

19. The Thirty-second Division had been taking part in the rolling up of the Soissons salient, which was bounded by Soissons to the west, Chateau-Thierry, and Reims. The southernmost boundary of the salient was at Chateau-Thierry on the Marne, with some German units across the river. The battle drove the Germans north to the Aisne River and alternatively was known as the Aisne-Marne offensive. The division's next action would lie to the north and west, between the branch of the Aisne known as the Oise, which ran east, and

continuation of the Aisne to the northeast—the Oise-Aisne offensive hence was
in this forked region, beginning August 18, ending September 6. American Battle
Monuments Commission, *32nd Division Summary of Operations in the World War*
(Washington, D.C., 1943), 6–32.

20. The French guns were Chauchats. When the United States entered the war
the number of machine guns in U.S. Army stores was fifteen hundred, with four
makes. In the production of armaments that was attempted in following months,
down to the armistice in November 1918, almost all of the efforts to produce
planes, tanks, artillery, mortars, and rifles failed, with the exception of the
Eddystone Enfield, a poor reproduction of the inferior British Enfield, and the
Browning guns, which by the end of the war numbered 29,000 rifles and 27,000
heavies. Pershing forbade their use until near the end of the war, for fear the
Germans would capture and copy them. The Brownings were the guns of choice
in World War II and the Korean War.

21. Troops trained in the United States with broad-brimmed campaign hats
of the War of 1898 and the Mexican border mobilization of 1916–1917. The AEF
received the small soft hats known also in World War II, and for battle they wore
the short British-style helmets.

22. At this juncture the narrative turns to the Meuse-Argonne offensive, by
far the largest battle during American participation in World War I. The AEF lost
26,000 men killed, the most costly battle in the nation's military history. One
million men took part in the field armies, First and Second, directed by Pershing,
who was army group commander. Nine divisions opened the battle in the I, V,
and III corps, distributed left to right on a front extending from the Argonne
Forest in the west to the Meuse River near Verdun. The Thirty-second Division
at first was in reserve for V Corps, whose divisions, left to right, were the Seventy-
ninth, Thirty-seventh, and Ninety-first. On September 30 the Thirty-second
relieved the Thirty-seventh, and on the night of October 3–4 it relieved the
Ninety-first. Fighting took place in the neighborhood of Romagne, the present-
day location of a cemetery containing 14,000 graves. The division captured
Romagne on October 14, was relieved October 20, and reentered the line as part
of III Corps on the east bank of the Meuse, November 9. *32nd Division: Summary
of Operations*, 33–68.

23. Baker's chronology is out of order, for the division did not get relieved until
October 20.

24. As mentioned in note 22, the Thirty-second Division did not go back into
the line until November 9. By that time there had been spectacular movement on
the sectors of I and V corps, where an offensive launched on November 1 led to
a breakthrough. III Corps, turning into the east bank of the Meuse, proceeded
much slower.

25. They returned to the line two days before the armistice of November 11.

26. Baker is confusing the Battle of Verdun in 1916 with American defense of Chateau-Thierry two years later. Americans had not participated at Verdun, which was an epic struggle because of huge casualties suffered both by the German attackers and French defenders, usually estimated as half a million on each side. At Chateau-Thierry on the Marne, American machine gunners from the Third Division prevented a German breakthrough across the river.

27. The false armistice, a widespread but erroneous report of peace, came several days before the real one. The author again blurs chronology, for the Thirty-second Division reentered the line two days before war's end.

28. For the Army of Occupation, the Third Army, General Pershing chose only divisions that had seen the most action. The men of the AEF always believed that the First Division, the first in France, saw the most action, followed by the Second. Both were regular army divisions. In fact the Thirty-second achieved the same number of battle honors as the First and one more than the Second. So proudly reported a guard officer, Captain Charles S. Coulter. Coulter, "National Guard Service in World War," *Infantry Journal*, XXX (January 1927), 97.

29. It was the thirteenth.

30. It was the area in the vicinity of Dierdorf and Rengsdorf.

31. A Chick Sales was an outhouse. It was named after the humorist, a vaudeville figure, who was the author of a little book entitled *The Specialist* in which as an alleged carpenter he described the virtues and defects of several models.

FIVE

Recollections of a World War II Combat Medic

BERNARD L. RICE

SHE SOBBED, "I DON'T WANT you to go!" The young man fought back his own tears as he wiped the salty stream from his wife's face. A dozen about-to-be soldiers stood in the predawn fog by the Red Car interurban in Van Nuys, California. Most were exchanging good-byes with parents, friends, or family. Red eyes were everywhere. I had said my last good-byes the night before at Ducky Dingler's rooming house, but my eyes, too, were misty.

The conductor picked up his light and with sadness in his voice said, "Boys, it's time to go." He waved his light, a bell on the front of the car clanged as the last hasty kisses were exchanged. Silent men filed into the car and sat down. Wheels squealed and the little knot of well-wishers vanished into the fog. There were no dry eyes as we moved down Van Nuys Boulevard. This was the last chance for tears, for in a few hours we would all be soldiers. And soldiers did not cry, did they? Little did we know. It was January 2, 1943. Our date of return was unknown.

Thirty-nine months later I came back to my old boarding house on Van Nuys Boulevard. Ducky Dingler had a bed for me. The morning after I returned, the San Fernando Valley was again engulfed in fog. After breakfast I went out to Ducky's front porch and lay down in her porch swing and daydreamed about buying civilian clothes. I drifted off to sleep.

Then I heard them. German jet bombers! And a voice came to me: "Red, what in the world are you doing?" That was Ducky's voice, but what was she doing over here in Germany? She had no business in combat. Slowly I realized I was back in Van Nuys, on Ducky's porch, with paint and wood under my fingernails from digging into her floor with my bare hands.

As I slept, the fog had dissipated, and a flight of Lockheed P-80 jets had taken off from Burbank.[1] In my sleep the noise of those American jet fighters became the only jet fighters I had ever seen, the German Messerschmitt 262s.[2] I was scared to death of them and had tried to dig a hole with my bare hands to hide in. I tried to explain this to Ducky, but I was certain she did not understand at all. I know she thought, "I am going to have to watch this kid. He's crazy."

In the following pages I will describe a few of the incidents that changed a twenty-year-old airplane lover into a man who could be scared by the sound of a jet. During those thirty-nine months I was to find out how the Army worked and how men reacted to high stress as my buddies and I were bombed, strafed, shelled, mortared, sniped at, and on occasion forced into playing God.

I'M IN THE ARMY NOW

I went to war a Hoosier, born in Elkhart, raised in Osceola and Mishawaka. My father was a baker, but during the depression he often worked at manual labor. My dream of a college education and of becoming a chemist had to be financed by my own earnings. After graduation from Mishawaka High School in 1940, I worked as a physical testing technician in the laboratories of the Ball Band Plant of the United States Rubber Company.[3] For the next two years I tested materials used in flying boots, rubber fuel tanks for airplanes (some for Jimmy Doolittle's raiders who bombed Tokyo in April, 1942), military raincoats, deep-sea diving suits, rubber boots, tennis shoes, and more. I started at fifty cents an hour and soon received a two-and-a-half-cent raise. I paid my mother five dollars a week for room and board, bought a 1937 Ford, and enrolled at the Indiana University extension at South Bend. Working with aviation products whetted my appetite for flying, so I learned to fly a Piper J-3 Cub, soloing on October 10, 1941.[4] My instructor, Zenith Barber, soon after left to ferry military airplanes to overseas bases and encouraged me to try to do the same.

Then came America's entry into the war. Not having enough flying time to qualify as a ferry pilot, I decided to become a celestial navigator. In April, 1942, I sold my 1937 Ford and bought a one-way bus ticket to Van Nuys, California. I enrolled in the Pan-American College of Celestial Air Navigation at the Van Nuys Metropolitan Airport where I studied aerial navigation under Alan Zweng.[5] I supported myself by testing gasoline tanks for P-38s at Timm Aircraft, which was located at the same airport.

I developed a hernia that fall and had corrective surgery on October 1. Navigating was now on hold. Then my draft number came up, and I reported for induction on December 28. All body openings were poked, probed, and examined. The internist saw the red scar on my belly and inquired about it. After my explanation, he said, "Well, Son, we can't put you on active duty for ninety days after hernia surgery. You will be sworn in today and report for active duty on January 2, 1943, at Fort MacArthur, California." This was not what I had planned. Could I now plan anything?

The main gate of Fort MacArthur loomed out of the mist.[6] A corporal met us. He was God personified for the next three days. He told us, "You WILL draw your GI clothing. Then you WILL send your civilian clothing home or donate it to charity. Then you WILL get your haircut. DO NOT PLAN for your future. The Army will do that. And remember, the Army always has 'contingency plans' to take care of any emergency."

Then he asked if there were any questions. I said, "I can fly and navigate. How do I get into the Air Force from here?"

"The Air Force is filled up, buddy. Everybody wants to fly. I want to fly. If an opening comes up, I am going to get it!" He continued, "You will take your tests and wait to see what the Army thinks it can do with such a sorry looking batch of misfits. But don't think for a moment that we are going to throw any of you back. We ain't. In about three days you will be assigned to a camp for your basic training. We are going to make fighting men out of each of you. It's going to be hard on you but harder on us poor corporals who have to teach you poor dumb slobs."

They issued us GI clothing. One of our group, promptly nicknamed "Fashion Plate," resplendent in his obviously tailored "zoot-suit," yelled out, "Hey, sergeant, you made a mistake here! I don't wear boxer shorts; I wear jockey shorts."

The supply sergeant just rolled his eyes heavenward and yelled back, "There ain't no jockey shorts in this man's Army!"

Fashion Plate muttered under his breath, "That's uncivilized. Kee-rist! Boxer shorts always ride up on me."

Then came the shot line. Rumors and jokes about horse needles floated back to us. We embellished them, adding blunt needles, and passed them on to the guys behind. Soon we all knew the cold hand of doom was waiting just down the hall. We were handed a piece of paper and told, "If you lose this, you will have to take your shots all over again!" Before we knew what was happening, a medic scratch-scratched our left biceps, and as we stepped forward, zip-zap, unseen medics stabbed needles into both arms. Then we were told to dress. I raised my arms to slip on my new olive drab undershirt, and the next thing I knew I was lying on the floor wondering where in the world all those soldiers had come from! Years later I recalled those unconscious seconds as the happiest moments of my army career.

On my third day in the Army, at exactly three o'clock, a sergeant posted lists on the bulletin board alongside the toilet and showers. There was much shoving and pushing and neck-stretching as everybody tried to learn his fate at the same time. There was mine: "Pvt. Rice, Bernard L., Camp Wallace, Texas. Coast Artillery, 26th Anti-Aircraft Training Battalion." I was not going to fly airplanes. Oh, no, I was going to shoot them down! This was the first in a long series of lessons on how the Army operated.

After my basic training, I was selected by competitive examination to attend the Army Specialized Training Program (ASTP) and assigned to New Mexico A & M to study basic engineering.[7] We were to remain privates or privates first class (pfcs) until we finished the program; then we would be commissioned second lieutenants.

A year later, however, the ASTP was disbanded abruptly, and we were shipped to the 12th Armored Division, which was preparing to go overseas.[8] In early 1944 the 12th had received a call for volunteers for a hazardous duty assignment. Several hundred men had volunteered and participated in the invasion of Normandy, June 6, 1944. The depleted ranks of the 12th were filled with about one thousand ASTP men. Most of those who had volunteered to leave the division were privates or pfcs, leaving the 12th top-heavy in rank. We ASTP men found we had no chance for advancement. I asked to be placed in the field artillery so I could fly their observation planes, which were Piper Cubs gone to war. The pilot and observer radioed corrections to the aiming of our big guns. When my orders came, however, they read, "Company C, 82nd Medics."

I BECOME A PILL ROLLER

The 82nd Armored Medical Battalion had been activated as a unit of the 12th on September 15, 1942, at Camp Campbell, Kentucky. Most of the men in the 82nd had been with it since its formation. They had received their basic and advanced medical training at Campbell.[9]

The 82nd provided medical support for the 12th Armored. The large vehicles—such as tanks and half-tracks, tank retrievers, and self-propelled guns—and other specialty vehicles plus their fuel posed hazards different from those in standard infantry divisions. In addition to tending the wounds inflicted by enemy weapons, we were faced with treating casualties from vehicular accidents and burns.

All training, equipment, and treatment techniques were under the direction of our division surgeon, Colonel Alf T. Haerem. He worked with medical personnel in the headquarters of the army corps to which the 12th was assigned.

Figure 5.1 Members of the Eighty-Second Armored Medical Battalion. The
battalion had been activated as a unit of the army's Twelfth Armored Division
in September 1942. Bernard Rice joined the battalion as a combat medic
in November 1944. Courtesy 12th Armored Museum, Abilene, Texas.

The 82nd was headed by a battalion headquarters that supplied the division
with medical equipment and drugs, performed major repairs to all our medical
vehicles, and maintained medical records of casualties as they flowed through
the battalion. There were three letter companies—A, B, and C—composed of
about 120 men each. Each company had two treatment platoons that operated
the mobile medical and surgical facilities. Composed of four doctors and about
one dozen technicians, a treatment platoon stabilized the sick and wounded
men so that they could be transported farther to the rear, usually to an evacuation hospital. One of the doctors was a dentist who had an assistant.

Each letter company had ten ambulances. During training and in the first
weeks of combat, the ambulance platoon carried casualties from the forward
aid stations to the treatment station. Later, as we swept across Germany, we
fought as a "task force" composed of a company of tanks, a company of infantry,
an artillery battery, plus specialists from ordnance, engineering, and signal
companies. One or more of our ambulances usually brought up the rear.

The ambulances of C Company were directed by First Lieutenant Bill Roark,
who was assisted by Second Lieutenant Joseph L. Pittari. Staff Sergeant Arthur Long helped manage the platoon. Under Long were two sergeants, Clyde

Robinson and Clarence Fread, and Corporals Chester Higgs, Tom Rhodes, Byron Young, and Alan Horowitz. The ambulance drivers were either privates first class or technicians fifth class.[10] Each ambulance driver had an assistant driver or aid man. Once in combat, an aid man who survived thirty days or more with an infantry, tank, reconnaissance, or artillery unit became a combat medic. He could be a private, private first class, or technician fifth class.

I well remember my chagrin at being told I was to be a "pill roller." As we trained to save the lives of the wounded, injured, and sick, however, I began to accept the role. We learned which injury to treat first and how to stop the flow of blood, how to sew and protect damaged tissue, and how to administer morphine and blood plasma. We could splint a broken bone using army equipment or improvise when issued equipment was not available. We were also taught the value of prophylaxis, the prevention of disease.

We spent the summer of 1944 in intensive training. We attended classes on medical and surgical techniques and worked on field problems with a combat command. We transferred simulated casualties over rough terrain from the "battlefield" to our treatment stations. There were also real casualties from injuries and accidents during this time. One man was nearly cut in half when his "grease gun," a new machine pistol, went off by itself while lying on the back seat of a jeep. Another ran through a barbed wire fence, severely slashing his throat.

On September 3, 1944, we boarded a troop train and were sent to Camp Shanks, New York. From there we boarded the navy troopship *Tasker H. Bliss* and landed at Avonmouth, England, on October 1. After five weeks of further training at a British army base at Tidworth's Windmill Hill, we were given our assignments; mine was to drive Lieutenant Bill Roark, our ambulance platoon leader.[11]

We waited on the docks at Southhampton to board Landing Ship Tanks (LSTs) on November 11. In those days we all observed a moment of silent prayer at 11:00 a.m. on that date in remembrance of those who had died in wars. As the somber notes of taps echoed off the hulls of ships at the wharf, we wondered what our fate would be. How many of us would be among those being revered a year later? I thought, "I'm going to miss you guys."

Our LSTs crossed the English Channel and were the first military cargo to go up the Seine River to Rouen, France, where we arrived in mid-November. Assigned to the 7th Army, we convoyed across France to Luneville. In the first week of December we went into combat for the first time on the Maginot Line near Bitche. We relieved the 4th Armored Division, destined to fight the Germans in the Ardennes in a few days.[12]

Our training period may have been over, but now we were truly learning. We quickly discovered war was not what we had experienced on maneuvers.

HERRLISHEIM

We were finally in combat. Now our casualties were real. We bandaged and carried men torn by bullets and shrapnel. Our tank warfare expert, Lieutenant Colonel Montgomery Meigs, was decapitated when he stuck his head from the turret of his tank to direct the attack. On our first day of combat, two out of ten C Company ambulances were fired on and one medic, Louis Kaducak, was wounded. It was an ominous beginning.[13]

In mid-December the Germans broke through the Allied lines in the Ardennes Forest in an attempt to retake the major port of Antwerp. This was called "The Battle of the Bulge."[14] The 12th, meanwhile, had been assigned the task of eradicating a small pocket of Germans at the Gambsheim bridgehead along the Rhine River north of Strasbourg. We were told this area was defended by a few hundred ill-equipped Wehrmacht. A quick victory here would give this green division experience and confidence for future combat.

However, Hitler knew the Allies had rushed all their reserves north to the Bulge. When it became obvious the Germans would not recapture Antwerp, he decided to smash into our weakened southern front from the Gambsheim pocket. He set up "Operation Nordwind," to be led by Heinrich Himmler. Nordwind was to push the French out of newly freed Strasbourg, breach the gap in the mountains at Saverne, then push on toward the sea.[15]

Supreme Commander Dwight D. Eisenhower, keenly aware of his lack of reserves, wrote General Jacob L. Devers, 21st Corps commander, that in the event of a German attack in the south he should straighten the Allied lines and withdraw all American and French forces from the Alsatian plain. This would strengthen the front, place the Allied forces in a better defensive position, and free up two divisions that could be used as reserves. This decision would come back to haunt Eisenhower.[16]

In early January, Himmler assembled the 553rd Volksgrenadier Infantry Division, the 10th SS Panzer Grenadier Division (Liebestandarte Adolph Hitler), the 17th SS Panzer Grenadier Division, 31st Panzer Division, and several smaller battle groups in the Black Forest across the Rhine opposite us. These units were ferried across the Rhine at night.[17]

The panzer divisions were equipped with the newest German Tiger and Panther tanks, whose guns could blast through an American Sherman tank's front armor from five thousand yards away. The Sherman's guns could not

penetrate the frontal armor on these German tanks, but if they had the opportunity to attack from the side at ranges of two thousand to four thousand
yards, they could blow the tracks from the Tigers and Panthers. This was not
an even match.

The Germans had discovered early in the war that our Sherman tanks would
burn when hit at a rear sprocket. When Shermans appeared, the Germans
called out, "Here come the Ronsons!" ("Ronson" was a famous American cigarette lighter.)

Working with these disadvantages, we used our tanks primarily against
infantry and avoided tank-versus-tank battles. Our tank destroyer battalions
and infantry with bazookas were to take care of the German tanks. The bazooka was a rocket-propelled projectile that could burn a hole through the
thick armor of the Tiger tank. (The Germans had earlier developed the Pan-
zerfaust which destroyed our tanks the same way.) The TDs (tank destroyers)
manned "Hellcat" vehicles that had a large bore gun mounted on a Sherman
tank chassis.[18]

The Germans moved across the Rhine at night into the Gambsheim area
and hid in the wooded area known as the Stainwald. In the meantime, the 12th
was preparing to attack the supposedly small German force. We were about to
find out what hell really was.

When German prisoners of war told of the build-up taking place in the
south, Devers ordered all divisions, French as well as American, to retreat to
the Vosges Mountains. This would abandon Strasbourg and the surrounding
area, an act condemning three hundred thousand loyal Frenchmen to death
when the Germans strode back into the area. French commander Charles de
Gaulle found this unacceptable, and he ordered his men to hold Strasbourg at
any cost. De Gaulle also telegraphed British Prime Minister Winston Churchill
and President Roosevelt to request their support in halting the planned withdrawal. Roosevelt deferred the query back to Eisenhower who was furious at
de Gaulle's insubordination.[19]

Things came to a head on January 3. Churchill flew to France and met with
de Gaulle and Eisenhower. Both de Gaulle and Eisenhower later wrote accounts of that meeting. De Gaulle related that Eisenhower opened the meeting
by stating his reasons for the withdrawal: the Bulge, the emergence of German
jet- and rocket-powered fighter planes, and the new German Panther tanks.
While Allied ground troops would be slaughtered if the armies met on the
flat plains, the Panthers would be at a disadvantage in the Vosges Mountains.
Moreover, the Germans had attacked in the Colmar pocket just south of the
12th Division over the previous two days.[20]

When de Gaulle told Eisenhower he could not condemn thousands of Frenchmen to certain death, Eisenhower responded with, "You give me political reasons . . . to change military orders."

De Gaulle argued, "Armies are created to serve the policy of states. And no one knows better than you yourself that strategy should include not only the given circumstances of military technique, but also the moral elements. And for the French people and the French soldiers, the fate of Strasbourg is of an extreme moral importance."[21]

De Gaulle wrote that Churchill chimed in, "All my life I have noted the significance Alsace has for the French. I agree with General de Gaulle that this fact must be taken into consideration."[22]

Eisenhower pressed de Gaulle further, asking what the French First Army would do if the Americans cut off all the supplies to the French. De Gaulle replied that the French people might be forced to deny the Allies the use of the roads and railroads if the war was not conducted in the best interests of France. He wrote later: "Rather than contemplate the consequences of such possibilities, I felt I should rely upon General Eisenhower's strategic talent and on his devotion to the service of the coalition of which France constitutes a part."[23]

De Gaulle won his point. Eisenhower telephoned General Devers that the retreat was to be cancelled immediately. Eisenhower, in his account of the conference, wrote: "He [Churchill] sat in with us as we talked but offered no word of comment. After de Gaulle left, he quietly remarked to me, 'I think you have done the wise and proper thing.'"[24]

The 12th Armored Division stayed and fought. Not only were we badly outnumbered, we were also not equipped to dig in and hold against an enemy attack. An armored division's strength is its ability to move, strike, and then move again.

The "Hell of Herrlisheim" lasted eight days before troops from the 36th Infantry Division relieved us. In memory, everything runs together, but here are incidents I cannot forget.

We attacked over a broad, flat, frozen plain covered with snow. The plain ended at the Stainwald. We whitewashed all our tanks and other front line vehicles so they would blend in with the snow. The tankers soon found Sherman tanks uncontrollable on the snow-covered ice.

The infantry had no picnic either. Soldiers fell while running over those flat and slippery fields. It was impossible to dig in. They waded or swam the ice-clogged ditches and canals that crisscrossed the plain. Sometimes they used the canals as trenches. Some infantry platoons were cut off and sliced up piecemeal. Others were captured intact as they were overwhelmed.

The casualty list of the 1st Squad, 2nd Platoon, C Company, 56th Armored Infantry at Herrlisheim tells the story of those foot soldiers. Of the eleven men, Platoon Sergeant Leslie T. Silvering and Privates First Class Alex A. Palma and William P. Desmond were killed. Priest, Knox, Hinojosha, Pilings, and Platoon Corporals Dewitt and Oaks were wounded. Only T 5 Conkling and Simmons went unscathed.

I helped the medics of the 56th Infantry pick up some wounded along the canal near Rohrwiller. Dozens of burned-out and flaming tanks screened the field with smoke. We evacuated our wounded under fire and came back into town. Then I saw an ASTP buddy, Joe Lentz, of South Bend, climbing aboard a halftrack, his M-1 rifle slung over his back. I ran over and said, "Be careful, Joe. I just came back from the canal. It is hotter than hell up there."

He looked down at me and said, "Don't worry. I'll be OK."

About an hour later someone walked into the aid station and told us that the last halftrack had been ambushed and that all aboard had been killed. I felt pretty bad about Joe. But this story has an epilogue. Two years later I thought I saw the ghost of Joe Lentz walking toward me in downtown South Bend. This was no ghost, just one bitter man. He said that he had been wounded and left for dead by someone from the 12th. He was later picked up by a medic from the 36th Infantry.

One night at the 56th Infantry aid station, two wounded were brought in. One, a lieutenant, had his left arm severed just below the shoulder. He was conscious and talking. The other GI had several holes in his abdomen and was unconscious. The aid station surgeon, Captain William Zimmerman, said, "Let's get the arm first." I applied sulfa powder and helped bandage the stump. I lit a cigarette for the lieutenant and placed it between his trembling lips. "Thanks," he whispered. He sat on a litter with his back against a box.

We then worked on the lad with the belly wounds. There was little hope for him. There were vital organs in that area, and he had so many holes. We sprinkled sulfa powder all over his belly and put on a compression bandage.[25]

We heard a "clunk" and checked the lieutenant. He was lying on the floor, dead. The GI with the belly wounds, however, lived and returned to his company a few months later. You never bat a thousand when you play God. At Herrlisheim, hell and health met at the hands of the combat medic and were forever after united.

Late one night Colonel Ingrahm Norton, commander of the 56th Infantry, came into the aid station. Captain Zimmerman offered him a canteen cup of hot coffee. As the colonel hugged the warmth of the stainless steel container, he passed his haggard eyes over the scene: our sparse aid station, an unconscious wounded GI on a litter. He had already passed the pile of bodies awaiting the Graves Registration team. After a few minutes the captain asked how things were going.

The colonel spoke in halting phrases. "I can account for . . . about 100 men . . . of the 56th . . . right now." He choked back dry sobs as he spoke. He was a very miserable man.[26]

Aid stations treated more than body wounds. Combat took its toll on the mind, too. It was not that everybody went crazy, but many men needed a kind word and a little reassurance. It was not easy to accept the loss of buddies that you had slept, eaten, worked, and played beside for months or years. Even the most hardy had difficulty facing the fact that they might die in the next hour, the next day, the next week.

Into this Hell the hand and voice of the chaplain was sometimes the best medicine. The following is a condensation of a recollection by First Lieutenant Lee Ghormley of the 66th Infantry about a night at Herrlisheim:

> God, it's cold. Today is tomorrow and yesterday is today and Rohrwiller is Bischwiller and Herrlisheim is Hell on earth. A Sergeant moved along the remnants of his platoon, selecting one, then another, for a short rest back at the 82nd Medical Battalion Aid Station in Bischwiller.
>
> There, those tired and bearded men of mercy, the Medics, moved about, zephyr-like, administering aid, comfort and relieving the pain of the wounded, frozen and exhausted. Saving lives, that's what they were doing. God Yes, saving lives!
>
> In another room, a group of tired, cold men with hollow hearts and sunken eyes, sat and smoked a cigarette in peace. These were the darkest days of that grim, horrible war for most of the men; for many, their last.
>
> They were gathered around a Chaplain frying cheeseburgers on a small stove. He placed them into grimy hands, offering words of encouragement, reminders of home or some sincere tribute to a fallen or missing comrade; speaking their language, renewing their faith and fanning the embers of the will to live within the bodies of bearded things that had almost forgotten that they were men, human beings.
>
> A GI muttered, "This is the best kind of religion." Grimy, battered GIs, most of whom had not smiled in days, looked at each other and grinned. They were ready to go back up. The Chaplain had done his work well.[27]

Private first class Robert Hooper, my ambulance driver, was Pennsylvania Dutch. He looked like Bing Crosby and played the guitar. He would sing "He's Too Old to Cut the Mustard Anymore" and "The Big White Bird" as he drove. The crew of a German eighty-eight millimeter gun would fire at vehicles as we sped along a short stretch of road. Eventually Hooper was dodging wrecks along the way. We would both sing to take our patients' minds off the danger of a shell that might blast us into oblivion at any instant. Hoop always got us through.

One night after taking a load of wounded back to our clearing station, a primitive emergency room, Hoop had to service the ambulance. Captain Campbell asked me to hold the plasma bottle while he amputated the leg of a badly shattered young man. As Campbell proceeded with the surgery, I felt tunnel vision setting in and knew it was just a matter of time until I passed out. I focused on the eyes of a surgical technician and prayed he would notice me. As my legs buckled, he rushed up and grabbed the plasma bottle as I fell. In a couple of minutes, I got up and drank a cup of hot coffee. Hoop stuck his head in the door and hollered for me, and we went back for another load of wounded.

A tired bunch of survivors left the Herrlisheim area. As we pulled out, we realized we had neither changed clothes nor slept for eight days. How did we stay awake? Well, if you were as scared as we were, you would not sleep either!

After the battle the 12th was rated by the 7th Army as "at one-third effective strength and unsuitable for combat." We immediately received 13 officers and 1,089 enlisted men as replacements.[28]

The 82nd Armored Medical Battalion was awarded the Presidential Meritorious Service Unit Plaque for its role during Herrlisheim. The 12th was awarded a battle star.

As an inexperienced and green division, we had made a lot of mistakes but not as many as the enemy. We also learned a lot. We had been outnumbered and had possessed inferior tanks. We may have bent, but the Germans did not break through our thin line. Hitler did not get his Atlantic port. The battle of Herrlisheim did not receive much notice in the press. All the correspondents were up north covering the big story, the mop-up of the Germans in the Ardennes. Had the Germans broken through our lines, all the correspondents would have flocked down to cover the story. But the Germans had taken notice: they now respectfully called us "The Suicide Division."[29]

IN THE FRENCH FIRST ARMY

After Herrlisheim we were assigned to the French First Army, commanded by General Jean de Lattre de Tassigny, later Marechal de France. This was one of the few times in United States history that American troops served under a foreign flag. Our mission was to drive the Germans from the Colmar pocket.

Hooper and I took Lieutenant Riley and a billeting party of three into the city of Colmar. Later we found we were the first six GIs to enter that historic town. Riley picked the University of Colmar building for our treatment station.

That night a small group of German soldiers who had holed up in a building across the street from us tried to escape in the darkness. Within a few moments we had several casualties right on our doorstep. Later, huge shells from a railway gun across the Rhine dropped into our area. One shell hit the roof of our building. Tile and bricks rained down upon our ambulance.

The next day Hoop and I supported the 17th Infantry Battalion. We served alongside the French Moroccan troops. They fought from horseback, and we witnessed what may have been the last cavalry charge on the western front. It was quite a sight as a few hundred white-robed men armed with long rifles mounted their steeds and raced down the hill onto a plain to charge a German outpost.

During this action, ambulance driver T 5 Lawrence Keller and his aid man, Fred Santoro, were wounded when a shell dropped beside their ambulance. Fred jumped into the ditch and discovered he was next to an old high school buddy whom he had not seen in years. Surprised, Fred yelled, "Joe, what in the world are you doing here?!"[30]

After smashing the Colmar pocket, the 12th rested and trained near Nancy, France. C Company, 82nd Medics spent a couple of weeks in the small village of Basse Vigneulle on the Maginot Line. While here, I had a serious discussion with our combat command surgeon, Major Pennock, about getting an aerial ambulance. I knew the Germans had one called a Storch. I told Pennock that I could fly patients back in minutes in relative comfort compared to the hours it took to drive over rough fields and torn-up roads. The groans of the wounded as we jostled them in the ambulance told us we were compounding the injuries that they had already received. Pennock told me to keep my eye open for a Storch, and if I found one, to hold it and notify him.

WITH PATTON'S THIRD ARMY

On March 17, 1945, we were transferred to the 3rd Army. All division markings were removed from our vehicles and all 12th Armored patches were removed from our clothing. We were now "The Mystery Division" spearheading Patton's drive to the Rhine.

We broke through the German lines near Trier heading east. Patton's strategy was simple: once you were on the move, keep going. Keep the enemy off balance, never give him time to dig in, and set up a line of defense. Just keep going until you ran out of gasoline or until you met too much resistance. Once more, we went without sleep, but this time it was only for three days.

It was here that we observed the close cooperation between the ground troops and the P-47s of the 9th Air Force. The planes came in right over the trees and shrubs and strafed the German convoys fleeing ahead of us.

Until now we had not realized the wide range of German modes of transportation. They had many bombers, the Messerschmitt Me 262 jet fighter and the Me 163 rocket-powered fighter, yet a lot of their ground equipment was horse-drawn. After a pass by four P-47s, the roadside was littered with dead and dying horses. Many were still harnessed to struggling survivors. Once, we cut a struggling horse free from its dying mate after giving aid to the German wounded.

When the drive to the Rhine was over, we had captured thousands of German soldiers. Our losses were light. We joined up with the French on March 24 and reverted back to the 7th Army.

NO TURNING BACK

We crossed the Rhine on the pontoon bridge at Worms on March 28. Now there was no turning back. We had to attack and keep moving east. The only alternative, as we saw it, was drowning in the Rhine.

Our first objective was Würzburg. Hooper and I were sent along with the 92nd reconnaissance squadron. Most of the time we were miles ahead of the main body of troops. Evacuating the wounded led to some harrowing moments.

Three B Company men never forgot George Wenrick, of A Company 714th Tank Battalion, and George never forgot them. In one horrible instant George's lower jaw had been removed by a burst from a German machine pistol. Sergeant Frank Thomas, T 4 Richard Hendry, and Pfc. Menzo Van Slyke found him.

They tried to lay George down so they could determine the extent of his injuries and stop the bleeding, but George kept struggling to sit up. Menzo then realized that George's unsupported tongue was falling back into his throat, blocking his air.

Once more Hell and heroism met at the fingertips of a combat medic. Menzo stuck a safety pin through the tip of George's tongue and closed it. Then he tied the safety pin to a shirt button with a piece of string. This kept George's tongue from strangling him when laid down. Then they were able to stop the bleeding.

Back in the states surgeons reconstructed a new jaw from George's hip bone. Muscle and skin from his abdominal wall were sculpted into facial tissue. It took them six years to form George's new face.

Figure 5.2 The Twelfth Armored Division crossing the Rhine River on a pontoon bridge, March 1945. Courtesy 12th Armored Museum, Abilene, Texas.

Menzo Van Slyke was written up for a Silver Star for saving George's life, but a combat command surgeon vetoed it because the proper antiseptic procedures had not been followed![31]

Lieutenant Bill Roark, our ambulance platoon leader, decided to give his driver, Corporal Byron Young, a rest and asked Private Kenny Zaraco to drive him. Zaraco wondered if he could finish his coffee first. Roark replied that he would find someone else. Company Clerk Loren Cluff jumped at the chance to drive the jeep, but his superior, Lieutenant George Reilly, objected because Cluff had to file a report. Roark then asked Corporal Tom Rhodes of Rochester, Indiana, if he could drive. Tom responded, "Sure, Sir."

They picked up Sergeant Arthur Long and took off for the front. They came to a fork in the road, and Tom took the left fork because he had been at that same route the evening before. Roark told Tom to stop, back up, and take the righthand road. Tom told Roark he had taken the left fork the day before, but Roark insisted he was correct and ordered Tom to go right. About a half mile down the road, German soldiers popped up from foxholes along the road. They were captured. Eventually Long escaped, but Tom and Roark were not freed until the end of the war. Lieutenant Joe Pitari, our assistant platoon leader, now took over the ambulance platoon.

I was with the 17th Infantry near Lorsch, Germany, on April 6, 1945. Two Messerschmitt 262 jet fighter-bombers dived in on us. As I lay facedown on the bank of a small stream, one of their bombs lifted me off the grass. When I finally shook the cobwebs from my brain, I heard the familiar call of "Medic!" I helped pull a wounded GI from a burning halftrack. During the next few minutes the wounded man and I discovered we had both worked for Timm Aircraft back in Van Nuys in the summer of 1942. He had a bad leg wound and a perforated belly. He could have no water. As we evacuated him, he begged for a drink. All I could do was wet his lips with a handkerchief dipped in water. He died shortly after we got him back to the treatment station. I wished I had eased his last moments with a drink, but I would have felt responsible for his death. I still have nightmares about him.

April 8, 1945, was a bad day for A Company, 82nd Medics. They set up a large canvas tent marked with red crosses on its top as a treatment facility. A Luftwaffe pilot strafed the tent, killing both Captain John E. Edge and his patient and wounding another medical officer and four technicians.

Still in early April, as we penetrated deeper into Germany, litter bearers brought into our station two wounded GIs whose jeep had run over a land mine. Both were so badly hurt that I did not immediately recognize my platoon leader, Lieutenant Joe Pittari, and his driver, motor pool Staff Sergeant Fran Charpentier. Charpy had volunteered to drive Pittari, so Corporal Young once more could have a few hours rest. Pittari died of his wounds, but Charpy recovered and lived another fifty years.

A task force of the 12th raced to the Danube and captured the bridge at Dillingen. Hellcats poured over it and secured the ground on the other side. Our task force, situated a few miles south, was not as fortunate. The Germans blew the bridge at Lauingen, and we had to wait for the engineers to put in a prefabricated steel Bailey bridge. I was assigned to give medical aid to the engineers for a few hours. While walking along the river bank, I spotted a strange object. I picked it up and hastily discarded it when I realized it was a human ear and a small section of hairy scalp!

I was relieved by one of the best combat medics I knew, Clarence Thornhill. He was a big, hulking young man from Alabama. He was fearless. We called him Churchill. He refused to crawl when lead was flying, saying, "If God wanted me to crawl, he would have put scales on my belly." Shortly after I left, an engineer was shot by a sniper on the opposite side of the river. Thornhill crawled onto a tank to radio for help when the sniper put a bullet through Thornhill's helmet. I sketched his sheet-draped body and helmet as it lay in the aid station.

As this was happening, I had my own problem. The first thing we did upon entering a town was to order all small arms to be turned in at a central spot. Fine hunting rifles and fowling pieces were later smashed by a Sherman tank. This day, a small boy was carrying a shotgun to the collection point. He had it over his shoulder, barrel down. It accidentally discharged, striking another boy about eight or ten years old in the right leg. Luckily, the gun was loaded with small bird shot, not buck shot. Hearing the shot, I ran out and carried the wounded lad in for treatment. The captain said we should not treat him as this was a case of one civilian shooting another. He directed me to a hospital located on a side street a few blocks down the street. I gave the lad a stick of Wrigleys Doublemint chewing gum and he quieted down. I picked him up and started for the hospital. Glancing down a side street, I saw a red cross on a flag flying in front of a building and walked to it. The ground was covered with snow, and the stone steps were icy. The building entrance was one story up from the street. As I carefully ascended, I paid no attention to what was above me until a pair of German boots came into my line of sight. I looked up into the eyes of a German soldier with his rifle at his side.

Still thinking this must be the civilian hospital, I was taken by surprise. I asked the soldier to bring his officer. He stepped inside and returned in a moment with a German medical doctor who spoke English. I explained my mission, and he told me to bring the lad in; he would remove the shot and bandage the leg. I followed him into a corridor and soon discovered wounded German soldiers standing at each doorway. I knew right then that the wounded boy was my ticket out of there. I followed the doctor to a small operating room where he removed the shot while I kept the boy calm. It did not take long, although the lad began to cry. I sure did not want to walk the gauntlet with a crying German boy. I gave him another stick of gum; he quit crying; and with the German doctor leading the way, we walked back down the corridor to the front door. By now my presence must have been known to everybody, for the corridor was lined with German wounded. I kept my head high, looked straight ahead, and walked out, negotiating the slippery steps with deliberate care and walked to the main street of town. I turned the corner and only then did my legs turn to rubber! I had blundered into the German military hospital by mistake.

That night Hooper and I were sent to an interrogation center in Dillingen, where a wounded German soldier awaited evacuation to a hospital. We found our patient lying on a litter, fear etched on his face. As we picked up the litter, one of the intelligence officers who had been questioning the wounded man remarked, "I'd like to shoot that son of a bitch." I thought to myself, "Somebody beat you to him, don't you see?" Apparently the German had not cooperated with his questioner. After we loaded him into the ambulance, I shined my flashlight onto his face, and he smiled his thanks. He was just another wounded man, glad the war was over for him. He was no threat to anyone.

On April 12 Hooper and I were winding among some small hills in our ambulance. A jeep driver told us a plane had been shot down ahead of us. Hoop and I raced past the line of vehicles and found one of our Cub artillery spotter planes in a small meadow alongside the road. (You may remember that flying a spotter plane was the duty I had asked for a year before.) A shell had hit the plane just behind the observer, who received a sucking chest wound, and the pilot was also in pretty bad shape with head wounds. We sprinkled the hole with sulfa powder, plugged the chest hole with vaselined gauze, and taped it securely. We then treated the pilot's wounds and bandaged him. Both men appeared to be survivors when we transferred them to an evacuation hospital ambulance, so I figured we had saved their lives. In 1986, however, another artillery pilot, Pete du Pont, told me that both had later died. Had someone been looking over me?

DACHAU

On April 26 strange people wearing ragged clothing began straggling to the 12th Division's rear. They were obviously fleeing something. Up close we saw that they were emaciated; their bodies were just skin over bone. They spoke in high-pitched, almost birdlike voices. They carried nothing. They could hardly put one foot ahead of the other. Their only clothing was thin, striped rags although the air was cold.

Words cannot describe their eyes. They, too, had seen death daily, but not as we had. They had been staring at their own deaths for years. The death they saw, however, was a light at the end of a very dark tunnel.

This was our first encounter with the German concentration camps. The people we met were inmates who had escaped from a satellite of the Dachau camp as the Germans retreated.[32] We were not prepared for this. We had seen death almost daily during the previous five months, but the dead up to now were mostly one or two at a time. Even our bloodiest battle could not prepare us for Dachau. There we found hundreds of dead. Some lay in grotesque piles, some neatly stacked like cordwood, others thrown helter skelter into a pit.

This was Hitler's "Final Solution," eliminate all of Europe's Jews and anyone else who opposed Hitler. Words cannot describe what we saw nor the feelings of revulsion we felt.

Combat Medic Fred Santoro, of Sandusky, Ohio, said the task force he was supporting opened the gates at a railroad siding that led into Dachau. He saw boxcars loaded with bodies.

Ambulance driver Alan Starck from Darian, Illinois, and his aid man, Pfc. Edmund Sorola from San Antonio, Texas, arrived at a locked gate. Starck opened it. He thought he was a liberator, the finest person in the world. He was promptly ordered by a lieutenant to close that gate! Al's protests that these people should not become "our captives" bounced off deaf ears.

As I approached the camp, a building was burning inside an open gate. The German guards had herded a bunch of captives into a barracks and set it on fire only minutes before. Then the guards had vanished, blending into the civilian population. Some survivors told of their mothers, fathers, and children being burned alive. An occasional moan from the pitiful pile of scorched bodies and the twitch of an arm or leg testified that not all had met their final moment of doom.

The jumble of black, scorched bodies lying in the smoking embers contrasted with the hundreds of white, naked bodies nearby. The Germans probably intended to dispose of these bodies in a nearby crematorium. A horse-drawn wagon, minus the horse, stood partially loaded alongside a stack of bodies. Had a guard run off with the horse?

The next day Pfc. Al Pheterson, of Rochester, New York, who had been in the ASTP with me, entered that same gate. Al had a camera. He knew that if he asked an officer for permission to take pictures, he would be told, "No," so he just took pictures without asking. Later he developed them himself at a German photo lab. He brought the negatives back home with him. I met him on June 19, 1997, at our annual reunion in Louisville. He asked me if I would like to see his scrapbook. I did. There were the scenes I had been trying to bury for fifty-two years. The burned bodies. The dead lying in the area.

The events in the following paragraphs occurred after we passed through, but the stories were told around the division.

The administrators of the Landsberg camp had fled. A search team, however, soon found the camp commandant and brought him back. He said he had been responsible only for what happened outside of the enclosure. He blamed a doctor as the real culprit.

Colonel Edward Seiller, the head of the 12th Armored Division military government team rounded up a bunch of local civilians and brought them into the camp. They, of course, protested their ignorance of what had gone on inside the camp. Seiller asked them why they could not smell the camp as we could. Did these "good Germans" feel the same horror and revulsion that swept through us? We wondered.

Seiller then produced the camp commandant, stood him among the partially burned corpses, and told the Germans that this man was responsible for the deaths.[33]

The civilians, seeing our strength and feeling that Hitler's dream of a "Thousand Years of Enlightenment" was now over, made quite a show of wanting to kill the camp commandant right on the spot. What else should we have expected?[34]

Once we crossed the Rhine, the division was covering a wide front. There were many roads heading east and south, so they split the combat commands into task forces, usually a company each of infantry, tanks, and artillery. These task forces were then assigned an objective and a route and were under the command of the ranking officer. Usually each task force had an ambulance attached to it. We stayed with the task force as much as possible but had to leave it occasionally to take wounded back to the rear.

I FIND MY STORCH

May 1 found us on the autobahn south of Munich. As we drove alongside a German airfield, I was amazed to see hundreds of airplanes of all types sitting on the ground. The task force stopped as the lead tank met some resistance. Huge snowflakes drifted gently down upon everything, making a fairyland of the war zone. I enjoyed the enchanting moment.

Then, faintly through the snow, I saw a red cross on an airplane. My brain could not believe what my eyes were telling it. There was a German ambulance plane, the Feisler Storch. At last Major Pennock and Pfc. Rice would have their aerial ambulance. I left Hooper in the ambulance and ran to the plane. I stuck my bare hand under the cowling and felt the warm cylinders. It had been flown within the past half hour. I crawled up into the fuselage, noted a stretcher in place behind the pilot's seat, and sat down. As I studied the instruments, I saw the gas gauge read empty. That was why the pilot did not fly it away.

My concentration was broken by a strange noise. Glancing out the left window, a Sherman tank was roaring down on me. It was crushing the tails of the planes into the mud. I jumped out and tried to stop the tank driver. I was yelling at the wind. He could not hear me. The tank ran over the Storch's tail, and I watched the steel tubes bend, then poke through torn fabric. Tank treads flattened the aft of the plane into instant junk. There went my dream of an aerial ambulance. It made no practical difference, for our fighting days were numbered and we would evacuate just a few wounded in the following days.

WERNER VON BRAUN

On May 2 Colonel Frederick P. Fields, 714th Tank Battalion, commanding Task Force Fields of the 12th was about to move out of Benediktbueren, Bavaria, when a gray jeep slid to a stop in the foot of snow beside him. He looked down at a United States Navy captain and his pea-jacketed driver. Our navy? In southern Germany? The captain said he needed a battalion of tanks and a battalion of infantry to capture and secure a German supersonic wind tunnel guarded by an SS unit up in the mountains.

When Fields said he did not have a force that large, the captain showed him some impressive letters signed by President Roosevelt, Admiral Ernest King, General George Marshall, Generals Eisenhower and A. M. Patch, each requesting that all possible aid be given to the captain.

Fields assigned him one platoon of tanks and one platoon of infantry, requesting they keep in radio contact with him. He then left as he had been assigned to capture Innsbruck, Austria. He lost radio contact with his splinter group soon after. Later, Fields ran into a blown bridge that he could not get around, and as he had no bridge building equipment with him, he backtracked into Kochel.

There on the veranda of a hotel was the navy captain, talking to a civilian with a broken arm. The captain introduced Fields to Dr. Werner von Braun. Von Braun showed Fields his wind tunnel, but Fields was not very impressed. He told me a few years before he died that it looked like a lot of junk to him. But he did remember that von Braun complained loudly that someone had stolen his bicycle!

That was how the men of the 12th happened to capture the rocket scientist who decades later would help the United States place men on the moon. He was just one of the estimated eight thousand Germans taken prisoner that day by the 12th.[35]

OVERTIME

Did you know that World War II went into overtime? It did for the 12th.[36] This story features Captain John C. Lee, Jr., Lieutenant Harry Basse, two tank crews from the 23rd Tank Battalion, and four infantrymen.

Captain Lee was the commanding officer of B Company, 23rd Tank Battalion. His unit stopped at Kufstein, where a captured German major told Lee several important French people were captives in Castle Itter near Wörgl, Austria. Lee and the German left in a jeep and approached Wörgl under a flag of truce. The German soon convinced the commandant in Wörgl that the war was over, many American tanks were coming, and this was the time to surrender. Lee decided to rescue the people in Castle Itter.

The duo returned to Kufstein, crawled into Lee's tank, "Besotten Jinny," and led six other tanks and a half-dozen infantrymen toward Wörgl. German soldiers surrendered to them, and Lee's men found explosives wired to the bridge into town. The prisoners defused the explosives and threw them into the river below.

"Besotten Jinny" and Lieutenant Basse's "Boche Buster" crossed the quivering bridge. They decided the engineers would have to reinforce it before another tank could pass over. Lee took four infantrymen atop his two-tank task force and headed into Wörgl. The rest of his troops returned to notify the engineers of the bridge.

Once in town, Lee left "Boche Buster" and three infantrymen in command of Tech Sergeant William Elliot to secure the town. Lee and his tank crew, Basse, the German major, and the remaining infantryman took off in "Besotten Jinny" for Castle Itter.

"Boche Buster" was to relay radio messages between "Besotten Jinny" and headquarters back in Kufstein. The infantryman led the way around the curving mountain road. He discovered that the SS had set up a roadblock just short of the castle. Rather than sit and fight it out, Lee decided to charge the roadblock. Firing his guns to keep the German defenders' heads down, he ran the gauntlet of fire and sped up the road. "Besotten Jinny" slid to a stop in the driveway of the castle, blocking the entrance.

An eighty-eight millimeter gun concealed in the brush along the mountainside fired at the tank. Lee fired back. "Besotten Jinny" was hit six times. The last shell hit the gas tank and flames erupted. As the crew bailed out of the burning tank, they grabbed the thirty-caliber machine gun and some ammunition. A hail of SS bullets followed the men as they dashed to the castle gate. It opened at once, and they felt safe behind those stone walls.

Then they met the "important people" they had come to rescue. There were two former French premiers, Edouard Daladier and Paul Reynaud; Madam Alfred Cailliau, a sister of Charles de Gaulle; French Generals Leon Jouhax, Maxime Weygand, and Maurice Gustave Gamelin; Madam Weygand; former French minister M. Caillaux; Jean Borotra, tennis star and French minister of sports and Madam Borotra; French fascist Colonel de la Roehe; Michel Clemenceau, son of the French leader during World War I, and a few others who were lesser known.

To this impressive list must be added some unnamed but very important people. There was a second German major and his dozen Wehrmacht soldiers who had guarded these prisoners for many months. They had surrendered to the inmates just before the American tank arrived at the castle gate. These German soldiers were afraid the SS would now kill them for not continuing to fight, so they volunteered to help fight off the SS that were attacking the castle from all sides. Captain Lee immediately gave the Germans their rifles and assigned them to windows where they began to take a toll on their former brothers-in-arms.

It was a strange alliance of American, French, and German peoples: soldiers, diplomats, politicians, and ordinary citizens, fighting together in common defense against a hated, vicious, and unscrupulous enemy.

That night the battle tapered off, and little firing took place. With the dawn the SS moved in. They were crack shots, and the number of wounded within the castle began to mount. The ladies within tended to the wounded and tried to rouse someone at the telephone exchange in Wörgl. As the morning wore on, the situation became truly serious. Their only link to the outside world was that one telephone line into the castle, but no one in Wörgl was answering.

When things looked bad, Jean Borotra volunteered to jump over the castle wall, run forty yards across an exposed field to the woods, and dash through the mountain pass to contact the troops in Wörgl. Lee vetoed the plan, saying it was suicide.

Half an hour later, however, their ammunition was low; there were more wounded; and the German major who had led them to the castle had been shot in the head and killed as he fought alongside Lieutenant Basse. Lee concluded that they might all be annihilated if help did not arrive soon. So Borotra took off.

As Borotra disappeared over the wall, the women yelled that someone in Wörgl had opened the telephone line. They would be rescued after all! But before they could utter a word, the line went dead. Borotra's dash was not suicide, for he was reported to be with the rest of the released captives that night at a hotel on the shore of Lake Constance where they were welcomed back by General Jean de Lattre de Tassigny.[37]

That little coalition within Castle Itter had held off the SS for sixteen hours before they saw Sherman tanks working their way up the road. Lee assumed the tankers coming up the road did not know who was in the castle. But he knew his tankers would see the burned out hulk of the "Besotten Jinny" and, assuming the castle was still a German stronghold, simply blast away at him.

Lee and General Weygand teamed up on the thirty-caliber machine gun and opened fire into the woods far ahead of the lead tank. This message was understood. Sergeant Elliot in the lead tank had his ninety-millimeter gun trained on the castle when he recognized the sound of the American machine gun and decided it was a signal instead of a threat.

The relief column, assisted by men from the 36th Infantry Division, broke through at 3:00 p.m. on May 5. They rounded up the surviving SS and took them prisoner. Lee and his men returned to Kufstein to learn that the Germans had signed a surrender document and that the war was to end at noon on May 5. These men of the 12th had gone into "overtime" by three hours!

This was the last combat sortie on the southern front of the European theater in World War II.

PEACE

What a time. Hoop and I sat down and tried to figure how many days we had spent behind the German lines. We agreed that it was up to thirty, but from there on our memories differed. But we had survived. We had to drink to that! (Just about everybody drank. Some drank to forget what they had seen, and some drank to forget what they had done. Some fellows said only a fool had a hangover: you should never sober up in the first place!) We quickly worked our way through that phase of life and settled down to occupation duty in a small town of Sneidheim, just north of Heidenheim.

Late that summer I was notified that I had qualified for the Combat Medic Badge, which later led to my being awarded a Bronze Star by direction of President John F. Kennedy.

The 12th was then broken up, and the GIs sent to various military outfits. I went to the 47th Medical Battalion of the 1st Armored Division, then based at Mannheim, Germany. Most of the men of the 1st had seen combat in North Africa and Italy and in the invasion of southern France. They had earned their trip home and left early that summer. I spent a couple of months in Idstein before moving to Bensheim.

My turn to go home came in February. I arrived in Antwerp, Belgium, ready to board a ship when they declared me "essential." I had to work at the dispensary at the port until another surgical technician came through with fewer points. After a delay of a couple of weeks, I boarded the *Robin Victory* bound for New York. I was now a part of the three-man medical staff of the *Robin*. After a stormy crossing, we passed the Statue of Liberty and disembarked at Hoboken, New Jersey. After a fast train ride to Fort Dix, I was informed that they would fly me to California that night on an Air Transport Command DC-4. During the last days in the Army, I finally got to fly—as a passenger. That was okay with me. I was discharged on March 23, 1946, and spent the day riding a bus back to Van Nuys, California. I returned to Indiana the next week.

LOOKING BACK

December, 1997, will mark the fifty-fifth anniversary of my induction into the Army. Looking back, it seems as though I am watching a young man I used to know go off to war. I had no idea when I left home that I would share experiences that would last a lifetime. I am amazed at the depth of feelings born of those days in combat. For the first thirty-five years after the war, I tried desperately to forget. I was only partially successful; there was much that refused to be forgotten. When I was contacted in 1980 to attend a reunion of the 82nd Medics, I had no interest in stirring up old memories. My wife Norma, however, wanted to meet the men I had mentioned over the years. We went. I found it to be good therapy. I learned that I had handled things pretty well by myself, although not as well as Tom Rhodes and Art Long, who cannot recall much about being prisoners of war. I met once again Truman Stivers; Max Eagelfeld, a genius who could not dig his own foxhole; Eddie Sorola; Sergeant Curtiss Slaughter, who was never born but quarried from solid granite; and others. Many more are simply among the missing.

At our first reunion I asked one of my old sergeants why he had sent Hooper and me out on what looked like suicide missions, those days with the reconnaissance troopers when we had to fend for ourselves in enemy-infested territory. His answer was simple: you kept coming back!

BERNARD L. RICE worked as a chemical engineer for nineteen years with Bendix Aerospace, Mishawaka, Indiana, and thirteen years with Dwyer Instruments, Michigan City, Indiana. He retired to live in Osceola, Indiana.

NOTES

This article appeared in volume 93, no. 4 (December 1997).

1. The P-80 was the first operational jet fighter in the United States Army Air Corps. It did not see combat until the Korean War, when it was designated the F-80.

2. The Messerschmitt 262 (Me 262) was the world's first operational jet fighter-bomber. It was much faster than the American piston-engine fighters, but its time in the air was limited. A controversy over how the plane was to be used delayed development and production of the Me 262. Hitler wanted it to

be equipped as a fighter-bomber in order to use it against the Allied invasion of France. Others in the German government envisioned it as strictly a fighter plane. Had it been used as a fighter plane earlier, the Me 262 could have caused great damage to Allied bombers and their fighter escorts. Jeffrey Ethell and Alfred Price, *The German Jets in Combat* (London, 1979), 10–71.

3. The Ball Band Plant in Mishawaka once employed over three thousand workers. During World War II the plant manufactured gas masks, flying boots, gasoline bladders for aircraft, self-sealing gasoline tanks for most bombers and fighters, raincoats for soldiers, a nylon-resin composition called V-board to support fuel cells in aircraft, and deep-sea diving suits for the Navy. After the war the company name was changed to Uniroyal.

4. The Piper J-3 Cub was one of the best planes for primary training in the early 1940s. It was a high-winged, fabric-covered aircraft. Early versions were powered by a fifty-horsepower Franklin or Continental engine. Instrumentation was sparse: oil temperature and pressure, engine rpm, airspeed, and altimeter. The Cub could be stalled, spun, and looped, and most students performed all of these maneuvers before flying it alone. It cost me four dollars an hour to fly with an instructor and three dollars an hour to fly it solo.

5. Alan Zweng ran the Pan-American College of Celestial Air Navigation in the 1940s. His father and Admiral P. V. H. Weems developed a system of aerial navigation based on the use of an octant to measure the angle of a star, moon, or sun above the horizon. The Zweng school was located at the Van Nuys Municipal Airport, but in the late summer of 1942 the owners moved it to a new location near Universal City.

6. Named for General Arthur MacArthur, the father of General Douglas MacArthur, Fort MacArthur was located on the Palos Verde peninsula in the town of San Pedro. During World War II it was the reception center for men entering the Army from southern California.

7. The Army Specialized Training Program was created at the urging of educators and industrialists who were worried about a dearth of well-trained technicians and engineers in the United States. President Franklin D. Roosevelt, worried that the program would become a way for the wealthy to keep their sons out of combat, insisted that admission be by competitive examination and available only to men with IQs of 115 or higher. During preparations for the invasion of France, much of the ASTP was disbanded in order to free more men for combat duty. Most ASTP soldiers were scattered among combat units then in the final stages of training in the United States. ASTP men in the medical schools continued to study and did earn their degrees and commissions as promised.

8. Armored divisions were all nicknamed. The 1st Armored was "Old Ironsides," the 3rd was "Hell on Wheels," and the 12th was "Hellcats." We went

from one extreme to another, from the "Sword and Lamp of Knowledge" of the ASTP to "Hellcats." It was quite a change for all of us.

9. Medics, both officers and enlisted men, had myriad stories about their training at Camp Campbell. A strong bond between these men was apparent when we arrived. One of our first lectures was on the history of the 82nd Armored Medical Battalion by the C Company commanding officer, Captain Walter Wiggins. All of us newcomers to the 82nd had a lot of catching up to do even though we had had first aid courses in basic training and more while in the ASTP. We sewed up orange peels as they were supposed to be a realistic substitute for human flesh. At least we learned how to thread a needle properly and could bring the edges of the orange peel together even if they were a bit mismatched. We were divided into two-man teams, and we practiced giving shots and drawing blood from each other. Believe me, there was a lot of squirming on the part of the guy being shot or stuck.

10. Men who had taken courses in the various medical or surgical specialties were rated as skilled technicians, and their rank was noted as technician fifth, fourth, or third class. They were referred to as T5, T4, or T3. A T5 was equivalent to a corporal, a T4 to a sergeant, and a T3 to a staff sergeant.

11. Located between Southampton and Salisbury, Tidworth Barracks was originally a training camp for the British army. After the United States entered the war, American forces occupied a tent city called "Windmill Hill." When my unit stayed there, the equipment was in bad repair. We heard that we were the last men to occupy the site, since with the invasion of France, American forces arriving in Europe could go directly to the mainland.

12. The 7th Army was the spearhead of the Allies' 6th Army Group, which had invaded southern France from the Mediterranean in August, 1944. After quickly securing beachheads on the Riviera and taking the port city of Marseilles, the 6th Army Group had driven north toward Grenoble and beyond. American forces had reached Dijon in mid-September and then had turned northeast to link up with George Patton's 3rd Army, which had raced across northern France. The Allies had then struck east toward the Rhine River. In late November the 7th Army had led the 6th Army Group in taking Strasbourg. Robert Leckie, *Delivered from Evil: The Saga of World War II* (New York, 1987), 757–58; L. F. Ellis, *Victory in the West:* Vol. II, *The Defeat of Germany* (London, 1968), 165.

13. The death of Meigs is noted in Kenneth Bradstreet, ed., *Hellcats* (Paducah, Ky., 1987), 61. The details of his death are still being debated by men who were there. The most popular version says that Meigs, having lost several tanks to accurate German fire from pillboxes on the Maginot Line, had surveyed the situation and concluded that he could not take the assigned pillboxes from his position on the front. He asked Major General Rodrick R. Allen, commanding general of the 12th Armored, to request permission for his tanks to attack

through the lines of the infantry division next door. He was refused and told to stay within the 12th's boundaries. Leaving the meeting, Meigs was reported to have said, "I'm a dead man." Men within the tank told many times of the terror felt within the tank as the headless body dropped back inside with blood spurting from the neck arteries.

My driver, Hooper, and I were fired upon by a German eighty-eight millimeter gun while we were returning with our first load of wounded that first day. Fortunately, either the gun crew was inexperienced or Hooper's slow-down-speed-up tactics threw off the gunners' aim, for all of the shells fell behind us. The ambulance carrying Louis Kaducak was not as lucky. Kaducak was in the passenger seat, and medic Andy Clemente was lying on a litter behind the driver. A piece of shrapnel slammed into the side of the ambulance, whizzed above Clemente's head, and imbedded itself into Kaducak's back just above the left kidney. Kaducak, however, returned to duty a few weeks later and rejoined us.

14. For the Battle of the Bulge, see Charles MacDonald, *A Time for Trumpets: The Untold Story of the Battle of the Bulge* (New York, 1985); Robert E. Merriam, *Dark December: The Full Account of the Battle of the Bulge* (New York, 1947); John Strawson, *The Battle for the Ardennes* (New York, 1972).

15. Bradstreet, *Hellcats*, 67.

16. Dwight D. Eisenhower, *Crusade in Europe* (New York, 1948), 362–63.

17. Bradstreet, *Hellcats*, 77.

18. Shelby Stanton, *Order of Battle, U. S. Army, World War II* (Novato, Calif., 1984), 64–65, 337; Keith E. Bonn, *When the Odds Were Even* (Novato, Calif., 1994), 58. Two of my ASTP buddies, the Mancill twins, Robert and Allan, were a bazooka team in C Company, 66th Armored Infantry Battalion. Allan was killed on February 16, 1945, and Robert was captured the same day near Weyersheim, France.

19. Charles de Gaulle, *The Complete War Memoirs of Charles de Gaulle* (3 vols., New York, 1955), III, 164–67.

20. *Ibid.*, 169. Although the 6th Army Group had successfully pushed the Germans across the Rhine in an area around Strasbourg, there remained a substantial German bridgehead east of the Rhine to the south of the city. This was known as the Colmar pocket, since the city of Colmar was at its center. Ellis, *Defeat of Germany*, 165.

21. De Gaulle, *Complete War Memoirs*, III, 169–70.

22. *Ibid.*, 171.

23. *Ibid.*

24. Eisenhower, *Crusade in Europe*, 362–63.

25. Combat medics provided very basic first aid. We were to protect wounds from infection, control pain, and stabilize the wounded man so that he could

be transported back to a medical clearing station where he could receive
emergency medical care from a physician or surgeon and other trained medical
personnel. The combat medic had to adjust to the rapid transition from periods
of relative quiet to the hellacious, feverish activity of diagnosis, stabilization,
and evacuation of the wounded under enemy (and sometimes friendly) fire.
We had minimal equipment. All training and supplies were predicated on the
assumption that there would be no running water. Each soldier carried an all-
purpose Carlyle bandage on his belt. The combat medic carried several Carlyles
plus packets of sulfa powder, a few morphine syrettes, and a supply of emergency
medical tags. If possible, the medic would fill out a form (EMT) so that the
next person treating the wounded would know what the injury was and what
treatment had been given, for often the wounded would be unconscious upon
arrival at the next station. The empty morphine syrette was attached to the EMT
or the patient's clothing to insure that the patient did not receive a second dose.
Bleeding was stopped with pressure and the wound securely bandaged. The
tourniquet was used sparingly to prevent oxygen starvation to limbs. Sucking
chest wounds were not readily treated by the combat medic for the vaselined
gauze used to stop the flow of air through the hole was not always available.
Broken bones were immobilized with whatever the environment provided. First
choice was an army medical splint, followed by sticks, rolled papers, or a blanket,
each bound tightly to immobilize the joint above and below the fracture. Sulfa
powder was sprinkled on open wounds. Water was not given to wounded men
with abdominal perforations, for that could lead to partially digested material
within the abdominal organs being flushed out into the abdominal cavity,
compounding the problems and even causing the death of the man. Combat
medics were told that when they were faced with a situation for which they had
not received training, they should still do something. Chances were that you
would do the right thing even if you did not know why. We were instructed never
to let a man die because we did nothing.

26. Many of the missing men had been surrounded in Herrlisheim. Some were
captured, a few escaped, and many were killed.

27. Bradstreet, *Hellcats*, 92.

28. *Ibid.*, 77.

29. *Ibid.*

30. In 1985 the widow of Jean de Lattre de Tassigny, Marechal de France, sent
me a picture of her late husband with a handwritten note: "Bernard L. Rice, En
souvenir de la victoire de Colmar-2 Fevrier 1945. G. de Lattre. 1985."

31. In the early 1950s George Wenrick went to the 12th Armored Division
Association reunion in Chicago. In an elevator he met Menzo Van Slyke. By
this time George had a new face. Neither man forgot this meeting, but it was
another thirty-five years before they met again. In 1988 the 82nd Medics held

their reunion in Columbus, Ohio. George Wenrick and his wife, Sarah, attended our reunion, and he and Menzo met again. George came because he wanted to thank Menzo, Hendry, Thomas, and the 82nd Medics for saving his life. It was an emotional reunion.

32. Dachau, located about ten miles northwest of Munich, was one of the first concentration camps established by Nazi Germany. It opened in March, 1933, and originally housed political opponents of the Nazis and criminals. With the rise of systematic persecution of Jews and the beginning of German expansion, Dachau's inmate population swelled with Jewish prisoners and those who resisted German expansion. During the war, Dachau became an important source of slave labor, especially in arms industries. Thirty-seven subsidiary camps, along with other smaller installations, were built to house armaments workers. Toward the end of the war Dachau received large numbers of inmates from other camps the Germans were forced to abandon as they retreated. Plans were drawn up for the killing of all prisoners, but before they could be carried out, elements of the American 7th Army began to overrun the Dachau camps. The main camp was liberated on April 29, 1945. Israel Gutman, ed., *Encyclopedia of the Holocaust* (4 vols., New York, 1990), I, 339–43. See also Paul Berben, *Dachau, 1933–1945: The Official History* (London, 1975); Feig Konnilyn, *Hitler's Death Camps* (New York, 1981); Marcus J. Smith, *Dachau: The Harrowing of Hell* (Albuquerque, N.M., 1972).

33. Bradstreet, *Hellcats*, 115.

34. In 1986, at the 12th ADA Reunion aboard the Hotel Queen Mary, Long Beach, California, I met Harold Gordon and his wife of Salinas, California. The 12th had liberated Harold while he was a captive of the Nazis at the Landsberg camp. He addressed the assembled Hellcats and thanked us for the last forty-one years of his life. Harold has since written a book about his life in a concentration camp, his struggle to get himself and his father to the United States, and his meeting with his wife. Harold Gordon, *The Last Sunrise, a True Story: Biography of a Ten-Year-Old Boy in Nazi Concentration Camps during World War II* (Salinas, Calif., 1989).

35. Personal conversation with Colonel Frederick P. Fields. His story is documented in Bradstreet, *Hellcats*, 175.

36. Bradstreet, *Hellcats*, 53, 175.

37. *Ibid.*, 122.

SIX

A Hoosier Soldier in the British Isles

LAWRENCE B. McFADDIN

[EDITOR'S NOTE: OUR AVERAGE READER may question the propriety of printing these two little gems in a historical magazine, though surely no one would question the desirability of having them in print. It seems, however, that history has come to be a very inclusive study, and that there are those who believe that intellectual history is the very heart of all history. If this is even approximately true, one need not explain the appearance of these items here.

The experience of many an American in the British Isles during the present war may build a foundation of friendship which will make impossible in the future the prejudice with which so many Americans have regarded our English brethren in the past. A young man like Larry McFaddin cannot be influenced by the cheap political practice of twisting the British Lion's tail as preceding generations of Americans have been influenced. These delightful week-ends will long be remembered. The kindness with which our boys have been treated can never be forgotten. May we not hope that a tradition is being developed like that between the United States and Canada which will make war between the United States and the British Isles impossible.

The author enlisted when a junior at Indiana University December, 1942. He served in the Office of Strategic Service in England and recently has transferred to Germany. The trip to Scotland was made October 15–23, 1944, and the one to St. Ives, May 22–31, 1945. The letters were written on a very old typewriter, the servicemen standing in line to use it and hurrying to make way for others. None of the mistakes are serious, and the manuscript is printed without change.]

SCOTLAND

Perhaps I should call it my "Highland Fling;" perhaps I shouldn't attempt to title the past week. Regardless, it shall always be a memorable seven days—a week of wonderful enjoyment and disassociation from the countless things that make life seem complicated, in spite of their relative unimportance.

Monday, John Meloney and I were in London, completely equipped for our trip to the North. We were to meet Fraser Stokes and Don Dunbar later in the day. The day beginning our furloughs had arrived suddenly, for it had been a furlough unexpected (but none the less appreciated!) We had been warned numerous times by rugged Scotchmen of treacherous bogs in the moors, blinding mists in the mountains, and dangerous ledges, and especially of the cold there in Scotland—all of the warnings only made the anticipation greater, and we sincerely hoped we might scare up a ghost or two in an old castle!

I spent a short time with Hugh that morning and learned that he was planning a trip to Edinburg later in the week. John and I then went to St. Jame's Palace to meet "Sir Norman," (a title which he used only when formality necessitated it—he preferred "Speedy"). We had a wonderful dinner at the "Trocadero," just off Piccadilly Circus. He's a good fellow—a nice sense of humor and a person who has had a great number of interesting experiences all over the world. We spent several amusing minutes standing on the Circus (an appropos name!) and watching the people, who never stopped passing by.

A couple of hours later we met Fraser and Don at the station and fortunately, got seats on the train. The only part of the night I remember is, at each awakening, finding myself in a different position, each more impossible than the previous. I had visions of never standing up again! By morning we were well into Scotland, for we had passed through Perth quite early. The Scots swear that the air is purer right over the border, and somehow it did seem different. It was a beautiful day—perhaps that alone accounted for the difference.

The country was already becoming pretty rugged, altho the real highlands were much farther north. Already I could feel the barrenness of them, for from a distance they appear quite bald. We were too late for the real autumn season—the heather had turned brown by frost and rain, but there was a sober loveliness in the hills that somehow almost equaled the vivid colors of early fall. The birch trees, which were sparce, however, were bright yellow, and the spruce, of course, retained their year-round dark green. The hues here on th[e] hills were very much alive—the large ferns had turned a dark rust. We still were traveling on the Dee side of the mountains.

We changed trains at Aviemore, and in a few minutes were in Boat of Garten, the village of our destination. It's a funny little town of two or three streets and very plain, but secure, looking houses. Years ago, so the good folk said, there was a boat which made the crossing of the Spey on which the town is located. Progress, however, caught up, and a bridge was built. The name remained the same. Incidentally, we never discovered the bridge, and the river is much too narrow to warrant much more than a canoe. We stopped at MacDonald's grocery to find the way to Lynchurn, the home of Mrs. Grant, where we were to stay. The farm is half an hour's walk from town past a little mill pond and a bakery. We had learned of Lynchurn through Lady Ross and her daughter in Oxford, for they often spent their vacations there.

The four of us stopped at a farm on the way, and apparently frightened the good farmer's wife, for she disappeared and returned with husband, offspring, and Granny. In wonderful Scotch brogue, Granny told us how to reach Mrs. Grant's. Our reception along the road was mostly that of barking dogs, disinterested cows, and friendly, but suspicious, glances from the people.

The farm house is way up on a hill—a beautiful spot. The river Spey runs through the valley just below it, and for miles around you can see the ranges of the Carn Gorm [Cairngorm] mountains. Mrs. Grant was at the door to meet us—such a wonderful little person—friendly and amusing, a delightful small caricature: gracious with the gift of real sincerity. She showed us first our sitting room—a nice comfortable room with a wonderful fire in the hearth. Already I had fallen in love with the place. Our rooms upstairs were lovely—two tremendously large rooms and one small one at the front of the house. It seemed the windows only framed the view to the front. The tile washstands were classic, and very lovely. However, I'll take my water hot! Which, by the way, I did; for we had our own bath.

And speaking of this very essential room, I think the bathtub deserves special mention. It was the biggest one I've ever seen—terrifically deep (speaking in relative terms, of course!) and long enough to lie completely flat. Really a wonderful idea! Too bad most of us are space-savers. And speaking again of essentials, the "W C" was without doubt the coldest object upon which I have ever rested. There was no central heating, and my teeth played a beautiful stacatto.

When we went down there were milk and gingerbread waiting for us—real milk—that wonderful cow! It was the first glass I had drunk since leaving the States. Soon afterward we had dinner—scotch broth, fried chicken, brussel sprouts, carrots, two pitchers of milk—and hot gingerbread with cream so thick you had to help it along with a spoon. That alone looked like paradise to us, and it was only the beginning. Fresh eggs (I hadn't seen one for weeks!),

lamb chops, steak, roast duck, more chicken, hot deserts—all in our own dining room. Perhaps you can better understand our deep affection for Lynchurn!

The first afternoon there, we dozed around the fire, had a delicious tea at 4:00
and dinner at 8:00 (by kerosene lantern!) Then we sat around the fire and talked
for several hours. It was a wonderful feeling of being completely away and yet
closer to the things I consider priceless than I had felt for weeks. We talked of
home, of course, and for a few too short days Lynchurn almost became home.

Wednesday morning we got up early, had a wonderful breakfast, and started
out for Mt. Carn Gorm, several miles away. In Aviemore we met a Mr. Mackay,
who possessed the village taxi, and he drove us to the hunting lodge at the foot
of the mountain. The lodge itself is on Loch Morlich, a lovely lake right up the
mountains. From there we took the path along the stream which followed a
narrow ravine up the rise. The heather was thick there, and in some patches
was still bright purple. The climb itself after reaching a certain level becomes
uninteresting unless you look—stop every short while to look back. The view
is beautiful—much too lovely for my description. Far up on the peak we could
see the snow and clouds which made the top invisible. During the entire climb,
as we looked back we could see a rainbow, which seemed to begin in the loch
and end at the foot of the mountain facing Carn Gorm. And yet, as we watched,
we could see it move slowly—it seemed to follow us up the mountain side. Far
below were the lodge and the loch—the black aberdeen-angus cows appeared
as small dots. Intermittently we got a little of the rain from the storm we could
see on a distant range. There the peaks were far more rugged and looked ugly
and dark.

A short distance from the top we stopped and looked at a curious formation
of weathered stones. The air was cold and the wind almost strong enough to
knock one over. Apparently I had overrated myself as a mountain climber—our
pace had been swift, and I was completely winded. The other three went ahead,
and I liked the sensation of being alone there. It was that wonderful sense of
freedom and complete, yet perhaps momentary, independence and at the same
time the fee[l]ing of utter insignificance. I ran several hundred yards down
the slope to the pile of stones. The wind was blowing so strongly that I could
scarcely hear myself shout. I tried to eat my lunch there, but my hands became
numb. The sun on the levels below looked much better.

I went down a different way, disregarding the path and the stone trail markers. On one level were dozens of clear springs on the mountain. The beds were
of small quartz stones, and the water clearer than I've ever seen. Strange how
natural a thing water becomes; yet the water [in] those springs actually tasted
better than I've ever known. Farther down the slope, I stopped at the loveliest

Figure 6.1 The Cairngorms in the Scottish Highlands. In October 1944,
Bloomington, Indiana, native Lawrence B. McFaddin, on leave
from working in London for the Office of Strategic Service, visited
Scotland with friends. Raphael Tuck & Sons photo postcard.

spot there. The entire slope is covered with thick heather and ferns. Directly
below me, several hundred feet, was the stream we had followed. It was a wonderful spot—the peak, no longer visible and no longer inviting, behind; the
valley below; and the mountains all around. I fell asleep on the heather a short
time and was awakened by a "pack" of congenial dogs followed by an elderly
man. Farther down the trail were another fellow and a horse. They were going
up to bring down the two deer they had shot the previous night.

It was an unforgettable day, and the beds at Lynchurn seemed even softer.

Thursday Don left for Dufftown in search of some relatives. That morning we
hiked along the Spey and in the evening went up into the hills behind the farm
to watch the sunset. The hills were lighted up beautifully, and in an instant,
when the sun disappeared behind the mountains in the back, became dark
and indiscernible. The clouds for several moments were lovely—and suddenly
dark and chilling.

The next day was rainy, in standard Scottish fashion, and we spent a lazy day
inside, sleeping and eating—in general doing a beautiful job of doing nothing.

Saturday we traveled up to Inverness, primarily to see a Mrs. Gooch, the
grandmother of a Mary Grant, whom we have known for some time. What
a wonderful person she is—young to be a grandmother. She's head of the

Women's Volunteer Service in northern Scotland and has recently flown back from the Shetlands on a governmental survey. Such an active little person, drives with great enthusiasm, and doesn't miss a trick. She took us to lunch and drove us out to her present home, Castle Hill House. First we drove up Moray Firth towards the sea. We stopped at Culloden Moor, the famous battle ground of Prince Charlie and some dozen Scottish clans. "The Young Pretender" landed in western Scotland, in his quest of the "rightful" inheritance of the English throne and fought across the country to this spot, high above Inverness. Apparently the Grant clan played a smart game and watched the battle closely before choosing sides. And from the grave markers were quite successful. Apparently the MacIntoshes were extremely vulnerable! Incidentally, Prince Charlie slept in Castle Hill House the night before the battle. That was in the 1770's.[1]

At Castle Hill we met Mary's great-grandmother, who is 96 years old. She is truly a remarkable person. I sometimes feel my mind is less alert than hers is now. She was determined to learn our names and homes, for she expects us to pay a visit again. She told me how clearly she remembered seeing the troops leave Edinburg Castle for the Crimean war, in 1850's. We also met Mrs. Gooch's sister and a charming Miss Ellis. I've never seen such vitality in a woman her age—she had just been stag hunting the day before. We had tea with them in their lovely old home and then Mrs. Gooch drove us to our train. Her son-in-law is the Grant who owns such great tracts of land and several homes in Inverness Shire.

One doesn't have the opportunity to meet people like these often. My contacts here have been so wonderful, [I] shall never forget them. One can't easily forget the cordiality and friendliness we've received here in England and Scotland. I particularly like the Scotch people—the way they laugh, their frankness and complete friendliness. Sunday morning we hiked through the pine forests behind the farm. We walked through them just as the sun started slanting in. It was so lovely, it seemed almost a sacrilege to make any kind of noise. The ground was covered with thick moss growing through the years' carpet of pine needles. That afternoon we left—for all good things must end, and spent the night in Perth.

We arrived in Edinburg Monday morning and had made arrangements to leave on the night train to London. John left in search of a friend, and Fraser and I first walked up to Edinburg Castle. It was a good climb, for the massive castle is located on a steep hill, approachable from one direction, with three sheer bluffs on the other sides. The history of the castle is quite interesting, and, of course, I know but a sketch. The first parts are over nine centuries old;

yet the castle, through the strife of England and Scotland, has been sieged and sacked, and each time rebuilt. The entrance is through the courtyard in front—on which square public executions took place and witches were burned at the stake hundreds of years ago. Then across the old moat and up the winding stairs to the top. From here one can get a truly beautiful view of Edinburg, a city of spires and shrines. At the highest part of the castle stands the tiny chapel built by St. Margaret, Queen, in the 11th century. Under the altar lie her remains—she died upon hearing of the death of her husband and son. By far the most interesting to me was a small plot of ground jutting cut rather precariously from the castle side. Here is the "Soldier's Dogs' Burying Ground." The Scottish War Memorial within the castle is a beautiful shrine. The coats of arms are so vivid and bright, the atmosphere so light and reverent.

From the castle we walked along the famous "High" to Calton Hill, on which stand Nelson's Tower, the Observatory, and the Scotsmans' "Disgrace." (A building begun modelled after Athen's Parthenon and discontinued through lack of funds.) On the way we stopped at an old cemetery where are buried many of Scotland's illustrious. At the foot of a rather ostentatious tomb, I saw a small white stone, carved in the shape of a heart. On it were inscribed the words: "Here lies sweet Marion, asleep." I remember it above all the others; yet who Marion was, to whom death came so soon, I shall never know.

From there we walked to the Royal Palace of Holyroodhouse, the palace in Scotland for the royal family, who, by the way, had been there a fortnight previously. According to legend, it was built in recognition of luck while hunting during the days of Arthur. We walked through Mary Queen of Scots audience chambers, bedroom, and dressing rooms. Mary's bed, one of the few remaining pieces of furniture, looked terribly uncomfortable! As did her husband's, Lord Darnley. (Modern psychologists say this two-bedroom business definitely leads to marital dischord!)

The remains of the royal chapel are quite impressive and very lovely. They are of Norman architecture of the 12th century. The roof is no longer there, for it disappeared when Cromwell burned the palace. However, ancient stone lattice work is still standing. The floor is nothing but tomb markers. On the floor also were several stone caskets, and for the first time, I knew what tomb, stone-cold, meant.

After leaving the castle we walked up some funny little side streets and stopped in a Scotch Tartan shop to look at some plaids. Apparently the McFaddin clan set up permanent residence in Ireland, for none seem to exist in northern Scotland now. The closest I could find was the MacLean Clan, of which MacFayden is a part. In any case, "our" plaid is very colorful. I still can't visualize myself in a kilt, although I saw dozens of them. Fraser and I met John for tea. Could it be that I'm becoming a synthetic Britisher, demanding my tea at 4:00, pouring the milk first and feeling indignant if the milk isn't hot?

Later, we met Don and boarded the train for rainy London. Yes, a good week. A nice week to remember . . .

ST. IVES

"As I was going to S. Ives . . . ," I met no polygomist, but rather a number of people who must have known the charms of Cornwall which I was to discover. The night train was slow, but time was not important then, for I had eight days ahead—eight days which were completely mine. My first glimpse of the sea came when we entered Plymouth, the city which, a year previously, had seen hundreds of ships leaving for the invasion of the continent. It was early and grey and cold, and the water of the channel wasn't any color. A few hours later we reached St. Erth, a small Cornish inland village, just west of the pirate's playground of Penzance. There I caught a wonderful little two car train, bound for the coast . . . a little two car train with a holiday whistle.

In ten minutes, St. Ives was in view, a toy village on a peninsula stretching out into the sea. The Gulf Stream is blue, but St. Ive's Bay was bluer that day. Blue, and sunny, and beautiful. Pedn Olva, our hotel, was just a short walk from the small station. I had hoped that it would be near the water; that perhaps we could get a glimpse of the sea from there. I never expected a lovely place, built right in the rocks—the foundation of which was washed by the tides. Yet, there it was, facing the sea, on the sea. I had a late breakfast in the lounge; yet as hungry as I was, I sat and looked out the bay window at the water, and the beach below. The sun was out, and the boats were sailing—and London seemed a million miles away.

Bill had arrived earlier that morning and was already somewhere below, on the rocks, sunning himself. Our room overlooked the harbor. Beyond St. Ives we could see the Atlantic, and straight down were rocks and the sea. Three miles out in the bay was the lighthouse on a small island. I stood by the window and looked, knowing there could be no other place the same. Then I climbed down to the beach to look for Willy . . . it was difficult to walk, when I wanted to run. The sand was soft and fine, and the tide was beginning to come in, each wave reaching a little farther up the beach.

Our table in the dining room was in a small bay window, overlooking the garden in the back of the hotel. Beyond the garden and below were the beach and the water. Flowers on the table, a pitcher of ice-water (Londoners never drink water!) and excellent meals, usually topped with fresh strawberries and cream. The view alone was worth the sitting there, but the food made it even more attractive. After coffee in the lounge that first day, we embarked upon a week of contented laziness, which, unfortunately, didn't end with the expiration date of my furlough papers. The entire afternoon we sat on the beach, wondering if our good luck in finding this spot were true. Unknowingly (undoubtedly stimulated by the sea air) I went dashing down the hot sand into the water. I emerged, dripping, and a ghastly shade of blue. Never have I been in such freezing water. The effect was even more colorful the next day when I blossomed forth a brilliant lobster red.

Tea was each afternoon at 4:00—how delightful it was to sit on the terrace and think of nothing except how delightful it was! I longed for some color film to capture the scenes which can never be written on paper. The small garden is enclosed by immense lilac bushes and flowers grow up and down the rocks and walls of the terrace. The boats in the harbor were blue, and red, green and orange—wonderfully happy looking.

Early each morning after breakfast we would wander down the hill to the wharf. Narrow, little streets with gay little houses—white ones, blue, yellow, and green. From a distance, St. Ives looked strangely colorless in contrast with the sea. Yet in the streets was the color—yards full of roses, brightly colored doors with polished knockers. And in the grey, drab streets were colorful children. There were no plain children there, for they all seemed to have curly hair, and blue eyes—and inquisitive faces. How strange it is that these children will mature into the plain old women who sit on the waterfront and knit vests, and men who fish at night and sleep through the days.

Each morning we would stop on the wharf to watch the fishermen bring in the night's catch. The tide was out at that time of day, and a little one-horse cart brought the fish to the dock from the boats, lying absurdly awkward in the sand. St. Ives was more alive in early morning than any other time. The fish, skates, crabs, and lobsters, after being weighted were sold there on the wharf to the highest bidder. Housewives seemed to be in the majority, but the lobsters were carried away by the owners of the littled cafes that lined the waterfront. After the auction, only the cats seemed to remain feasting on fish heads—the fishermen went off to bed, and the wives took the day's food home.

"... each wife had seven bags; each bag had seven cats; each cat had seven kittens." I'm sure that those cats have been reproducing prodifiously ever since that Cornish verse was first composed. Hundreds of cats—in the windows in the doors, in the shops, in the boats—everywhere cats. They all seemed quite well pleased with themselves and their stations in life. Even the dogs in St. Ives

Figure 6.2 Wharf Road, St. Ives, Cornwall, England. McFaddin visited
the resort town in May 1945. Raphael Tuck & Sons photo postcard.

appeared to enjoy themselves more than dogs anywhere else. Centuries ago
they must have tired of chasing cats. A nondescript pack of them played each
morning on the beach, charging the waves and kicking up the sand.

In addition to being a fishing village, St. Ives is an artists' colony. In almost
every street were artists, sitting and painting scenes which were offered no
where else in England. The second day we came across an elderly painter, quite
at home sitting in a rowboat painting a harbor scene. The shops were full of
watercolors, and oils, lovely and expensive. During our week in the village, we
visited, I think, every gallery there.

At ten o'clock each morning, we could be found at the Shore Cafe, drinking
hot chocolate and eating ice-cream. After two or three days it became a ritual,
and at the stroke of ten, we'd head for the little room upstairs, over looking the
bay. After lunch each day we sprawled in the sun, a glorious English sun which,
for the first, time, warmed me completely. The days, which went so quickly,
were difficult to distinguish one from [the] other. However, though their patterns were almost identical, their designs were quite different. Each part of each
day there was something new to see, and, if not different, to be enjoyed again.

On the wharf in St. Ives is a magnificent pub. Countless are the "King's
Arms," "Dog and Badgers," "Running Horses," "Duke's Head," "Little White

Harts," and "Red Lions"—but there is only one "The Sloop," and it is in St. Ives. The ceilings slant, as in a ship's cabin—closing time is the ringing of a ships bell. Great oceans of mild and bitters flowed each night there, where gathered the town's illustrious. Adorning the walls of the largest room in the pub, are caricatures of the best known people in the village. What fun it was to sit there, with a glass of ale, and spot the people whose pictures were on the walls; the whiskered old fisherman, the bartender, the village fish dealer, the funny old woman who sat and screamed " 'ello mi love," at each newcomer.

Centuries ago, an Irish saint by the name of Ives, sailed from the Emerald Isle on a shamrock. He landed on this tip of Cornwall and built a chapel on the highest hill there. This building, reconstructed some years ago, still stands, viewing the town and the ocean. The hill on which it stands is called "The Island." A long time ago the sea washed over a part of the peninsula and isolated the hill—perhaps believing that in some future time the sea again will do the same, the people have never stopped referring to this piece of land as "The island." From the top can be seen the Atlantic Ocean, St. Ives Bay, and the Irish Sea. Miles of ocean—blue sea, and rocks, and white foam . . . hilly St. Ives and Carbis Bay, leading to rhododendron covered hills behind.

After lying contentedly in the sun for several hours after lunch, we would climb back up to the hotel for tea at four o'clock. This tea was usually augmented by another one at "The Copper Kettle" at four thirty—toasted scones, and bisquits, and jam. By early evening, the tide was well in, and the boats began to prepare for the night's fishing. All this we watched from the small tea room, which also faced the harbor. Then back up the narrow hilly street we'd go to Pedn Olva, dinner, and watching the sunset from the terrace.

We didn't do much—there wasn't time to take the side trips to Land's End and Penzance as we had originally planned. A week was much too short a time to be in paradise. Seven days were much too brief to hear enough of the waves at night, or see the boats sailing out with high tide and moonlight. Early in the morning, even before the gulls started screaming for day, I would sit up in bed and see the fishing boats returning. There weren't enough hours to feed the gulls, and watch them swoop down to catch bits of bread tossed in the air. Now, as I look out of the window and see the Rhine, Cornwall and St. Ives seem even farther away, more as if I remember them from an early imagination and not from having been there. Perhaps it was a continental fascination, a likeness to the Riviera which people claim exists, that made it so attractive. That I can't say. I only know it was different from the rest of England I knew. I feel as if it will retain an individuality which can belong to no other place. Sometime I'll go back just to know it's still there and the same, as it has always been. . . .

This article appeared in volume 41, no. 3 (September 1945). The editor who wrote the note that begins the article was Professor of History John D. Barnhart.

NOTE

1. This is obviously an error. Prince Charlie, the Young Pretender, landed on the west coast of Scotland, July 25, 1745. He was defeated at Culloden Moor, April 16, 1746.

SEVEN

"A Fair Chance To Do My Part of Work"

Black Women, War Work, and Rights Claims at the Kingsbury Ordnance Plant

KATHERINE TURK

MAMIE JOHNSON WAS AT HER wit's end. A widow who was unemployed during World War II, she had eagerly pursued a job at the Kingsbury ordnance plant, located more than forty miles away from her Gary, Indiana, home. The plant had been newly constructed to provide the troops with state-of-the-art weapons, and Johnson had visited the Kingsbury employment office at least eight times seeking a job. In a letter to President Franklin D. Roosevelt, she recounted her experiences there. After a good deal of pestering, she had been cleared for hire but could not pass the physical exam. Kingsbury's doctor told her she had high blood pressure. His advice, in her words, was to "see a doctor and get my pressure down then come back for a recheck." Crestfallen, Johnson visited her private physician that same day to confirm the diagnosis, but he insisted her blood pressure was fine. He rechecked her two days later, found her to be in good health, and gave her a letter declaring her fitness to work. She had forwarded that letter to plant authorities, she explained, but had not received a reply. Johnson was afraid that the rumors she had heard were true: "They just don't want to hire colored people at Kingsbury. They will tell them anything to get rid of them."[1]

Johnson's letter was forwarded to the President's Committee on Fair Employment Practices (FEPC), a federal agency created during World War II to receive and investigate complaints of racial discrimination in war industries. She was convinced that the government could and should do something to help her secure employment at Kingsbury. To prove that point, Johnson's letter referenced her status as a motivated worker, a dedicated citizen, and a disadvantaged woman alike: "I am a citizen of the United States[,] been here all my life[,] pays taxes here [and] am a widow. I wants to work."[2] To Johnson,

Figure 7.1 Women workers at the Kingsbury
Ordnance Plant, LaPorte County, Indiana. The plant,
built in 1941, offered dangerous but high-paying
jobs for men and women. African American women
faced consistent discrimination in obtaining jobs for
which they were qualified. Reprinted from William
P. Vogel, *Kingsbury: A Venture in Teamwork* (1940).

the chasm between her appeal and the FEPC response may have proved more
frustrating than her initial experiences at Kingsbury. "You must know how difficult it is to contradict a physician's diagnosis," wrote George M. Johnson, assistant executive secretary of the agency, whose rebuff of Ms. Johnson's claims
sidestepped the list of attributes that she felt should guarantee her a war job.
Further, since Kingsbury could prove that it had recently hired a number of
blacks for a variety of positions, Mr. Johnson explained, "it would be extremely
difficult to establish race discrimination in this case." Ms. Johnson was invited
to submit any additional evidence of discrimination she could produce, but her

case was considered closed. The sizeable gap between Ms. Johnson's aspirations and her respondent's answer reflected their different conceptions of fairness in employment practices and of the government's role in ensuring it.[3]

During World War II, the question of where and how one worked was laden with new meaning and increased significance. The rapid wartime expansion of the federal government—in terms of both its sheer size and its reach into people's lives—newly blurred the lines between civic and private obligations.[4] In particular, a job in a plant that produced materials for the war effort enabled a worker simultaneously to earn high wages and to contribute to American victory overseas. War jobs proved especially tantalizing and symbolic to African Americans as a means to demonstrate their patriotism and to participate in the ongoing struggle for racial justice that had been reinvigorated by the pressures of war.[5] Emboldened by the nation's escalating needs for industrial production and enraged by the hypocrisy of state-sponsored segregation, African American labor leaders pressured President Roosevelt to create a new federal agency to combat race discrimination. The FEPC, established in 1941, was mandated to field and investigate African Americans' claims of racist treatment in workplaces that were owned by or held contracts with the U.S. government.[6] Following on the heels of the seismic political and cultural shifts of the 1930s—which had been spurred by economic disaster and the strong federal response—many Americans believed that directing labor rights claims toward the national government was natural and appropriate.[7]

The onset of war prompted African American women to seek new employment opportunities, to redefine the rights and responsibilities commensurate with their citizenship, and to levy unprecedented demands upon the federal government.[8] Many such women, like Johnson, wrote to authorities in Washington about the Kingsbury ordnance plant.[9] One of seventy-two weapons factories constructed during World War II, Kingsbury was built in 1941 on 13,000 acres of northern Indiana farmland. War Department officials preferred such sparsely populated inland locations for ordnance manufacture because catastrophic accidents were so common. Yet the same factors that made La-Porte County geographically ideal meant that the 20,000 workers needed to staff Kingsbury would have to travel in from urban and rural areas for miles in every direction.[10] In the Calumet region, the skyrocketing steel economy had spurred four decades of rapid urbanization and burgeoning communities of southern African Americans who had migrated in search of good jobs and a freer social climate.[11] Once there, however, they encountered resistant whites who enforced segregation in education, employment, and public facilities. The racial conflicts that erupted at the Kingsbury plant thus reflected the swelling tensions between politicized blacks and hostile whites in northern Indiana.[12] At Kingsbury, racial hierarchy was policed and resisted at the intersection of new federal nondiscrimination policy, personal expectations, and the particular pressures of wartime work in a newly erected munitions plant.

In their letters to the government, black women who held or sought employment at Kingsbury juxtaposed their specific grievances against the new federal mandate for workplace equality and the national climate of shared sacrifice and political engagement. They recounted their perceptions of discriminatory treatment they had experienced at the plant, argued that their problems required assistance, and suggested ways by which government officials could set things right. Yet their correspondence with federal authorities reveals tensions between the women's own consciousness of their rights and the perspectives of the federal investigators to whom they pleaded their cases. The women reasoned outward from personal experiences, envisioning a state that was at once disinterested and discerning. While local FEPC branches took varying approaches to carrying out the agency's mandate, officials typically responded to Kingsbury workers' claims by referencing the number of African American workers in the plant—thus demonstrating that the employer hired some blacks for some positions—and giving credence to plant officials' professed good intentions in the name of preserving order and industrial output.[13]

Black women's claims for employment at Kingsbury also displayed a pattern that scholars have traced across many decades. In contrast to African American men, whose complaints prioritized access to better jobs, black women also demanded government and employer acknowledgement of their abilities, sacrifices, and limitations.[14] This different approach reflects black women workers' ambiguous position in employment law and policy, which placed them somewhere between black men—for whom equality was defined as increased access to jobs through the erosion of racial stigma—and white women, whose workplace rights were rooted in the ideology of protection and sex difference.[15]

Further, the pressures of war simultaneously created a powerful new impetus for black women's expansive definitions of fairness and legitimated state and employer assumptions that high production and industrial peace were more important than racial justice. Exposing the logic that underpinned black women's aspirations reveals the inherent challenges of enacting federal mandates for individual rights—the content and boundaries of which must be deployed, interpreted, and negotiated at the grassroots. While bureaucrats could define and measure fairness in the abstract, the project of implementing workplace equality was inherently local, context-specific, and dependent upon personal perceptions and experiences. To the black women employed or seeking employment at the Kingsbury ordnance plant, the state-protected right to meaningful work cemented their status as valued family members, as breadwinners, and as patriotic citizens—identities that they experienced as mutually constitutive and equally significant.[16]

Two coinciding trends in the early war years put the nation's industrial infrastructure in a bind: the men who predominated in heavy industry were increasingly drafted overseas just as the nation's need for those goods grew. The paucity of white male workers to fill both the abandoned and newly created jobs yielded a significant opportunity. As in World War I, female and African American workers previously barred from access to high-wage industrial jobs would be tapped to help produce the goods that were crucial to the war effort.[17] Five million women entered the American workforce between 1940 and 1944.[18] Work in a war plant was especially desirable and symbolic for African American women. Shut out of most types of employment, they worked for wages at much higher rates than did white women.[19] A 1940 survey of Northwest Indiana workers found black women concentrated in domestic service work even as their white counterparts labored in sizeable numbers in industrial, clerical, and semi-professional jobs.[20] Yet World War II transformed the region's economy. "Northwest Indiana was one huge engine," recalled a Gary resident, and the proportion of African Americans in the city's workforce increased from 14 percent to 22 percent between May and November of 1943 alone.[21] At the dawn of the war, the promise of the FEPC, the president's calls for national unity and sacrifice, and well-publicized local labor shortages convinced many African American women that good jobs were theirs for the taking.[22] Kingsbury worker Flora Campbell explained: "All over the radio is broadcasting, go to your employment house and tell them you want a war job."[23]

However, African American women in northern Indiana had reason to expect that they might encounter resistance in their quest for jobs at Kingsbury. Despite its proximity to Chicago, LaPorte County, Indiana, was both very rural and extremely white. In 1940, only 1,148 blacks resided in the 600-square-mile county, and "only about twelve or fourteen Negro families" resided in the town of LaPorte prior to the war. Thus, many area whites had never worked with or lived near blacks.[24] Further, the African American women who found and sought work at Kingsbury were no strangers to racial prejudice in their home community. Nearly all were residents of Gary, the booming industrial city that sat at the southern tip of Lake Michigan to the northwest of the plant. The area had been relatively barren until United States Steel selected the location for its new mill in 1906, but in just nine years, Gary's population grew from several hundred to more than 55,000.[25] The city's employment opportunities attracted increasing numbers of African Americans. Between 1910 and 1920, Gary's black population grew from 383 to 5,299; by 1930, blacks constituted 18 percent of the city's population; and by 1940, Gary had the largest ratio of African Americans to whites of any city north of the Mason-Dixon line.[26]

White residents of Gary reacted to their city's growing black population by enforcing racially segregated housing, education, and public parks and hospitals, and by barring African Americans from city jobs.[27] Labor shortages in World War I provided limited and temporary opportunities for African Americans at U.S. Steel. Black workers constituted 20.5 percent of total employment at the mill in 1923, but their representation was constant at 15 percent for the next decade. Blacks were segregated in dead-end and dangerous jobs at the plant—when they could secure employment at all. During the 1920s, the Klan played a strong role in city politics.[28] Early Gary residents recalled that blacks were not allowed outside after dark in certain areas of the city, and that African American residents were confined to "blighted areas with chicken coops, hog pens and outhouses."[29] Resident Arnold Greer recalled that "Gary was a very prejudiced place. A pregnant woman who was feeling sick was denied a drink of water at a drug store next to the Palace Theater."[30] In 1930, the Gary American wrote that local blacks were "subject to insult and discrimination . . . they are Jim Crowed in the schools; they have little or no recognition in politics, and denied many of the rights, which, as citizens and taxpayers, they are justly entitled to."[31]

In response to their ghettoization, Gary's black residents established social networks and organized around shared grievances.[32] Many women were active in local churches, sororities, and service clubs. Men could play on the town's African American baseball team, which battled teams from neighboring black communities, and in 1935, Gary hosted a golf tournament for African Americans only. In the 1920s and 1930s, Gary's nascent NAACP chapter organized boycotts against discriminatory employers; protested the showing of The Birth of a Nation (1915) at downtown theaters; and fought mostly unsuccessful battles against segregation in schools, parks, and pools, and against police brutality. Historians Raymond A. Mohl and Neil Betten argue that Gary's black population was politically divided between the NAACP's integrationist goals and the Marcus Garvey-inspired push for separatism—a split that helps to explain the community's lack of lasting progress in the pre-World-War-II era.[33] Yet while the black women who wrote to federal authorities about Kingsbury were more in line with the NAACP's approach, they claimed more than entrance into the plant's high-paying industrial jobs. In addition, they took advantage of new opportunities provided by the war—particularly a government that they perceived as newly listening and accountable to them—to demand expansive rights of access and accommodation they argued would enable them to participate fully in American society on their own terms.

As the nation mobilized for war, federal authorities identified northern Indiana as a prime location for ordnance manufacture. The region was far enough inland to escape an enemy attack upon either coast but well-placed to distribute goods to either theater of combat. If a tragic factory mistake should end in a devastating explosion, the area was sparsely populated and insignificant to the nation's infrastructure. LaPorte County was particularly well-situated: the area featured flat, even terrain, intersections of preexisting cross-country railroads, a network of state and county roads, and adequate well and river water.[34] The Kingsbury plant was built between 1940 and 1941 to be one of the largest shell-loading plants in the nation. It was erected on a twenty-square-mile plot, forcing the relocation of several farms and a cemetery.[35] Kingsbury was authorized by the War Department, but its construction and operation were contracted to a private company. Todd & Brown, a New York-based engineering and construction firm, built and ordered the plant for maximum efficiency and productivity.[36]

Staffing such an enormous operation in a rural area proved a formidable challenge. Todd & Brown initially sought 10,000 workers, and the entire population of LaPorte numbered only 16,000 in 1940. To accommodate the influx of labor, the War Department constructed a new town right outside the factory gates. Kingsford Heights consisted of more than 2,600 dormitories, trailers, and prefabricated homes. Todd & Brown also financed repairs to existing homes in LaPorte and encouraged area residents to rent spare rooms to Kingsbury workers.[37] Through the United States Employment Service and local labor unions, the plant recruited in towns and cities up to fifty miles away—including Gary, where employers faced new competition with Kingsbury's high wages.[38] Gary resident Mary Kay Maisel, who worked at U.S. Steel as a secretary while her husband served overseas, recalled that "All my friends were going to the ammunition plant in LaPorte, however, so I went with them."[39] Kingsbury operated buses from nearby towns, and workers like Maisel and her friends carpooled, generating "clusters of traffic" each morning on previously desolate rural highways.[40]

At Kingsbury, workers assembled and packaged the components of explosive weapons to be used in the war. Approaching the plant entrance, one would first notice its silhouette—punctuated by floodlight towers, several menacing

Figure 7.2 A view over the Kingsbury Ordnance
Plant. Railroads running on all four sides of
plant transported ordnance to both coasts for
shipment overseas; separated buildings ensured
that work would continue if an accident destroyed
part of the site. Reprinted from William P. Vogel,
Kingsbury: A Venture in Teamwork (1940).

brick buildings, five 200,000-gallon water tanks, and the "earth-covered concrete igloos" that stored TNT and chemicals. In the distance, one might also
see workers initiating controlled burns on the prairie land to destroy the explosive waste produced by ordnance manufacture. The twenty-square-mile
plant itself was traversed by eighty miles of railroad track. At its south end,
trains brought onto the grounds the crates of empty cases for bullets, bombs,
and other projectiles and the various powders and chemicals that would fill
them. Inside the plant, workers unloaded the metal casings and filled them
with explosive material. The shells were then fitted with fuses, boosters, and
detonators. When they had been checked and counted, they were loaded into

crates and onto train cars that would take them to their point of debarkation for the front lines.[41]

The work at Kingsbury was primarily assembly-line style and highly systematized. Each step built upon the last and was essential to the next worker's task further down the line. Careful work was crucial, as any mistake could be deadly. Yet the pressure to produce quickly for the raging war was made manifest by the conveyor belts that pushed components from one line operator to the next. Once a new worker was hired, he or she was medically examined and received a half-day of training and several lectures on plant regulations. From there, each worker was assigned to one of two ten-hour shifts. Kingsbury's employment and output grew rapidly. More than 2,000 workers joined the workforce in November 1941 alone, and in May 1942, Kingsbury's labor force reached its apex of more than 20,000. On an average day at the midpoint of the war, Kingsbury produced 180,000 fuses, 46,000 shells, and 500,000 rounds of ammunition.[42]

Work at Kingsbury was dirty, difficult, and dangerous.[43] In 1942, twenty-one-year-old Esther Sanders was hired at Kingsbury to weigh powder for bullets. She recalled that as she worked, she could hear other staff testing the bullets outside, a sound that frayed her nerves. She also spoke sympathetically of a coworker whose initially untreated powder burns required lifelong pain medication.[44] Kingsbury's automated assembly line forced workers to remain alert and productive despite tasks that might be physically taxing, repetitive, or both; the assembly lines were only dimly lit, and many of the materials had to be quickly assembled with tweezers. All workers had to wear protective clothing and shower before leaving, as one chemical component turned any exposed hair or skin orange. Further, because workers routinely handled explosive powders, they followed strict rules concerning where and when they could smoke. The plant's design reflected the potential for disaster—four separate buildings were partially underground so that if one exploded, the structural integrity of the others would not be compromised. The pressure of producing for the war only compounded the physical dangers that were endemic to ordnance work.[45]

In many key war industries, the flood of new groups of workers (primarily African Americans and women) into what were formerly white male spaces sent plant management scrambling to establish boundaries and norms of behavior that would keep production high and dissension among workers low. In 1941, Kingsbury's workforce was approximately one-third female, and by the end of the war women comprised 45 percent of the labor force. The number of African American workers also steadily increased, with many men working in the warehouse and at demolition jobs. Todd & Brown policies divided Kingsbury workers by race and gender.[46] Every job was coded male or female, and black or white. Plant officials expected to hire African Americans but capped their percentage of total employment around 10 percent. If a real shortage of workers for "white" tasks occurred, management asked the U.S. Employment Service to find more white workers to maintain the racial balance—eventually recruiting from as far away as Georgia, Colorado, New York, and North Dakota.[47] Plant management set aside two of the nine production lines at Kingsbury for African American workers. "We do not work with the white people," explained line operator Mrs. Willie Young. "We handle loose powder and the white women handle sealed powder."[48]

Black women's opportunities for employment at Kingsbury were extremely limited. When the assembly lines designated for African Americans were fully staffed, plant managers simply stopped hiring black women to do anything but janitorial work. While undesirable and low-paid, the work was a plant priority. Government fear of disease outbreaks in war plants led to a strict sanitation code developed by the Office of Civilian Defense and issued to each war employer. The regulations mandated: "Drinking fountains shall be thoroughly cleaned at least once each day"; "all toilets and urinals and all toilet room floors shall be cleaned once, at least each working day"; "all shower rooms shall be cleaned daily"; and "equipment subject to serious contamination or exposure shall be periodically and thoroughly cleaned." Though African American women preferred higher-paid work as line operators, their janitorial labor was crucial to Kingsbury's safety and productivity.[49]

Due to Todd & Brown policies, whites—especially white women—held all positions of authority over their African American counterparts. Most African American women workers answered immediately to a white "forelady" or to her African American assistant. Workers who overstepped the racial boundaries that kept this hierarchy in place could expect immediate punishment. African American women workers like Laura Washington Cyrus, an adopted daughter of Booker T. Washington who objected when her white forelady addressed her by her first name and acted as a self-appointed sub-forelady in that woman's absence, were fired for insubordination.[50] Such struggles for dignity and respect were easily construed as selfish acts that hindered the war effort.[51] The result was the conflation of strict factory discipline with the maintenance of the racial order.

Historian Karen Tucker Anderson has argued that while white men demanded authority over black coworkers, white women insisted upon distance, fearful that proximity could cause disease and contamination. Evidence suggests that white women at Kingsbury pursued both separation from and intimate control over their black counterparts. African American and white women workers did not intermingle at leisure time. On the job, they ate lunch and took breaks in separate areas. At white women's insistence, separate bathrooms were designated for women of each race. In the event of an air raid, workers knew to proceed to the bomb shelter specific to their race as well.[52] Further, blacks were not permitted to live in the onsite housing at Kingsford Heights, instead commuting by bus or car.[53] An internal FEPC communication documented federal authorities' awareness of the lack of local housing for African Americans and whites' hostility to potential black neighbors. "There seems to be opposition in the local community to the in-migration of negroes, and it is almost certain that defense housing for negroes in or near LaPorte would be opposed by local community leaders and local organizations," wrote one official in 1942. Ruth and C. L. Strickland, Gary residents who stepped away from their undertaking business to work for the war effort, drove five other passengers on the ninety-mile round trip to Kingsbury each day.[54]

While African American men faced similar types of segregation within the plant, their assumed ability to perform manual tasks opened many more job categories to them. Although most of these jobs called for unskilled physical labor, they allowed for greater mobility and provided for significant interaction with white workers doing similar types of work—loading, cleaning, guarding, and inspecting.[55] African American women, then, were uniquely stigmatized and subordinated at Kingsbury.

Day-to-day interactions between white women supervisors and African American women workers were fraught with friction. "The officials there are inclined to be what you may call hard boiled, with no regard as to how they speak to one. They do not seem to realize that the [Negro] employees are there for the one and same cause that they are," explained Willie Young. White women supervisors talked of having to "herd the operators," observed Ruth Strickland: "the majority of the supervisors have the feeling and idea that the colored people are animals."[56] Kingsbury worker Elizabeth Reed explained that her white overseer, "Dorothy Koch, [is] very arrogant. Once when the girls struck for better conditions she said in a speech to us that [since] we were making more money than we ever made in our lives and more money than we could get by scrubbing floors in Gary, then why not be satisfied." White women overseers had unchecked discretion over black women line workers, regulating the pace at which they worked, whether and when they took breaks, and what tasks they performed day-to-day. This intimate control over their bodies and their workplace experiences fueled black women's dissatisfaction with Kingsbury, setting it apart from other nearby plants. In her department at General American, another shell-loading plant in the area, Adrana Turner recalled that she and her fellow African American coworkers cooperated well with whites and that she enjoyed her job.[57] By contrast, black women at Kingsbury resented the daily indignities they suffered while performing the most dangerous and dead-end work in the plant.

In handwritten and typed letters, black women described their experiences and outlined their grievances and expectations for fair treatment at Kingsbury. A few women sent letters to the FEPC or to other government officials, but most addressed their claims directly to the White House. Writers expressed the hope that the Roosevelts would take action on behalf of individuals, thereby boosting the black community as a whole. Arguments for intervention highlighted themes of personal sacrifice, meritocracy, patriotism, and racial justice, values many Americans associated with the president and his wife Eleanor.[58] Ethel Jackson wrote to Mrs. Roosevelt that "Being citizen[s] of the United States I feel that we are entitled to any job offered us by the government. I appreciate and await your answer." Pernellia Hull concluded her letter to FDR "as a law abiding citizen with our country at heart and our boys on the front."[59] Other correspondents described their education, skills, and work experience as evidence that Kingsbury's policies of subordinating capable black women were "un-American" and thus required "immediate attention."[60]

Black women who described their experiences at Kingsbury to the president and first lady in personal terms were not taking uncalculated shots in the dark. For years, the Roosevelts had cultivated their reputations as political figures who were invested in the lives of individual Americans. Those with access to radios could hear FDR's distinctive baritone deliver speeches that decried corruption and lauded honest work. And in her weekly *Woman's Home Companion* column, Eleanor described her daily life, answered questions mailed to her by readers, and established her commitment to standing up for the dispossessed against poverty and faceless bureaucracy.[61] Thus many Americans, like the black women at Kingsbury, perceived the Roosevelts to be listening and interested in their struggles.[62] "I want to have a head to head talk with you," Flora Campbell's complaint letter began. Thelma Morgan opened her letter with, "Mrs Roosevelt, I know your time is pretty well taken up, but could you please spare a few moments to listen to my problem."[63] Irene Marks asked the president to contact Kingsbury on her behalf, claiming that "one has a hard time getting on unless someone pulls for them. So I am asking you to help me by sending a good word there for me or send me a letter to carry them. My application is in and a word from you would help me get in soon."[64] The president and his wife, they reasoned, were powerful friends who would be outraged by unfair labor practices in a war plant and would rectify the injustices occurring at Kingsbury.

In their letters to federal authorities, black women described the racism that was built into Kingsbury's employment policies and defined interactions among its workers. Echoing their male counterparts, women argued that their race should play no role in obtaining or holding a job, and that racism hampered efficiency and kept talented workers unfairly subordinated. They emphasized both their desire to cooperate and their demand to be treated as equal members of the community of respected Americans whose labor contributed to the war effort.

Complainants argued that racism unfairly limited their access to war work; race was irrelevant and only their qualifications and dedication to the cause were important. Ethel Stewart had recently moved to LaPorte from Chicago when she sought work as a typist at Kingsbury. In her 1942 letter to Mrs. Roosevelt, she elaborated her lengthy resume as evidence that racism plagued Kingsbury's hiring policies. Stewart had fifteen years of experience as a secretary at premier African American-owned businesses including the *Chicago Defender* and the Binga State Bank. Stewart explained that she had sent her application, complete with recommendations from several past employers, to Kingsbury one year earlier:

> Although I have made repeated telephone calls I have always been very
> courteously told that there was no opening yet, since production has not
> started. Nevertheless, a large number of [white] clerical people have been
> hired since that time, and even non-residents, [but] still there is no opening
> for me.

The FEPC should correct this unfairness, Stewart argued, because her race should not counteract her demonstrated ability to do the job for which she applied.[65] Other female Kingsbury applicants reported similar experiences. Mrs. F. H. Woods, upon applying for and being denied a job at Kingsbury, remarked, "it seems as if my color or race (Negro) is the only factor that prevents my receiving this position."[66]

African American workers demanded the same respect that Kingsbury officials afforded to whites. They argued that plant managers should acknowledge their skills and work experience as individuals, rather than limiting all black workers to the bottom of the factory hierarchy.[67] "Among the hundreds of Negro operators there are school teachers, embalmers, printers, secretaries, ministers, ex-businessmen and women, and men and women from all walks of life," according to Ruth Strickland. She told the FEPC that

> Of the two lines now operating and manned by Negroes, the highest position held by Negroes is sub-forelady or sub-foreman, but with no voice or authority. None of these people are chosen for their character, intelligence, schooling, earnestness or patriotism, or on their seniority in the plant.[68]

They also sought equal privileges to white workers, protesting, for example, when they were forced to work during allotted rest and meal periods even as white women's leisure time was never violated. Further, they observed that Kingsbury management seemed to prioritize subordinating blacks ahead of maximizing productivity, as the plant left white-coded jobs empty even as area blacks clamored for work.

When confronted with biased treatment, African American women at Kingsbury were more tolerant of racial separation than of arbitrary personnel decisions by the white supervisors who punished them with impunity. Hattie Gardner was a line worker at Kingsbury who voiced her complaint to the FEPC in terms of a grievance against her floor supervisor, Mrs. Schneider. "For three weeks she has continually picked on me," Hattie explained, and the plant personnel office had provided her no assistance. "They wouldn't give me a transfer to another lady," and she was instead terminated for her inability to cooperate with Mrs. Schneider. This was unfair, Hattie explained, for "This is the first time I have had trouble with anybody."[69] Hattie's coworker Elizabeth Reed had risen to the position of inspector on the detonator line, the highest position a black woman could hold at Kingsbury. "As such inspector," she explained, "I am the last to leave the line, which means that the other girls leave for lunch from five to seven min. before I do." When Elizabeth returned late from lunch on two occasions, "which was unavoidable," her "very arrogant" floor lady had her terminated for insubordination.[70] Willie Young similarly decried her white supervisors' unwillingness to treat black workers with respect: "There are some officials there that have never been in authority before. Some of them have never lived in a town where the Negro lived, and therefore don't cooperate with the Negro as they should."[71]

In April 1942, Kingsbury workers voted to unionize under the aegis of the American Federation of Labor (AFL). The election was close: of 5,193 eligible workers, 2,751 voted in the election; 1,621 voted for the union, while 1,130 voted against unionization. After the election, labor and management drew up seventeen individual contracts: three for railroad workers, one for line operators, and thirteen for workers in specialized crafts such as painting. Evidence suggests that the union functioned primarily to set wage rates and determine seniority, doing little to fight segregation or advocate on behalf of aggrieved black workers. Even so, Ruth Strickland, the chief union steward on the detonator line, had felt empowered by her position of authority to challenge the factory order.[72] She explained to FDR: "My duties as Chief Steward were to conduct grievances brought up by other stewards and operators. There were many grievances, but none that could not be reasoned out. Most of the causes were due to lack of understanding between the supervision and operators." When a fistfight broke out on the detonator line between the white foreman and a "young colored man," Strickland went above the foreman's head to protest because the line worker was fired but the foreman was not. She explained that the plant's internal fair employment "committee and the supervisors on the lines seem to have an arranged understanding."[73] In response to her complaint, Kingsbury management contended that "Mrs. Strickland has no respect for supervision and was constantly leaving her work without obtaining permission from her immediate supervisor."[74] Factory officials were reluctant to place black women in authority, and those who complained about racist personnel policies were typically fired, as Strickland was. The difference in management's eyes between complaining about or defying racist discrimination and subverting factory order was slight, perhaps nonexistent.

Black women's demands for meritocracy and freedom from stigma resembled those of their male coworkers at Kingsbury. The male and female complainants who wrote on behalf of their peers at Kingsbury sought equality of opportunity to prove their dedication to working hard and serving their country. In a petition to the FEPC, twenty-two male workers of the African American detonator line appealed to the president's new mandate for racial equality, declaring that "the spirit as well as the letter of section 8802 of the FEPC has been and continues to be flagrantly and ruthlessly violated and ignored daily." They explained that "well-qualified, capable and competent Negro men" were relegated to menial and unskilled occupations, excluded from positions as firemen, policemen, and even supervisors of other black workers. They went on to relate that the few blacks selected for supervisory roles were "the least competent and most ignorant . . . a mere stuge, for this prejudice[d] unsympathetic white building foremen."[75] Like African American women, men emphasized their patriotism. Kingsbury worker William Sneed wrote, "We the colored men and women are not being treated fair in the employment like other races and we are American[,] we love America[,] we all ways stand by America."[76]

Like their male coworkers, the African American women at Kingsbury argued that their status as American citizens and as qualified, dedicated, and capable workers should open desirable jobs to them. In their letters about Kingsbury, however, these women also drew attention to their particular needs, obligations, and struggles, referencing their burdens and sacrifices as women to explain why they deserved equal opportunity and fair treatment at work. The war generated unprecedented interdependencies between state and employer and newly politicized elements of women's private lives, giving new weight to their claims as mothers, wives, and breadwinners. In defining fairness by reasoning outward from their perceptions of their own needs and entitlements, black women articulated a vision of equality in which the government protected the self-sufficiency of all citizens—not turning a blind eye to women's domestic responsibilities, private struggles, and differences (from men and from each other), but accounting for them.

Many of the women who wrote to government officials about Kingsbury referenced their personal sacrifices as wives. During the Great Depression, employers had fired married women to preserve breadwinner status for men with dependents.[77] Now, women opined that the government should care for those whose husbands were serving overseas—not through social security or disability payments, but with a job to help the war effort.[78] In a letter to her former Chicago alderman, Eleanora Kincade explained, "My husband is eligible for the army and is subject to spill his blood for freedom the same as any other man beside many colored men are spilling their blood daily." Kincade was a white woman whom plant officials had forced to resign for opaque reasons—she suspected because her interracial marriage unsettled her coworkers. She asked, "because of the color of my husband does that disqualify me for having a job in the defense of our government[?] I am with in the law of our country—I am lawfully married."[79] Similarly, Willie Young felt especially entitled to a war job because her husband had lost his life during World War I.

> I was made a widow by our government. My husband was killed while employed in defense work in the war No. 1 at muscle shoals in Alabama. I feel as I being the widow of one whom gave all he had when he gave his life, I should have conciteration especially with the government. I explained that to the supervisor. I told her that she had a hand in the government and a part to play.[80]

To women like Kincade and Young, the government had inserted itself into the contract of marriage and thus owed wives something in return.

Other African American women workers cited their rights and personal sacrifices as mothers. Complainant Annie Kendrick reasoned that "if [my] boys can sleep on the ground with snak[e]s and water holes I am willing to try to do all I can." African American and white mothers, she wrote, should be given equal consideration for war jobs—black women "hafter give up there sons" just as white women did.[81] African American women also expressed their desire to help their men return quickly and safely. "We have sons husbands and brothers that are fighting for justice the same as other races," explained Pernellia Hull. "We women here are in the first line of defence and faceing the danger as any other women. . . . Our men are on the battlefields fighting for our rights."[82] In a telegram crafted to appeal to Mrs. Roosevelt's parental status, Hallie E. Hayes, president of the Gary Negro Mothers Union, wrote: "Our boys and girls are not given any consideration at the Kingsbury ammunition plant at LaPorte Indiana. Will you please help us."[83] The wives and mothers of black soldiers regarded the unfair treatment they experienced as especially abhorrent; they believed that their status lent their workplace complaints special force.

Black women who were breadwinners for their families also expected the government to provide work in light of those responsibilities. "I have two children and no husband," related Hattie Gardner, while Ruth Strickland described herself as "a mother of three children, 31 years of age."[84] Other complainants described their obligations to care for adult family members. Mrs. F. H. Woods recounted that she bore "the responsibility of supporting my mother who is seventy-one years of age and refuses to accept a pension because of her belief that the government has enough responsibility already."[85] Willie Young described her need for "a sufficient job" to provide for both her unemployed sister and her "aged mother whom have not been successful enough to get old age pension yet because of furnishing sufficient proof of her age. She is a widow." Young, who was also a widow, deplored Kingsbury management's practice of firing female breadwinners while employing multiple members of the same family. She wrote:

> In some cases there are four or five of one family working there, man wife son and daughters. And when it become[s] nessecery to lay some one off they don't look on the human side of life. They lay off single women and let the woman and her husband work. Instead of laying off the woman who have someone to support her.[86]

Young and others argued that their government should provide responsible, capable Americans—men and women—with the means to earn enough money to meet their financial obligations.[87]

Women also referenced their responsible local citizenship, believing that their civic-mindedness benefited their communities and their country and earned them the right to desirable employment. "I have lived in Gary for the past 18 years," Ruth Strickland wrote to FDR.[88] Mamie Johnson expressed a similar commitment to her community: "I live in Gary for 16 and a half years never has been in no kind of truble. I lived here at this address for 12 years and [I have] never caused any trouble in the community."[89] Ethel Stewart indicated that her husband had been a taxpayer in LaPorte County for thirty-five years; Merle Stokes Dunston explained that she was a twenty-year resident of and taxpayer in Gary as well as "an alert member of this community—active in its organizations, staff assistant volunteer of its Red Cross, speaker at its Forums on its Civilian Defense Committee and Disaster Preparedness Committee."[90] Pernellia Hull referenced her patriotic consumerism in her workplace rights claim. "I buy stamps and war bonds as far as I am able to help my country win this war," she explained, and thus, "I should be given a fair chance to do my part of work in the defense plant."[91]

Some complainants argued that their desire to work should outweigh their health problems, rejecting plant rationale that any physical limitations disqualified them from employment at Kingsbury. In her letter to the FEPC, Willie Young explained that constant standing aggravated her back problem. She was fired for asking to be transferred to a position where she could sit down, even though "at my age plus being in a certain state of life," standing all day was too difficult.[92] Young asked the FEPC to secure her a less taxing position at Kingsbury. Leila White expressed similar difficulty with the physicality of factory work. She was fired after she and her supervisor "had a little misunderstanding because of my not standing on the floor. [A]t that particular time I did not feel well to stand all day on my feet."[93] In her letter to the FEPC, Kathryn Webb, a matron at Kingsbury, described her supervisor's unwillingness to accommodate her physical limitations:

> [I] tried to get transferred to another line of work (operating dept) for over two months after being advised by my doctor, the scrubbing and waxing floors was too strenuous for me, as I've had one of my ovaries operated on, and the heavy lifting and mopping was causing me severe pains.[94]

In her complaint, fifty-four-year-old Annie Kendrick explained that she had been unable to obtain even a matron job at Kingsbury because she was perceived to be overweight. "The lady down at kingsbury employment told me that I was to heavy for the job well I was not as large as she was at least I am built in proportion to my high 5'7'1/2 weight about 200."[95] These women asked for the opportunity to prove themselves in jobs where their particular health issues would not impede their performance. They referenced their physical attributes not to minimize them, but to ask the government to compel their employer to accommodate them.

African American women workers responded to the discrepancy between their perceptions of fair treatment and the reality of work at Kingsbury through appeals to their union, their president, and the FEPC. None of these yielded meaningful results. FEPC officials knew that the AFL did little to help aggrieved black workers, admitting that their agency, not the union, stood as black workers' first line of defense.[96] Yet over and over, the FEPC answered women's handwritten claims with form letters urging them to reapply at Kingsbury or elsewhere. Women received one of four types of responses: that Kingsbury had hired many black workers and thus proving race discrimination would be impossible; that the FEPC was doing its best to open jobs at Kingsbury for qualified African American workers; that the employer's actions seemed unfair, but not racist; and—if the agency had asked Kingsbury to defend itself—that the worker had been fired or denied a job because, as Laura Washington Cyrus was told, "her services were unsatisfactory as far as her work with this firm was concerned."[97] In response to her complaint, Irene Marks received one of these standard replies:

> The records of this office indicate that the Kingsbury plant has already employed a number of Negroes and that it has committed itself to employ others. I suggest, therefore, that you continue your applications at the plant and also at the Employment Services office in your vicinity.[98]

In meetings between FEPC and Kingsbury officials, plant managers claimed that while they opposed race discrimination, they could not desegregate more jobs without risking a decline in factory output. "The production records of the negro lines have not been equal to those of the white lines," explained the plant personnel director in 1943, who blamed the discrepancy on "a higher degree of absenteeism, lack of punctuality, and generally sloppy work habits among negro workers."[99] The FEPC could only attempt to persuade officials otherwise. The commission's overall lack of power was compounded by tremendous pressure on the federal government to maintain industrial production. Thus, Todd & Brown set its own policies with impunity.

When the war ended in August 1945, Kingsbury officials began the process of shutting down the plant. Black women workers returned to their home communities and found that their wartime opportunities for high-paying factory jobs had been fleeting. Corinne, a high school senior in 1945, recalled that postwar prosperity was not shared equally by Gary residents: "The mills were booming, the stores on Broadway were remodeling, the returning soldiers were using the G. I. Bill to purchase homes, and everyone was hoping to buy a new car and replace their worn out appliances." While young white women in Gary were hired as secretaries and retail clerks, black women were all but shut out of those jobs. Corinne eventually found work behind the counter in the canteen of a steel mill, as a housemaid, and as a school janitor.[100] By 1950, 60 percent of all employed black women nationwide were in institutional and private household service jobs, compared with 16 percent of white working women. Only 5 percent of black women workers were in clerical or sales jobs; 41 percent were domestic servants in private homes.[101]

After the war, the racial animosity that had plagued northwest Indiana for decades reared up with renewed ferocity.[102] In 1945, several hundred white high school students in Gary boycotted their classes to protest school desegregation.[103] Even as schools were forcibly desegregated in the 1950s, residential patterns created de facto segregation, and the new proximities between blacks and whites created by urban renewal only ignited new conflicts.[104] The town of LaPorte also saw racial strife. In 1963, a group of African Americans tested a new statewide ban on race discrimination in state-licensed bars and restaurants. Their attempted "walk-ins" were met with locked doors, assaults with beer bottles, and gun-wielding tavern owners.[105]

Gary blacks fought postwar racism through a new vanguard community organization, the Gary Urban League (GUL). Founded in 1945, the GUL emphasized integration and colorblindness as the hallmarks of racial equality. Far from the Kingsbury women's claims that equality could be flexible and self-defined, the GUL fought to open jobs "on the basis of merit without respect to race or non-occupational qualifications."[106] In a 1950 speech to the Gary Welfare Council, GUL executive director Clifford Minton justified expanding workplace opportunities for blacks by appealing to the bottom line:

> Business enterprises and other institutions can never reach their highest
> efficiency in production, sales and service, without objective methods for
> selecting and upgrading workers Each year, Gary loses some of its best
> prospective negro citizens, because the normal channels of employment are
> not open to negro high school and college graduates.[107]

The GUL chipped away at segregation in schools, jobs, and public spaces, achieving most of its goals by the 1960s. In the same decade, however, Gary was devastated by seismic shifts in the global economy.[108] The city experienced industrial disinvestment, white flight, and a declining quality of life by the time black residents first outnumbered whites in 1970. Gary's black population rose to power just as the city entered its most troubled era.[109]

Perhaps ironically, black women workers had put forward bold demands in years that also saw a tremendous nationwide impetus toward labor discipline, cooperation, and productivity. The Second World War both reconfigured people's sense of belonging to the nation—empowering them to link their rights as workers, citizens, and family members—and created millions of new jobs that needed workers. African American women perceived an inherent flexibility in the FEPC mandates. They believed that their rights were partly defined by comparison to their male and white female counterparts. But they also argued that another essential element of fairness could only be measured in personal terms. They laid claim to their new government-protected rights vis-a-vis their powerful employers by referencing their status as citizens deserving of equality of opportunity, as women who had sacrificed heavily, and as individuals with their own abilities and limitations. The workplace rights claims of blacks and women alike got new teeth in 1964 when Title VII of the Civil Rights Act outlawed workplace discrimination based upon race and sex.[110] In its wake, Congress, the courts, and activists came to define equality in terms of access to what men and whites already had. The demands black women workers levied upon their government in the 1940s—that equality should guarantee desirable jobs to patriotic citizens regardless of their race or sex, and that fairness should be measured according to a worker's personal circumstances and economic status within her family—became much more difficult to justify in the postwar era of federal regulation and court decisions. The power of the Kingsbury women's personal appeals—which called for equality and fairness in equal measures—diminished even as state power to enforce anti-discrimination policies expanded.

KATHERINE TURK is Associate Professor of History at the University of North Carolina, Chapel Hill. She wishes to thank George Chauncey, Anthony Cotton, James Grossman, Betty Luther Hillman, James B. Lane, Polly Lennon, Steve McShane, James T. Sparrow, Amy Dru Stanley, the Center for Law, Society & Culture at the Indiana University Maurer School of Law, and the editors and anonymous reviewers of the *Indiana Magazine of History*.

NOTES

This article appeared in volume 108, no. 3 (September 2012).
    1. Mamie Johnson to President Franklin D. Roosevelt, LaPorte, Indiana, May 16, 1942, Kingsbury Ordnance Plant Folder 1, box 67, Active Cases, Records

of the Committee on Fair Employment Practice, Region VI, Record Group 228, National Archives and Records Administration, Chicago, Illinois (hereafter: FEPC-NARA). I have not added "*sic*" where spelling or grammatical errors occur in complainants' words. Instead, I have added parenthetical notes where complainants' meaning is potentially obscured.

2. Ibid.

3. George M. Johnson, Assistant Executive Secretary of FEPC, to Mamie Johnson, LaPorte, Indiana, June 3, 1942, Kingsbury Ordnance Plant Folder 1, box 67, FEPC-NARA.

4. D'Ann Campbell, *Women at War With America: Private Lives in a Patriotic Era* (Cambridge, Mass., 1984); James Sparrow, *Warfare State: World War II Americans and the Age of Big Government* (Oxford, U.K., 2011).

5. A wave of new scholarship interprets African American history through the frame of a "long civil rights movement," looking to the 1940s or earlier to excavate the roots and explain the outcomes of postwar activism. Jacquelyn Dowd Hall, "The Long Civil Rights Movement and the Political Uses of the Past," *Journal of American History* 91 (March 2005), 1233–63; Cornelius L. Bynum, *A. Philip Randolph and the Struggle for Civil Rights* (Urbana, Ill., 2010); Laurie B. Green, *Battling the Plantation Mentality: Memphis and the Black Freedom Struggle* (Chapel Hill, N. C., 2007); Tomiko Brown-Nagin, *Courage to Dissent: Atlanta and the Long History of the Civil Rights Movement* (Oxford, U. K., 2011); and Risa L. Goluboff, *The Lost Promise of Civil Rights* (Cambridge, Mass., 2007).

6. Roosevelt created the FEPC with Executive Order 8802 on June 25, 1941. The order stated: "There shall be no discrimination in the employment of workers in defense industries or government because of race, creed, color, or national origin." In 1943, Roosevelt issued Executive Order 9346, which required that all government contracts include a non-discrimination provision. Scholars have debated the FEPC's effectiveness in creating meaningful improvements for black workers in wartime, but most conclude that the agency represented a crucial precursor to the federal government's postwar efforts to protect minorities' workplace rights. See Eileen Boris, "Fair Employment and the Origins of Affirmative Action in the 1940s," *NWSA Journal* 10 (Autumn 1998), 142–50; William J. Collins, "Race, Roosevelt, and Wartime Production: Fair Employment in World War II Labor Markets," *American Economic Review* 91 (March 2001), 272–86; Andrew Edmund Kersten, *Race, Jobs and the War: The FEPC in the Midwest, 1941–46* (Urbana, Ill., 2000); Paul D. Moreno, *From Direct Action to Affirmative Action: Fair Employment Law and Policy in America, 1933–1972* (Baton Rouge, La., 1999); Merl E. Reed, *Seedtime for the Modern Civil Rights Movement: The President's Committee on Fair Employment Practice, 1941–1946* (Baton Rouge, La., 1991); and Megan Taylor Shockley, "*We, Too, Are*

Americans": African American Women in Detroit and Richmond, 1940–54 (Urbana, Ill., 2004).

7. The New Deal expanded government's role in individuals' lives and labor relationships. FDR personally encouraged Americans to look to the federal government as the powerful arbiter of fairness and citizens' rights. Lizabeth Cohen argues that feelings of common sacrifice, forged during the Great Depression, combined with the promise of the New Deal state to convince individual Americans of their entitlement to make personal claims upon governmental assistance. Lizabeth Cohen, *Making a New Deal: Industrial Workers in Chicago, 1919–1939* (New York, 1990). On the expansion of federally defined and protected workers' rights, see Nelson Lichtenstein, *State of the Union: A Century of American Labor* (Princeton, N. J., 2002). The 1930s also saw increased labor activism and workers' growing assertion that labor rights and civil rights were of a piece. See Michael K. Honey, *Southern Labor and Black Civil Rights: Organizing Memphis Workers* (Champaign, Ill., 1993); Green, *Battling the Plantation Mentality*; and Shockley, "We, Too, Are Americans."

8. In the early twentieth century, African American women remained clustered in low-paying, back-breaking, and often informal employment. On the rare occasions when they worked alongside white women, they seldom received equal pay. Jacqueline Jones, *Labor of Love, Labor of Sorrow: Black Women, Work, and the Family, from Slavery to the Present* (New York, 1985). Seventy-five percent of African American women who indicated an occupation in the 1920 U.S. Census worked in agricultural, domestic, and laundry work. Alice Kessler-Harris, *Out to Work: A History of Wage-Earning Women in the United States* (New York, 1982), 237. Of the nine thousand black women in Indiana who were reported as employed in the 1910 Census, more than seven thousand were servants or laundresses. Others worked as seamstresses, hairdressers, waitresses, and laundry operators. Emma Lou Thornbrough and Lana Ruegamer, *Indiana Blacks in the Twentieth Century* (Bloomington, Ind., 2000), 6; Shockley, "We, Too, Are Americans," 65. In creating the welfare state of the 1930s, bureaucrats and politicians drew new gendered distinctions between assistance and entitlements. See Linda Gordon, *Pitied But Not Entitled: Single Mothers and the History of Welfare, 1890–1935* (Cambridge, Mass., 1998); Alice Kessler-Harris, *In Pursuit of Equity: Women, Men, and the Quest for Economic Citizenship in 20th-Century America* (Oxford, U. K., 2001); and Theda Skocpol, *Protecting Soldiers and Mothers: The Political Origins of Social Policy in the United States* (Cambridge, Mass., 1995).

9. Cathy D. Knepper, ed., *Dear Mrs. Roosevelt: Letters to Eleanor Roosevelt Through Depression and War* (New York, 2004). On using women's letters as a primary source, see Regina Kunzel, "Pulp Fictions and Problem Girls: Reading

and Rewriting Single Pregnancy in the Postwar United States," *American Historical Review* 100 (December 1995), 1465–87.

10. William P. Vogel, *Kingsbury: A Venture in Teamwork* (New York, 1946), 5, 13, 19, 72.

11. Between 1910 and 1970, approximately seven million African Americans migrated from the American South to the North. James N. Gregory, *The Southern Diaspora: How the Great Migrations of Black and White Southerners Transformed America* (Chapel Hill, N. C., 2005); James R. Grossman, *Land of Hope: Chicago, Black Southerners, and the Great Migration* (Chicago, 1991); Nicholas Lemann, *The Promised Land: The Great Black Migration and How it Changed America* (New York, 1992); Kimberley L. Phillips, *AlabamaNorth: African-American Migrants, Community, and Working-Class Activism in Cleveland, 1915–45* (Urbana, Ill., 1999); and Isabel Wilkerson, *The Warmth of Other Suns: The Epic Story of America's Great Migration* (New York, 2010).

12. Raymond A. Mohl and Neil Betten, *Steel City: Urban and Ethnic Patterns in Gary, Indiana, 1906–1950* (New York, 1986); Thornbrough and Ruegamer, *Indiana Blacks in the Twentieth Century*; James B. Lane, ed., *Steel Shavings: Gary's First Hundred Years: A Centennial History of Gary, Indiana, 1906–2006* 37 (2006); and Isaac James Quillen, *Industrial City: A History of Gary, Indiana to 1929* (New York, 1986).

13. Collins, "Race, Roosevelt, and Wartime Production"; Kersten, *Race, Jobs and the War*. Boris's study of FEPC case files from World War II reveals that the local branches of the agency at times pressured employers to take affirmative steps to boost African Americans' overall representation in war plants. Boris, "Fair Employment and the Origins of Affirmative Action in the 1940s," 142. Despite women workers' demands, the FEPC did not take strong action at Kingsbury. On attempts to reconfigure American liberalism and worker rights in the aftermath of World War II, see Gareth Davies, *From Opportunity to Entitlement: The Transformation and Decline of Great Society Liberalism* (Lawrence, Kan., 1996); Nancy MacLean, *Freedom is Not Enough: The Opening of the American Workplace* (Cambridge, Mass., 2005); Allen J. Matusow, *Nixon's Economy: Booms, Busts, Dollars and Votes* (Lawrence, Kan., 1998); and John David Skrentny, *The Minority Rights Revolution* (Cambridge, Mass., 2002).

14. On black women's rights consciousness and activism, see Gloria T. Hull, Patricia Bell Scott, and Barbara Smith, eds., *But Some of Us Are Brave: All the Women are White, All the Blacks are Men* (New York, 1993). See also Eileen Boris, "Gender, Race and Rights: Listening to Critical Race Theory," *Journal of Women's History* 6 (Summer 1994), 111–24; Elsa Barkley Brown, "To Catch a Vision of Freedom: Reconstructing Southern Black Women's Political History, 1865–1880," in Vicki Ruiz and Ellen DuBois, eds., *Unequal Sisters: An Inclusive Reader in U.S. Women's History* (4th ed., New York, 2007); Glenda Elizabeth

Gilmore, *Gender and Jim Crow: Women and the Politics of White Supremacy in North Carolina, 1896–1920* (Chapel Hill, N. C., 1996); and Felicia Kornbluh, *The Battle For Welfare Rights: Politics and Poverty in Modern America* (Philadelphia, Pa., 2007).

15. On black women's experience of their race, class, and sex, see Kimberlé Crenshaw, *On Intersectionality: The Essential Writings of Kimberlé Crenshaw* (New York, 2012). On sex-specific protective labor legislation, see Kessler-Harris, *Out to Work*, chap. 7; Kathleen A. Laughlin, *Women's Work and Public Policy: A History of the Women's Bureau, U. S. Department of Labor, 1945–1970* (Boston, 2000); Susan Lehrer, *Origins of Protective Labor Legislation for Women, 1905–1925* (Albany, N. Y., 1987); Suzanne B. Mettler, "Federalism, Gender, & the Fair Labor Standards Act of 1938," *Polity* 26 (Summer 1994), 635–54; and Julie Novkov, *Constituting Workers, Protecting Women: Gender, Law and Labor in the Progressive Era and New Deal Years* (Ann Arbor, Mich., 2001).

16. On the intersections of labor rights and political rights within citizenship claims, see Evelyn Nakano Glenn, *Unequal Freedom: How Race and Gender Shaped American Citizenship and Labor* (Cambridge, Mass., 2002); Kessler-Harris, *In Pursuit of Equity*; and Judith N. Shklar, *American Citizenship: The Quest for Inclusion* (Cambridge, Mass., 1991).

17. On African American workers in war industry, see A. Russell Buchanan, *Black Americans in World War II* (Berkeley, Cal., 1977); Sally M. Miller and Daniel A. Cornford, eds., *American Labor in the Era of World War II* (Westport, Conn., 1995); and Neil A. Wynn, *The Afro-American and the Second World War* (New York, 1975). On women war workers, see Maureen Honey, *Creating Rosie the Riveter: Class, Gender, and Propaganda during World War II* (Amherst, Mass., 1984); Kessler-Harris, *Out to Work*; and Ruth Milkman, *Gender at Work: The Dynamics of Job Segregation by Sex During World War II* (Urbana, Ill., 1987).

18. Kessler-Harris, *Out to Work*, 273.

19. Jones, *Labor of Love, Labor of Sorrow*, 4. Karen Tucker Anderson's study of African American women war workers found that they typically made gains in feminized sectors such as textiles, nursing, and clerical work, but were often excluded from heavy industry. Thus, despite the new deluge of industrial jobs, on the national scale, black female jobseekers found more resistance than their white counterparts. Karen Tucker Anderson, "Last Hired, First Fired: Black Women Workers During World War II," *Journal of American History* 69 (June 1982), 82–97.

20. Gary Council of Social Agencies, "A Study of the Social and Economic Conditions of the Negro Population in Gary, 1944," p. 9, folder 3, box 3, CRA 160, Clifford E. Minton Papers, Calumet Regional Archives, Indiana University Northwest Library, Gary, Indiana.

21. Michael Marchese, "Economy," in James B. Lane, ed., *Steel Shavings: Home Front: The World War II Years in the Calumet Region, 1941–1945* 22 (1993), 45; Mohl and Betten, *Steel City* (New York, 1986), 76; Lane, ed., *Steel Shavings* 37 (2006), 153–54.

22. Nelson Lichtenstein, *Labor's War at Home: The CIO in World War II* (Cambridge, Mass., 1982); Honey, *Creating Rosie the Riveter*; Collins, "Race, Roosevelt, and Wartime Production"; Kersten, *Race, Jobs and the War*; Shockley, *"We, Too, Are Americans."*

23. Flora Campbell to President Franklin D. Roosevelt, January 22, 1943, Gary, Indiana, Kingsbury Ordnance Plant Folder 1, box 67, FEPC-NARA. The wartime economy created unprecedented new opportunities for Adrana Turner, who moved to northwest Indiana from Georgia in 1943 when she was eighteen. She worked frying donuts until she finished high school, when she found assembly line jobs at General American and Pullman-Standard. In 1945, she had saved enough money to buy a house in cash. Sanita A. Turner, "Working and Jitterbugging," *Steel Shavings: Families of the Calumet Region During the World War II Years, 1941–1945* 5 (1979), 8. Black employment at Gary's U.S. Steel plant peaked at 24.4 percent of the labor force in September 1945; this included an unprecedented number of black women. Mohl and Betten, *Steel City*, 76.

24. The town of LaPorte was a historic lakeside town whose main industries were ice harvesting and tourism. Max Parvin Cavnes, *The Hoosier Community at War* (Bloomington, Ind., 1961), 134; Kenneth J. Schoon, *Calumet Beginnings: Ancient Shorelines and Settlements at the South End of Lake Michigan* (Bloomington, Ind., 2003), 207–208; Joy Schultz, FEPC Field Investigator, to Elmer Henderson, Region VI Director, December 17, 1943, Kingsbury Ordnance Plant Folder 2, box 67, FEPC-NARA; "Conference with Mr. Joseph Trace, Manager, La Porte Office of United States Employment Service," Chicago, Illinois, Kingsbury Ordnance Plant Folder 2, box 67, FEPC-NARA.

25. Schoon, *Calumet Beginnings*, 155; Lane, ed., *Steel Shavings* 37 (2006), 15; Thornbrough and Ruegamer, *Indiana Blacks in the Twentieth Century*, 4.

26. A 1944 study commissioned by the Gary Urban League found that more African American residents of Gary had been born in Mississippi and Alabama than Indiana. "A Study of the Social and Economic Conditions of the Negro Population in Gary, 1944," p. 6, folder 3, box 3, CRA 160, Clifford E. Minton Papers; Mohl and Betten, *Steel City*. The city's population growth mirrored earlier statewide trends; in 1900, 73.5 percent of Indiana blacks lived in urban areas, and by 1910, the percentage had increased to 80.3. Historian Emma Lou Thornbrough credits primarily northern Indiana's rapid industrialization for this trend. Thornbrough and Ruegamer, *Indiana Blacks in the Twentieth Century*, 2; Cavnes, *Hoosier Community at War*, 162.

27. Mohl and Betten, *Steel City*, 61–62; Lane, ed., *Steel Shavings* 37 (2006), 40, 48–50; Manervie Smith, "A Little Girl's Dreams," in James B. Lane, ed., *Steel Shavings: Families of the Calumet Region: During the Depression of the 1930s* 3 (1977), 10; Sheila J. Brown, "Whites Upstairs, Blacks in the Basement," in Lane, ed., *Steel Shavings* 3 (1977), 28.

28. The Depression hit Gary blacks hardest, with blacks constituting half of the city's unemployed in 1930. Thornbrough and Ruegamer, *Indiana Blacks in the Twentieth Century*, 73; Mohl and Betten, *Steel City*, 74, 76; Edward Anderson, "Blacks at the Mill," in Lane, ed., *Steel Shavings* 3 (1977), 29; Lane, ed., *Steel Shavings* 37 (2006), 66. The Klan was active statewide in those years. An estimated one-quarter of all males born within the state of Indiana in the early twentieth century were Klan members. Thornbrough and Ruegamer, *Indiana Blacks in the Twentieth Century*, 48.

29. Herbert Steele, Katherine Eck, and Shirley Clay, "Gary's Central District," in Lane, ed., *Steel Shavings* 22 (1993), 39.

30. Arnold Greer, "Gary's Central District," in Lane, ed., *Steel Shavings* 22 (1993), 39.

31. Quoted in Mohl and Betten, *Steel City*, 65.

32. Lane, ed., *Steel Shavings* 37 (2006), 143; Mohl and Betten, *Steel City*, 56; "Gary, Indiana," *The Chicago Defender*, August 24, 1953, p. 3; "Delta Sorority Organizes Chapter in Gary, Indiana," *The Chicago Defender*, December 31, 1938, p. 13; "Alpha Kappa Alpha Sorors and Committee Campaign," *The Chicago Defender*, October 11, 1941, p. 17.

33. Mohl and Betten, *Steel City*, 80–82.

34. Kingsbury was the fourth ordnance site approved for World War II. Other sites included Ravenna, Ohio; Elwood, Illinois; and Burlington, Iowa. Vogel, *Kingsbury*, 17–19; Homer E. Marsh, "Local Labor Market Survey for the Michigan City-LaPorte-Kingsbury area in North Western Indiana: A Special Study," conducted by the Indiana Employment Security Division, 1941, Herman B Wells Library, Indiana University, Bloomington, Indiana.

35. Employment Security Division Report: LaPorte County, 1942–1946, "Survey of the Employment Situation in Relation to the Kingsbury Ordinance Development in La Porte County, IN as of April 1, 1941," Record Group L1581, Indiana State Archives, Commission on Public Records, Indianapolis, Indiana; Vogel, *Kingsbury*, 23.

36. Todd & Brown was a relatively young offshoot of the family company whose projects included construction of Rockefeller Center and the reconstruction of colonial Williamsburg, Virginia. Susan Heller Anderson, "Webster B. Todd is Dead at 89; Ex-Leader of Jersey Republicans," *New York Times*, February 10, 1989. The original estimated cost of operation for the plant's

first year was $26,000,000; its construction cost approximately $50,380,000. Vogel, *Kingsbury*, 5, 14, 26–27, 33.

37. Vogel, *Kingsbury*, 68, 78.

38. Robert Gyurko, "Women," in Lane, ed., *Steel Shavings* 22 (1993), 50; Vogel, *Kingsbury*, 65–66.

39. Mary Kay Maisel, "Women," in Lane, ed., *Steel Shavings* 22 (1993), 50–51.

40. Joan Cobb, "Women," in Lane, ed., *Steel Shavings* 22 (1993), 50; Vogel, *Kingsbury*, 8–9; *Peski v. Todd & Brown Inc.*, 158 F.2d 59 (7th Cir., 1946).

41. Vogel, *Kingsbury*, 5, 9, 36, 39.

42. Ibid., 5, 9–10, 36, 39, 57, 66, 75.

43. Even transportation to Kingsbury could prove deadly, as a Todd & Brown–operated bus had a fatal accident on its way to the plant. *Peski v. Todd & Brown Inc.*, 158 F.2d 59 (7th Cir., 1946).

44. Wanda Jones, "Making Ammunition," in Lane, ed., *Steel Shavings* 5 (1979), 10.

45. Joan Cobb, "Women," in Lane, ed., *Steel Shavings* 22 (1993), 50; Maryalice Roberts, former Kingsbury worker, quoted in "Generation of Heroes: Rosie the Riveter," WNDU News Center, June 2, 2004, online at http://www.wndu.com /news/generationofheroes/062004/generationofheroes_35545.php.

46. Memo re: meeting with Kingsbury officials March 13, 1942, Austin Scott, FEPC Field Representative, to Chicago FEPC Director Robert Weaver, March 14, 1942, Chicago, Illinois, Kingsbury Ordnance Plant Folder 1, box 67, FEPC-NARA. Historians have demonstrated that interactions on the factory floor during this period were characterized by hyper-awareness of workers' race and gender. See Eileen Boris, "'You Wouldn't Want One of 'Em Dancing With Your Wife': Racialized Bodies on the Job in World War II," *American Quarterly* 50 (March 1998), 77–108; Kevin Boyle, "The Kiss: Racial and Gender Conflict in a 1950s Automobile Factory," *Journal of American History* 84 (September 1997), 496–523. In fall 1944, the Farm Security Administration also transferred 150 Jamaicans to Kingsbury, where they worked in ammunition storage. Vogel, *Kingsbury*, 68, 71–72; Eleanora Kincade to Earl Dickerson, Chicago Alderman, July 29, 1942, Gary, Indiana, Kingsbury Ordnance Plant Folder 1, box 67, FEPC-NARA.

47. For example, in November 1943, Kingsbury employed 965 "non-whites" out of 8,257 total workers. Elmer Henderson Report, November 2, 1943, Kingsbury Ordnance Plant Folder 2, box 67, FEPC-NARA; "Discrimination Report," filed by Bernice Jena, LaPorte U.S. Employment Services Committee, filed October 20, 1942, LaPorte, Indiana, Kingsbury Ordnance Plant Folder 1, box 67, FEPC-NARA; Walter B. Swan to Eugene J. Brock, July 18, 1942, Kingsbury Ordnance Plant Folder 1, box 67, FEPC-NARA; Vogel, *Kingsbury*, 65–66.

48. Willie Young to Fair Employment Practices Region VI Office, June 7, 1943, Gary, Indiana, Kingsbury Ordnance Plant Folder 2, box 67, FEPC-NARA.

49. Ethel Jackson to Eleanor Roosevelt, March 20, 1942, Gary, Indiana, Kingsbury Ordnance Plant Folder 1, box 67, FEPC-NARA; Jones, *Labor of Love, Labor of Sorrow,* 240; Indiana State Board of Health and Indiana Division of Labor, "Sanitation Bulletin," Box 30: Labor, WWII History Commission Inventory, Record Group 1984046, Indiana State Archives.

50. Mrs. Laura Washington Cyrus affidavit, May 5, 1942, Michigan City, Indiana, Kingsbury Ordnance Plant Folder 1, box 67, FEPC-NARA; Supporting affidavit by Vivian Pensinger, June 6, 1942, South Bend, Indiana, Kingsbury Ordnance Plant Folder 1, box 67, FEPC-NARA.

51. Anderson, "Last Hired, First Fired," 86.

52. Cavnes, *Hoosier Community at War,* 134.

53. Ruth Strickland to Franklin Delano Roosevelt, August 27, 1943, Kingsbury Ordnance Plant Folder 2, box 67, FEPC-NARA.

54. Austin H. Scott to Dr. Robert Weaver, re: Field Report, Kingsbury Ordnance, March 23, 1942, Kingsbury Ordnance Plant Folder 1, box 67, FEPC-NARA; Ruth Strickland to Frances Perkins, U.S. Secretary of Labor, August 26, 1943, Gary, Indiana, Kingsbury Ordnance Plant Folder 2, box 67, FEPC-NARA.

55. Russell Jackson to FEPC, n.d., Kingsbury, Indiana, Kingsbury Ordnance Plant Folder 1, box 67, FEPC-NARA.

56. Willie Young to Fair Employment Practices Region VI Office, June 7, 1943, Gary, Indiana, Kingsbury Ordnance Plant Folder 2, box 67, FEPC-NARA; Ruth Strickland to President Franklin D. Roosevelt, August 27, 1943, Gary, Indiana, Kingsbury Ordnance Plant Folder 1, box 67, FEPC-NARA.

57. Sanita Turner, "Women," in Lane, ed., *Steel Shavings* 22 (1993), 55–56.

58. While the Roosevelts surely read some of the thousands of such letters written to them during the war years, White House staff forwarded without comment allegations of race discrimination in war work to the FEPC. Thereupon, the committee investigated complaints and mediated between workers and employers.

59. Ethel Jackson to Eleanor Roosevelt, March 20, 1942, Kingsbury Ordnance Plant Folder 1, box 67, FEPC-NARA; Pernellia Hull to President Franklin D. Roosevelt, February 16, 1942, Gary, Indiana, Kingsbury Ordnance Plant Folder 1, box 67, FEPC-NARA.

60. Mrs. Eugene Armstrong to Eleanor Roosevelt, undated, Kingsbury Ordnance Plant Folder 1, box 67, FEPC-NARA.

61. The letters from the public to First Lady Eleanor Roosevelt that are housed at the Franklin Delano Roosevelt Presidential Library in Hyde Park, New York, fill 3,000 boxes. Knepper, ed., *Dear Mrs. Roosevelt,* xx.

62. See Cohen, *Making a New Deal*, chaps. 5, 6; Knepper, ed., *Dear Mrs. Roosevelt*; and Jean Edward Smith, *FDR* (New York, 2008).

63. Flora Campbell to President Franklin D. Roosevelt, January 22, 1943, Gary, Indiana, Kingsbury Ordnance Plant Folder 1, box 67, FEPC-NARA; Thelma Morgan to Eleanor Roosevelt, March 27, 1942, Gary, Indiana, Kingsbury Ordnance Plant Folder 1, box 67, FEPC-NARA.

64. Irene Marks to President Franklin D. Roosevelt, March 26, 1942, Gary, Indiana, Kingsbury Ordnance Plant Folder 1, box 67, FEPC-NARA.

65. Ethel Stewart to Eleanor Roosevelt, March 20, 1942, Gary, Indiana, Kingsbury Ordnance Plant Folder 2, box 67, FEPC-NARA.

66. Mrs. F. H. Woods to Eleanor Roosevelt, July 31, 1942, Gary, Indiana, Kingsbury Ordnance Plant Folder 2, box 67, FEPC-NARA.

67. Nikhil Pal Singh writes that the quintessentially American concept of the "abstract individual subject"—a citizen freely acting within both the public and private spheres—has disadvantaged African Americans throughout U.S. history. He argues that "racial stigma has been applied to blacks as a group, preventing them from being perceived as qualitatively differentiated individuals," and thus not fully enabled to exercise the rights of citizenship. Nikhil Pal Singh, *Black is a Country: Race and the Unfinished Struggle for Democracy* (Cambridge, Mass., 2004), 23–24.

68. Ruth Strickland, C. L. Strickland, and R. L. Lloyd to Mr. F. V. Terrell, n.d., Kingsbury Ordnance Plant Folder 2, box 67, FEPC-NARA.

69. Hattie Gardner to Fair Employment Practices Committee, September 15, 1942, Gary, Indiana, Kingsbury Ordnance Plant Folder 1, box 67, FEPC-NARA.

70. Elizabeth Reed to Earl Dickerson, Chicago Alderman, n.d., Gary, Indiana, Kingsbury Ordnance Plant Folder 1, box 67, FEPC-NARA.

71. Willie Young to Fair Employment Practices Region VI Office, June 7, 1943, Gary, Indiana, Kingsbury Ordnance Plant Folder 2, box 67, FEPC-NARA.

72. Vogel, *Kingsbury*, 73–74.

73. Ruth Strickland to President Franklin D. Roosevelt, August 27, 1943, Gary, Indiana, Kingsbury Ordnance Plant Folder 1, box 67, FEPC-NARA.

74. Memo re: Ruth Strickland from Todd & Brown to Joy Schultz, FEPC Field Officer, December 30, 1943, Kingsbury, Indiana, Kingsbury Ordnance Plant Folder 1, box 67, FEPC-NARA.

75. Complaint and Petition Signed by Twenty-Two Male Workers of Unit E-1, Detonator Line, Kingsbury Ordnance Plant to Fair Employment Practices Committee, Kingsbury Ordnance Plant Folder 1, box 67, FEPC-NARA.

76. William Sneed to William Alexander, January 22, 1942, Kingsbury Ordnance Plant Folder 1, box 67, FEPC-NARA.

77. Kessler-Harris, *Out to Work*, 251.

78. For similar types of demands made by war wives, see Stephanie McCurry, "Citizens, Soldiers' Wives, and 'Hiley Hope Up' Slaves: The Problem of Political

Obligation in the Civil War South," in *Gender and the Southern Body Politic*, ed. Nancy Bercaw (Jackson, Miss., 2000), 95–124.

79. Eleanora Kincade to Earl Dickerson, Chicago Alderman, July 29, 1942, Gary, Indiana, Kingsbury Ordnance Plant Folder 1, box 67, FEPC-NARA.

80. Willie Young to Fair Employment Practices Region VI Office, June 7, 1943, Gary, Indiana, Kingsbury Ordnance Plant Folder 2, box 67, FEPC-NARA.

81. Annie Kendrick to Fair Employment Practices Committee Region VI, October 14, 1943, Gary, Indiana, Kingsbury Ordnance Plant Folder 2, box 67, FEPC-NARA.

82. Pernellia Hull to President Franklin D. Roosevelt, February 16, 1942, Gary, Indiana, Kingsbury Ordnance Plant Folder 1, box 67, FEPC-NARA.

83. Hallie Hayes, President, Negro Mothers Union, to Eleanor Roosevelt, January 30, 1942, Kingsbury Ordnance Plant Folder 1, box 67, FEPC-NARA.

84. Hattie Gardner to Fair Employment Practices Committee, September 15, 1942, Gary, Indiana, Kingsbury Ordnance Plant Folder 1, box 67, FEPC-NARA; Ruth Strickland to President Franklin D. Roosevelt, August 27, 1943, Gary, Indiana, Kingsbury Ordnance Plant Folder 1, box 67, FEPC-NARA.

85. Mrs. F. H. Woods to Eleanor Roosevelt, July 31, 1942, Gary, Indiana, Kingsbury Ordnance Plant Folder 2, box 67, FEPC-NARA; Willie Young to Fair Employment Practices Region VI Office, June 7, 1943, Gary, Indiana, Kingsbury Ordnance Plant Folder 2, box 67, FEPC-NARA.

86. Willie Young to Fair Employment Practices Region VI Office, June 7, 1943, Gary, Indiana, Kingsbury Ordnance Plant Folder 2, box 67, FEPC-NARA.

87. This was perhaps the earliest instance in which working women would have demanded that the government provide them a "family wage," typically a man's claim and frequently out of reach to African Americans. Historian Alice Kessler-Harris argues that the war accelerated the dismantling of the logic of the family wage as a male prerogative because women were increasingly providing for their families in what had previously been men's jobs. Alice Kessler-Harris, *A Woman's Wage: Historical Meanings & Social Consequences* (Lexington, Ky., 1990), 94.

88. Ruth Strickland to President Franklin D. Roosevelt, August 27, 1943, Gary, Indiana, Kingsbury Ordnance Plant Folder 1, box 67, FEPC-NARA.

89. Mamie Johnson to President Franklin D. Roosevelt, LaPorte, Indiana, May 16, 1942, Kingsbury Ordnance Plant Folder 1, box 67, FEPC-NARA.

90. Ethel Stewart to Eleanor Roosevelt, March 20, 1942, Gary, Indiana, Kingsbury Ordnance Plant Folder 2, box 67, FEPC-NARA; Merle Stokes Dunston to Robert Weaver, FEPC Executive Secretary, February 18, 1942, LaPorte, Indiana, Kingsbury Ordnance Plant Folder 1, box 67, FEPC-NARA.

91. Pernellia Hull to President Franklin D. Roosevelt, February 16, 1942, Gary, Indiana, Kingsbury Ordnance Plant Folder 1, box 67, FEPC-NARA.

92. Willie Young to Fair Employment Practices Region VI Office, June 7, 1943, Gary, Indiana, Kingsbury Ordnance Plant Folder 2, box 67, FEPC-NARA.

93. Leila White to Harry Baron, FEPC Administrative Assistant, n.d., Gary, Indiana, Kingsbury Ordnance Plant Folder 1, box 67, FEPC-NARA.

94. Kathryn Webb to Fair Employment Practices Committee Region VI Office, May 14, 1942, Gary, Indiana, Kingsbury Ordnance Plant Folder 1, box 67, FEPC-NARA.

95. Annie Kendrick to Fair Employment Practices Committee Region VI, October 14, 1943, Gary, Indiana, Kingsbury Ordnance Plant Folder 2, box 67, FEPC-NARA.

96. Ruth Strickland to President Franklin D. Roosevelt, August 27, 1943, Gary, Indiana, Kingsbury Ordnance Plant Folder 1, box 67, FEPC-NARA.

97. F. E. LeBaron, Labor Relations Division, Todd & Brown, to George M. Johnson, July 28, 1942, Kingsbury, Indiana, Kingsbury Ordnance Plant Folder 1, box 67, FEPC-NARA.

98. Robert C. Weaver, FEPC, to Irene Marks, March 29, 1942, Kingsbury, Indiana, Kingsbury Ordnance Plant Folder 2, box 67, FEPC-NARA.

99. Joy Schultz to Elmer W. Henderson, December 18, 1943, re: Conference with Col. Schubart, Commanding Officer and Mr. Hodgins, Kingsbury Ordnance Plant Personnel Director, December 18, 1943, Kingsbury Ordnance Plant Folder 2, box 67, FEPC-NARA.

100. Marcy Weinstein, "Fulfilling a Dream," in James B. Lane, ed., *Steel Shavings: Work Experiences in the Calumet Region* 7 (1981), 11–12.

101. Jones, *Labor of Love, Labor of Sorrow*, 235, 256–57.

102. Postwar Gary also saw massive labor strife and a rise in crime and divorce rates. James B. Lane, "Anxious Years," in James B. Lane, ed., *Steel Shavings: The Postwar Period in the Calumet Region, 1945–1955* 14 (1988), 1.

103. Lane, ed., *Steel Shavings* 37 (2006), 169–73; Mohl and Betten, *Steel City*, 59.

104. Leroy Henderson, "Trying to Join the Cub Scouts," in James B. Lane, ed., *Steel Shavings: Race-relations in the Calumet Region: During the 1960s* 6 (1980), 1.

105. "Trouble in La Porte," July 8, 1963, *Gary Post-Tribune*, in Lane, ed., *Steel Shavings* 6 (1980), 5.

106. Clifford E. Minton address to Gary Urban League, "Indiana's Past, Present, Future," 1956, pp. 1, 4, folder 1, box 2, Clifford Minton Papers.

107. Clifford E. Minton address to Gary Welfare Council, Gary YMCA, October 16, 1950, re: "Essential Factors in a Democratic Society," folder 4, box 2, Clifford Minton Papers. The Urban League held several oversubscribed trainings for clerical workers in 1959. Gary Urban League Clerical Workshop, 1959, folder 33, box 3, Clifford Minton Papers; "Urban League Sponsors Two Workshops for Clerical Workers," *Gary Post-Tribune*, February 13, 1959, folder 33, box 3, Clifford Minton Papers.

108. Mohl and Betten, *Steel City*, 7.

109. Lane, ed., *Steel Shavings* 37 (2006), 223–24; Ed Mores, "Automation," in Lane, ed., *Steel Shavings* 7 (1981), 15; Petronia Radcliffe, "Store Closings," in James B. Lane, ed., *Steel Shavings: Life in the Calumet Region: During the 1970s* 9 (1983), 15; Mohl and Betten, *Steel City*, 6. On postwar Gary, see Andrew Hurley, *Environmental Inequalities: Class, Race, and Industrial Pollution in Gary, Indiana, 1945–1980* (Chapel Hill, N. C., 1995); Sandra L. Barnes, *The Cost of Being Poor: A Comparative Study of Life in Poor Urban Neighborhoods in Gary, Indiana* (Albany, N. Y., 2005); Edward Greer, *Big Steel: Black Politics and Corporate Power in Gary, Indiana* (New York, 1979).

110. Cynthia Harrison, *On Account of Sex: The Politics of Women's Issues, 1945–1968* (Berkeley, Cal., 1988); MacLean, *Freedom is Not Enough*; Serena Mayeri, *Reasoning from Race: Feminism, Law, and the Civil Rights Revolution* (Cambridge, Mass., 2011); Skrentny, *Minority Rights Revolution*.

DAWN E. BAKKEN is Associate Editor of the *Indiana Magazine of History*, a scholarly journal of state and midwestern history. She is the author of *On This Day in Indianapolis*.

CPSIA information can be obtained
at www.ICGtesting.com
Printed in the USA
LVHW091305261021
701592LV00004B/68

9 780253 056849